The Flask Mega-Tutorial

Miguel Grinberg

2018-03-01

ii

Contents

Preface   **v**
    1   Who This Book Is For   v
    2   Requirements vi
    3   About The Example Application vi
    4   How To Work With The Example Code vii
    5   Conventions Used In This Book viii
    6   Acknowledgements ix

1 Hello, World!   **1**
    1.1   Installing Python   2
    1.2   Installing Flask   2
    1.3   A "Hello, World" Flask Application   5

2 Templates   **11**
    2.1   What Are Templates? 12
    2.2   Conditional Statements 15
    2.3   Loops 15
    2.4   Template Inheritance 17

3 Web Forms   **21**
    3.1   Introduction to Flask-WTF 21
    3.2   Configuration 22
    3.3   User Login Form 24
    3.4   Form Templates 25
    3.5   Form Views 26
    3.6   Receiving Form Data 28
    3.7   Improving Field Validation 30
    3.8   Generating Links 32

4 Database — 35
- 4.1 Databases in Flask — 35
- 4.2 Database Migrations — 36
- 4.3 Flask-SQLAlchemy Configuration — 37
- 4.4 Database Models — 38
- 4.5 Creating The Migration Repository — 40
- 4.6 The First Database Migration — 41
- 4.7 Database Upgrade and Downgrade Workflow — 42
- 4.8 Database Relationships — 43
- 4.9 Play Time — 45
- 4.10 Shell Context — 48

5 User Logins — 51
- 5.1 Password Hashing — 51
- 5.2 Introduction to Flask-Login — 53
- 5.3 Preparing The User Model for Flask-Login — 53
- 5.4 User Loader Function — 54
- 5.5 Logging Users In — 55
- 5.6 Logging Users Out — 56
- 5.7 Requiring Users To Login — 57
- 5.8 Showing The Logged In User in Templates — 59
- 5.9 User Registration — 60

6 Profile Page and Avatars — 65
- 6.1 User Profile Page — 65
- 6.2 Avatars — 68
- 6.3 Using Jinja2 Sub-Templates — 71
- 6.4 More Interesting Profiles — 72
- 6.5 Recording The Last Visit Time For a User — 74
- 6.6 Profile Editor — 76

7 Error Handling — 81
- 7.1 Error Handling in Flask — 81
- 7.2 Debug Mode — 83
- 7.3 Custom Error Pages — 85
- 7.4 Sending Errors by Email — 87
- 7.5 Logging to a File — 90
- 7.6 Fixing the Duplicate Username Bug — 91

8 Followers — 93
- 8.1 Database Relationships Revisited 93
  - 8.1.1 One-to-Many 93
  - 8.1.2 Many-to-Many 94
  - 8.1.3 Many-to-One and One-to-One 95
- 8.2 Representing Followers 95
- 8.3 Database Model Representation 96
- 8.4 Adding and Removing "follows" 98
- 8.5 Obtaining the Posts from Followed Users 99
  - 8.5.1 Joins 101
  - 8.5.2 Filters 102
  - 8.5.3 Sorting 103
- 8.6 Combining Own and Followed Posts 103
- 8.7 Unit Testing the User Model 104
- 8.8 Integrating Followers with the Application 107

9 Pagination — 109
- 9.1 Submission of Blog Posts 109
- 9.2 Displaying Blog Posts 111
- 9.3 Making It Easier to Find Users to Follow 112
- 9.4 Pagination of Blog Posts 115
- 9.5 Page Navigation 118
- 9.6 Pagination in the User Profile Page 120

10 Email Support — 123
- 10.1 Introduction to Flask-Mail 123
- 10.2 Flask-Mail Usage 125
- 10.3 A Simple Email Framework 126
- 10.4 Requesting a Password Reset 126
- 10.5 Password Reset Tokens 128
- 10.6 Sending a Password Reset Email 130
- 10.7 Resetting a User Password 131
- 10.8 Asynchronous Emails 133

11 Facelift — 135
- 11.1 CSS Frameworks 135
- 11.2 Introducing Bootstrap 136
- 11.3 Using Flask-Bootstrap 137
- 11.4 Rendering Bootstrap Forms 139
- 11.5 Rendering of Blog Posts 140

11.6 Rendering Pagination Links 140
11.7 Before And After 141

12 Dates and Times 143
12.1 Timezone Hell 143
12.2 Timezone Conversions 144
12.3 Introducing Moment.js and Flask-Moment 145
12.4 Using Moment.js 146

13 I18n and L10n 151
13.1 Introduction to Flask-Babel 151
13.2 Marking Texts to Translate In Python Source Code 153
13.3 Marking Texts to Translate In Templates 155
13.4 Extracting Text to Translate 156
13.5 Generating a Language Catalog 156
13.6 Updating the Translations 160
13.7 Translating Dates and Times 160
13.8 Command-Line Enhancements 162

14 Ajax 167
14.1 Server-side vs. Client-side 167
14.2 Live Translation Workflow 168
14.3 Language Identification 169
14.4 Displaying a "Translate" Link 170
14.5 Using a Third-Party Translation Service 171
14.6 Ajax From The Server 174
14.7 Ajax From The Client 176

15 A Better Application Structure 181
15.1 Current Limitations 181
15.2 Blueprints 183
    15.2.1 Error Handling Blueprint 183
    15.2.2 Authentication Blueprint 185
    15.2.3 Main Application Blueprint 186
15.3 The Application Factory Pattern 186
15.4 Unit Testing Improvements 190
15.5 Environment Variables 192
15.6 Requirements File 193

16 Full-Text Search — 195
- 16.1 Introduction to Full-Text Search Engines — 195
- 16.2 Installing Elasticsearch — 196
- 16.3 Elasticsearch Tutorial — 197
- 16.4 Elasticsearch Configuration — 199
- 16.5 A Full-Text Search Abstraction — 201
- 16.6 Integrating Searches with SQLAlchemy — 204
- 16.7 Search Form — 207
- 16.8 Search View Function — 210

17 Deployment on Linux — 213
- 17.1 Traditional Hosting — 213
- 17.2 Creating an Ubuntu Server — 214
- 17.3 Using a SSH Client — 215
- 17.4 Password-less Logins — 216
- 17.5 Securing Your Server — 218
- 17.6 Installing Base Dependencies — 219
- 17.7 Installing the Application — 220
- 17.8 Setting Up MySQL — 222
- 17.9 Setting Up Gunicorn and Supervisor — 223
- 17.10 Setting Up Nginx — 225
- 17.11 Deploying Application Updates — 227
- 17.12 Raspberry Pi Hosting — 228

18 Deployment on Heroku — 229
- 18.1 Hosting on Heroku — 230
- 18.2 Creating Heroku account — 230
- 18.3 Installing the Heroku CLI — 230
- 18.4 Setting Up Git — 231
- 18.5 Creating a Heroku Application — 231
- 18.6 The Ephemeral File System — 232
- 18.7 Working with a Heroku Postgres Database — 232
- 18.8 Logging to stdout — 233
- 18.9 Compiled Translations — 234
- 18.10 Elasticsearch Hosting — 235
- 18.11 Updates to Requirements — 235
- 18.12 The Procfile — 236
- 18.13 Deploying the Application — 237
- 18.14 Deploying Application Updates — 238

19 Deployment on Docker Containers — 241
- 19.1 Installing Docker CE — 242
- 19.2 Building a Container Image — 243
- 19.3 Starting a Container — 246
- 19.4 Using Third-Party "Containerized" Services — 248
  - 19.4.1 Adding a MySQL Container — 249
  - 19.4.2 Adding a Elasticsearch Container — 251
- 19.5 The Docker Container Registry — 252
- 19.6 Deployment of Containerized Applications — 253

20 Some JavaScript Magic — 255
- 20.1 Server-side Support — 256
- 20.2 Introduction to the Bootstrap Popover Component — 258
- 20.3 Executing a Function On Page Load — 259
- 20.4 Finding DOM Elements with Selectors — 260
- 20.5 Popovers and the DOM — 260
- 20.6 Hover Events — 262
- 20.7 Ajax Requests — 263
- 20.8 Popover Creation and Destruction — 265

21 User Notifications — 267
- 21.1 Private Messages — 267
  - 21.1.1 Database Support for Private Messages — 268
  - 21.1.2 Sending a Private Message — 269
  - 21.1.3 Viewing Private Messages — 270
- 21.2 Static Message Notification Badge — 272
- 21.3 Dynamic Message Notification Badge — 273
- 21.4 Delivering Notifications to Clients — 274

22 Background Jobs — 281
- 22.1 Introduction to Task Queues — 281
- 22.2 Using RQ — 282
  - 22.2.1 Creating a Task — 283
  - 22.2.2 Running the RQ Worker — 283
  - 22.2.3 Executing Tasks — 284
  - 22.2.4 Reporting Task Progress — 285
- 22.3 Database Representation of Tasks — 286
- 22.4 Integrating RQ with the Flask Application — 288
- 22.5 Sending Emails from the RQ Task — 290
- 22.6 Task Helpers — 291

CONTENTS

    22.7 Implementing the Export Task 293
    22.8 Export Functionality in the Application 296
    22.9 Progress Notifications 297
    22.10 Deployment Considerations 301
        22.10.1 Deployment on a Linux Server 301
        22.10.2 Deployment on Heroku 301
        22.10.3 Deployment on Docker 302

23 Application Programming Interfaces (APIs)   305
    23.1 REST as a Foundation of API Design 306
        23.1.1 Client-Server 307
        23.1.2 Layered System 307
        23.1.3 Cache 307
        23.1.4 Code On Demand 308
        23.1.5 Stateless 308
        23.1.6 Uniform Interface 308
    23.2 Implementing an API Blueprint 310
    23.3 Representing Users as JSON Objects 312
    23.4 Representing Collections of Users 315
    23.5 Error Handling 317
    23.6 User Resource Endpoints 318
        23.6.1 Retrieving a User 318
        23.6.2 Retrieving Collections of Users 319
        23.6.3 Registering New Users 321
        23.6.4 Editing Users 322
    23.7 API Authentication 323
        23.7.1 Tokens In the User Model 324
        23.7.2 Token Requests 325
        23.7.3 Protecting API Routes with Tokens 328
        23.7.4 Revoking Tokens 330
    23.8 API Friendly Error Messages 330

Preface

Back in 2012, I decided to start a software development blog. Because I am a do-it-yourselfer at heart, instead of using Blogger or WordPress, I sat down and wrote my own blog engine, using a then little known web framework called Flask. I knew I wanted to code it in Python, and I first tried Django, which was (and still is) the most popular Python web framework. But unfortunately Django seemed too big and too structured for my needs. I've found that Flask gave me as much power, while being small, unopinionated and unobtrusive.

Writing my own blog engine was an awesome experience that left me with a lot of ideas for topics I wanted to blog about. Instead of writing individual articles about all these topics, I decided to write a long, overarching tutorial that Python beginners can use to learn web development. And just like that, the Flask Mega-Tutorial was born!

The book that you have in your hands is a new edition of the original tutorial, revised, updated and expanded in 2017 thanks to the support of almost 600 Kickstarter backers.

1 Who This Book Is For

This book will take you on a journey through a realistic web development project, from start to end. If you have just a little bit of experience coding in Python and understand how the web works at a high-level, you should have no trouble using this book to learn how to develop your own web applications using Python and Flask.

The tutorial assumes that you are familiar with the command line in your operating system. If you aren't, then I recommend that you learn how to execute programs, create directories, copy files, etc. using the command line before you begin.

If you have learned Flask with my original Mega-Tutorial, this new edition will introduce you to new features in Flask that did not exist when I wrote the original articles, as well as give you an updated look at important topics such as authentication, full-text search and internationalization. In addition to the revised content, this version of the tutorial includes new chapters that cover topics that have become relevant in recent times, such as APIs, background jobs and containers.

2 Requirements

The example code that accompanies this book can be used on any platform on which Python runs, so Mac OS X, Linux and Microsoft Windows are all valid choices. I have tested all the code extensively on Python 3.5 and 3.6, so these are the versions I recommend you to use. Unless specifically noted, the code also runs on Python 2.7, but keep in mind that Python 2.7 will not be supported past the year 2020, so you should seriously consider migrating to Python 3 as soon as possible.

If you are using a Microsoft Windows computer, you probably know that the world of web development is dominated by Unix-based workflows, and you may rightly feel that you are at a disadvantage. That should not be a major concern when you work with this book, because when necessary, specific instructions that apply to Windows users are noted. My assumption is that if you are working on Windows you will be using the command prompt to work with your application. If you prefer to use PowerShell, you will need to translate commands to the appropriate syntax for that shell.

This may be hard to accept if you work on Windows, but I think you will have a better experience if you force yourself to learn Unix, which can be done right on your Windows computer without making any drastic configuration changes. My recommendation is that you install Unix tools on your Windows system and adopt the Unix workflow. If you are interested in doing this, one option is the Windows Subsystem for Linux (WSL)[1], an officially supported feature of Windows 10 that adds an Ubuntu Linux system that runs in parallel with your Windows operating system and includes Python 3.5. If your system is not compatible with WSL, then another very good option is Cygwin[2], an open-source POSIX emulation layer that includes Windows ports of a large number of Unix tools, including Python. I have worked with Python under both WSL and Cygwin and find them perfectly adequate for web development work.

3 About The Example Application

The application that I'm going to develop as part of this tutorial is a nicely featured microblogging server that I decided to call *Microblog*. Pretty creative, I know.

---

[1] https://msdn.microsoft.com/en-us/commandline/wsl/about
[2] https://cygwin.org

Just so that you have some idea of what you will learn if you follow this tutorial, these are some of the topics that I will cover:

- User management, including secure password handling, logins, user profiles and avatars.
- Database management and database migration support
- Handling of user input via web forms
- Pagination of long lists of items
- Full-text search
- Email notifications to users
- HTML templates
- Working with dates and times
- Internationalization and localization
- Installation on a production server
- Working with Docker containers
- Application Programming Interfaces
- Push notifications
- Background jobs

I hope this application will serve as a template that you can use for writing your own web applications.

4 How To Work With The Example Code

I have released the complete source code for this project on the following GitHub repository: https://github.com/miguelgrinberg/microblog. There is a commit in this repository for each chapter.

The way I envision you will work through this tutorial is by writing the application on your own, based on the instructions provided in the text, at least for the first few chapters. You can certainly copy and paste portions of code from the text or from GitHub to save some typing, but I think it is important that you familiarize yourself with the task of coding a Flask application by writing the code yourself, instead of just downloading the files from GitHub (unless explicitly instructed to do so).

The GitHub repository can serve as a reference if you get lost and can't get the application to work. You can compare your files against the code in the repository link provided with each chapter if you get stuck with a problem you can't solve.

5 Conventions Used In This Book

This book frequently includes commands that you need to type in a terminal session. For these commands, a $ will be shown as a command prompt. This is a standard prompt for many Linux shells, but may look unfamiliar to Microsoft Windows users. For example:

```
$ python hello.py
hello
```

In a lot of the terminal examples, you are going to be required to have an activated *virtual environment* (do not worry if you don't know what this is yet, you will find out very soon!). For those examples, the prompt will appear as `(venv) $`:

```
(venv) $ python hello.py
hello
```

You will also need to interact with the Python interactive interpreter. Examples that show statements that need to be entered in a Python interpreter session will use a >>> prompt, as in the following example:

```
>>> print('hello!')
hello
```

In all cases, lines that are not prefixed with a $ or >>> prompt, are output printed by the command, and should not be typed.

6 Acknowledgements

This project would not have been possible without the amazing support of my Kickstarter backers. My deepest thanks go to Dhritiman Sagar, Alex Anderson, Bahrom Matyakubov, Dave Finnegan, John Gann, John W. O'Brien, Kojo Idrissa, Mark Anders, Raph, Fredrik Dahlgren, Jorge García García, Todd Twiggs, Pietro P Peterlongo, Chris Davis, Alexandre Harano, Bob Jordan, Chris Dent, Chris Jones, CptJason, Daniel Abeles, Daniel Plas Rivera, Dipanjan Sarkar, Eric Chou, Eric Ho, Graham Williamson, jiho Bak, John Sobanski, Kai Mies, Len Sumnler, Marc P. Rostock, Michael Sim, Nick Brandaleone, Nnamdi E. Anyanwu, R. Da Costa Faro, Reimund Klain, Scott Strattner, SNC Cloud Dev (twitter.com/snc_clouddev), T81, Tobias Siebenlist, Viet Le, Ed Wachtel, Shivas Jayaram, JVA, GenLots.com, Martin Thorsen Ranang, DFW Python, Allan Swanepoel, Andrej Stabenow, Anthony Bourguignon, Aron Filbert, Auke Bakker, Bryson Tyrrell, Chuck Woodraska, Colin R. Crossman, Dario Varotto, Dax Morrow, Eric G. Barron, Everett Toews, Fisherworks, flasky mcflaskface, Iain Hunter, Jeremy Barisch Rooney, Jesse Liles, Jindrich K. Smitka, Jing Sheng Pang, Karthik Ramakrishnan, Kevin Porterfield (KP), Leonel Decunta, Martynas Budvytis, Mathew Divine, Matt Makai (Full Stack Python), Matt Trentini, Michael from Talk Python, Nana B Okyere, Nathan Sanders, Nduka Obinna Azubuike, Neal Duncan, Philip Penquitt, Rémi Debette, Romer Ibo, Ryan Hagan, Scott Andrew Underwood, Stephan Simon, Steve Bartell, Timothy DAuria, Vitaly Popovich, Yi Luo and the remaining 484 backers.

Chapter 1

Hello, World!

Welcome! You are about to start on a journey to learn how to create web applications with Python[1] and the Flask[2] framework. In this first chapter, you are going to learn how to set up a Flask project. By the end of this chapter you are going to have a simple Flask web application running on your computer!

All the code examples presented in this book are hosted on a GitHub repository. Downloading the code from GitHub can save you a lot of typing, but I strongly recommend that you type the code yourself, at least for the first few chapters. Once you become more familiar with Flask and the example application you can access the code directly from GitHub if the typing becomes too tedious.

At the beginning of each chapter, I'm going to give you three GitHub links that can be useful while you work through the chapter. The **Browse** link will open the GitHub repository for Microblog at the place where the changes for the chapter you are reading were added, without including any changes introduced in future chapters. The **Zip** link is a download link for a zip file including the entire application up to and including the changes in the chapter. The **Diff** link will open a graphical view of all the changes that were made in the chapter you are about to read.

The GitHub links for this chapter are: Browse[3], *Zip*[4], *Diff*[5].

---

[1] https://python.org
[2] http://flask.pocoo.org
[3] https://github.com/miguelgrinberg/microblog/tree/v0.1
[4] https://github.com/miguelgrinberg/microblog/archive/v0.1.zip
[5] https://github.com/miguelgrinberg/microblog/compare/v0.0...v0.1

1.1 Installing Python

If you don't have Python installed on your computer, go ahead and install it now. If your operating system does not provide you with a Python package, you can download an installer from the Python official website[6]. If you are using Microsoft Windows along with WSL or Cygwin, note that you will not be using the Windows native version of Python, but a Unix-friendly version that you need to obtain from Ubuntu (if you are using WSL) or from Cygwin.

To make sure your Python installation is functional, you can open a terminal window and type `python3`, or if that does not work, just `python`. Here is what you should expect to see:

```
$ python3
Python 3.5.2 (default, Nov 17 2016, 17:05:23)
[GCC 5.4.0 20160609] on linux
Type "help", "copyright", "credits" or "license" for more information.
>>> _
```

The Python interpreter is now waiting at an interactive prompt, where you can enter Python statements. In future chapters you will learn what kinds of things this interactive prompt is useful for. But for now, you have confirmed that Python is installed on your system. To exit the interactive prompt, you can type `exit()` and press Enter. On the Linux and Mac OS X versions of Python you can also exit the interpreter by pressing Ctrl-D. On Windows, the exit shortcut is Ctrl-Z followed by Enter.

1.2 Installing Flask

The next step is to install Flask, but before I go into that I want to tell you about the best practices associated with installing Python *packages*.

In Python, packages such as Flask are available in a public repository, from where anybody can download them and install them. The official Python package repository is called PyPI[7], which stands for Python Package Index (some people also refer to this repository as the "cheese shop"). Installing a package from PyPI is very simple, because Python comes with a tool called `pip` that does this work (in Python 2.7 `pip` does not come bundled with Python and needs to be installed separately).

To install a package on your machine, you use `pip` as follows:

---

[6] http://python.org/download/
[7] https://pypi.python.org/pypi

1.2. INSTALLING FLASK

```
$ pip install <package-name>
```

Interestingly, this method of installing packages will not work in most cases. If your Python interpreter was installed globally for all the users of your computer, chances are your regular user account is not going to have permission to make modifications to it, so the only way to make the command above work is to run it from an administrator account. But even without that complication, consider what happens when you install a package as above. The `pip` tool is going to download the package from PyPI, and then add it to your Python installation. From that point on, every Python script that you have on your system will have access to this package. Imagine a situation where you have completed a web application using version 0.11 of Flask, which was the most current version of Flask when you started, but now has been superseeded by version 0.12. You now want to start a second application, for which you'd like to use the 0.12 version, but if you replace the 0.11 version that you have installed you risk breaking your older application. Do you see the problem? It would be ideal if it was possible to install Flask 0.11 to be used by your old application, and also install Flask 0.12 for your new one.

To address the issue of maintaining different versions of packages for different applications, Python uses the concept of *virtual environments*. A virtual environment is a complete copy of the Python interpreter. When you install packages in a virtual environment, the system-wide Python interpreter is not affected, only the copy is. So the solution to have complete freedom to install any versions of your packages for each application is to use a different virtual environment for each application. Virtual environments have the added benefit that they are owned by the user who creates them, so they do not require an administrator account.

Let's start by creating a directory where the project will live. I'm going to call this directory *microblog*, since that is the name of the application:

```
$ mkdir microblog
$ cd microblog
```

If you are using a Python 3 version, virtual environment support is included in it, so all you need to do to create one is this:

```
$ python3 -m venv venv
```

With this command, I'm asking Python to run the `venv` package, which creates a virtual environment named `venv`. The first `venv` in the command is the name of the Python virtual environment package, and the second is the virtual environment name that I'm going to use for this particular environment. If you find this confusing, you can replace the second `venv` with a different name that you want to assign to your virtual environment. In general I create my virtual environments with the name `venv` in the project directory, so whenever I `cd` into a project I find its corresponding virtual environment.

Note that in some operating systems you may need to use `python` instead of `python3` in the command above. Some installations use `python` for Python 2.x releases and `python3` for the 3.x releases, while others map `python` to the 3.x releases.

After the command completes, you are going to have a directory named *venv* where the virtual environment files are stored.

If you are using any version of Python older than 3.4 (and that includes the 2.7 release), virtual environments are not supported natively. For those versions of Python, you need to download and install a third-party tool called virtualenv[8] before you can create virtual environments. Once virtualenv is installed, you can create a virtual environment with the following command:

```
$ virtualenv venv
```

Regardless of the method you used to create it, you should have your virtual environment created. Now you have to tell the system that you want to use it, and you do that by *activating* it. To activate your brand new virtual environment you use the following command:

```
$ source venv/bin/activate
(venv) $
```

If you are using a Microsoft Windows command prompt window, the activation command is slightly different:

```
$ venv\Scripts\activate
(venv) $
```

When you activate a virtual environment, the configuration of your terminal session is modified so that the Python interpreter stored inside it is the one that is invoked when you type `python`. Also, the terminal prompt is modified to include the name of the activated virtual environment. The changes made to your terminal session are all temporary and private to that session, so they will not persist when you close the terminal window. If you work with multiple terminal windows open at the same time, it is perfectly fine to have different virtual environments activated on each one.

---

[8]https://virtualenv.pypa.io

Now that you have a virtual environment created and activated, you can finally install Flask in it:

```
(venv) $ pip install flask
```

If you want to confirm that your virtual environment now has Flask installed, you can start the Python interpreter and *import* Flask into it:

```
>>> import flask
>>> _
```

If this statement does not give you any errors you can congratulate yourself, as Flask is installed and ready to be used.

1.3 A "Hello, World" Flask Application

If you go to the Flask website[9], you are welcomed with a very simple example application that has just five lines of code. Instead of repeating that trivial example, I'm going to show you a slightly more elaborate one that will give you a good base structure for writing larger applications.

The application will exist in a *package*. In Python, a sub-directory that includes a *__init__.py* file is considered a package, and can be imported. When you import a package, the *__init__.py* executes and defines what symbols the package exposes to the outside world.

Let's create a package called `app`, that will host the application. Make sure you are in the *microblog* directory and then run the following command:

```
(venv) $ mkdir app
```

The *__init__.py* for the `app` package is going to contain the following code:

Listing 1.1: *app/__init__.py*: Flask application instance

```
from flask import Flask

app = Flask(__name__)

from app import routes
```

---
[9]http://flask.pocoo.org/

The script above simply creates the application object as an instance of class `Flask` imported from the flask package. The __name__ variable passed to the `Flask` class is a Python predefined variable, which is set to the name of the module in which it is used. Flask uses the location of the module passed here as a starting point when it needs to load associated resources such as template files, which I will cover in Chapter 2. For all practical purposes, passing __name__ is almost always going to configure Flask in the correct way. The application then imports the `routes` module, which doesn't exist yet.

One aspect that may seem confusing at first is that there are two entities named `app`. The `app` package is defined by the *app* directory and the *__init__.py* script, and is referenced in the `from app import routes` statement. The `app` variable is defined as an instance of class `Flask` in the *__init__.py* script, which makes it a member of the `app` package.

Another peculiarity is that the `routes` module is imported at the bottom and not at the top of the script as it is always done. The bottom import is a workaround to *circular imports*, a common problem with Flask applications. You are going to see that the `routes` module needs to import the `app` variable defined in this script, so putting one of the reciprocal imports at the bottom avoids the error that results from the mutual references between these two files.

So what goes in the `routes` module? The routes are the different URLs that the application implements. In Flask, handlers for the application routes are written as Python functions, called *view functions*. View functions are mapped to one or more route URLs so that Flask knows what logic to execute when a client requests a given URL.

Here is the first view function for this application, which you need to write in a new module named *app/routes.py*:

Listing 1.2: *app/routes.py*: Home page route

```
from app import app

@app.route('/')
@app.route('/index')
def index():
    return "Hello, World!"
```

This view function is actually pretty simple, it just returns a greeting as a string. The two strange `@app.route` lines above the function are *decorators*, a unique feature of the Python language. A decorator modifies the function that follows it. A common pattern with decorators is to use them to register functions as callbacks for certain events. In this case, the `@app.route` decorator creates an association between the URL given as an argument and the function. In this example there are two decorators, which associate the URLs `/` and `/index` to this function. This means that when a web browser requests either of these two URLs, Flask is going to

1.3. A "HELLO, WORLD" FLASK APPLICATION

invoke this function and pass the return value of it back to the browser as a response. If this does not make complete sense yet, it will in a little bit when you run this application.

To complete the application, you need to have a Python script at the top-level that defines the Flask application instance. Let's call this script *microblog.py*, and define it as a single line that imports the application instance:

Listing 1.3: *microblog.py*: Main application module

```
from app import app
```

Remember the two `app` entities? Here you can see both together in the same sentence. The Flask application instance is called `app` and is a member of the `app` package. The `from app import app` statement imports the `app` variable that is a member of the `app` package. If you find this confusing, you can rename either the package or the variable to something else.

Just to make sure that you are doing everything correctly, below you can see a diagram of the project structure so far:

```
microblog/
  venv/
  app/
    __init__.py
    routes.py
  microblog.py
```

Believe it or not, this first version of the application is now complete! Before running it, though, Flask needs to be told how to import it, by setting the `FLASK_APP` environment variable:

```
(venv) $ export FLASK_APP=microblog.py
```

If you are using the Microsoft Windows command prompt, use `set` instead of `export` in the command above.

Are you ready to be blown away? You can run your first web application, with the following command:

```
(venv) $ flask run
 * Serving Flask app "microblog"
 * Running on http://127.0.0.1:5000/ (Press CTRL+C to quit)
```

After the server initializes it will wait for client connections. The output from `flask run` indicates that the server is running on IP address 127.0.0.1, which is always the address of your own computer. This address is so common that is also has a simpler name that you may have seen before: *localhost*. Network servers listen for connections on a specific port number. Applications deployed on production web servers typically listen on port 443, or sometimes 80 if they do not implement encryption, but access to these ports require administration rights. Since this application is running in a development environment, Flask uses the freely available port 5000. Now open up your web browser and enter the following URL in the address field:

```
http://localhost:5000/
```

Alternatively you can use this other URL:

```
http://localhost:5000/index
```

Do you see the application route mappings in action? The first URL maps to `/`, while the second maps to `/index`. Both routes are associated with the only view function in the application, so they produce the same output, which is the string that the function returns. If you enter any other URL you will get an error, since only these two URLs are recognized by the application.

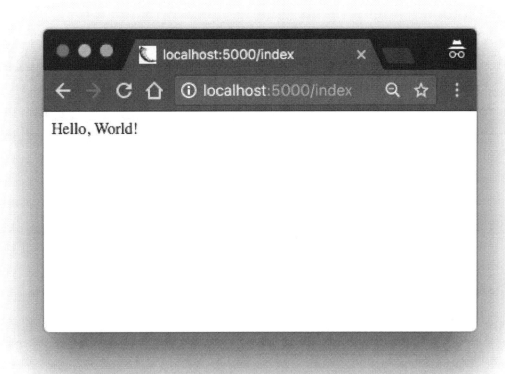

When you are done playing with the server you can just press Ctrl-C to stop it.

Congratulations, you have completed the first big step to become a web developer!

Chapter 2

Templates

After you complete Chapter 1, you should have a fully working, yet simple web application that has the following file structure:

```
microblog\
  venv\
  app\
    __init__.py
    routes.py
  microblog.py
```

To run the application you set the `FLASK_APP=microblog.py` in your terminal session, and then execute `flask run`. This starts a web server with the application, which you can open by typing the *http://localhost:5000/* URL in your web browser's address bar.

In this chapter you will continue working on the same application, and in particular, you are going to learn how to generate more elaborate web pages that have a complex structure and many dynamic components. If anything about the application or the development workflow so far isn't clear, please review Chapter 1 again before continuing.

The GitHub links for this chapter are: Browse[1], Zip[2], Diff[3].

---

[1] https://github.com/miguelgrinberg/microblog/tree/v0.2
[2] https://github.com/miguelgrinberg/microblog/archive/v0.2.zip
[3] https://github.com/miguelgrinberg/microblog/compare/v0.1...v0.2

2.1 What Are Templates?

I want the home page of my microblogging application to have a heading that welcomes the user. For the moment, I'm going to ignore the fact that the application does not have the concept of users yet, as this is going to come later. Instead, I'm going to use a *mock* user, which I'm going to implement as a Python dictionary, as follows:

```
user = {'username': 'Miguel'}
```

Creating mock objects is a useful technique that allows you to concentrate on one part of the application without having to worry about other parts of the system that don't exist yet. I want to design the home page of my application, and I don't want the fact that I don't have a user system in place to distract me, so I just make up a user object so that I can keep going.

The view function in the application returns a simple string. What I want to do now is expand that returned string into a complete HTML page, maybe something like this:

Listing 2.1: *app/routes.py*: Return complete HTML page from view function

```python
from app import app

@app.route('/')
@app.route('/index')
def index():
    user = {'username': 'Miguel'}
    return '''
<html>
    <head>
        <title>Home Page - Microblog</title>
    </head>
    <body>
        <h1>Hello, ''' + user['username'] + '''!</h1>
    </body>
</html>'''
```

If you are not familiar with HTML, I recommend that you read HTML Markup[4] on Wikipedia for a brief introduction.

Update the view function as shown above and give the application a try to see how it looks in your browser.

---

[4] https://en.wikipedia.org/wiki/HTML#Markup

2.1. WHAT ARE TEMPLATES?

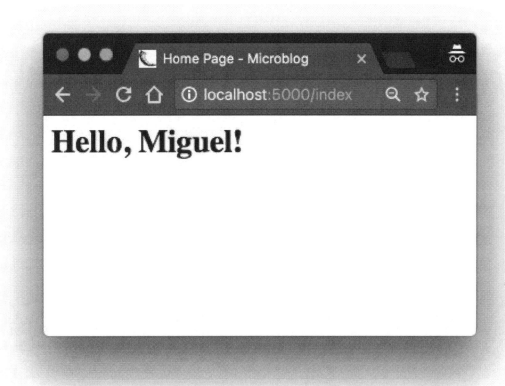

I hope you agree with me that the solution used above to deliver HTML to the browser is not good. Consider how complex the code in this view function will become when I have the blog posts from users, which are going to constantly change. The application is also going to have more view functions that are going to be associated with other URLs, so imagine if one day I decide to change the layout of this application, and have to update the HTML in every view function. This is clearly not an option that will scale as the application grows.

If you could keep the logic of your application separate from the layout or presentation of your web pages, then things would be much better organized, don't you think? You could even hire a web designer to create a killer web site while you code the application logic in Python.

Templates help achieve this separation between presentation and business logic. In Flask, templates are written as separate files, stored in a *templates* folder that is inside the application package. So after making sure that you are in the *microblog* directory, create the directory where templates will be stored:

```
(venv) $ mkdir app/templates
```

Below you can see your first template, which is similar in functionality to the HTML page returned by the `index()` view function above. Write this file in *app/templates/index.html*:

Listing 2.2: *app/templates/index.html*: Main page template

```html
<html>
    <head>
        <title>{{ title }} - Microblog</title>
    </head>
    <body>
        <h1>Hello, {{ user.username }}!</h1>
    </body>
</html>
```

This is a mostly standard, very simply HTML page. The only interesting thing in this page is that there are a couple of placeholders for the dynamic content, enclosed in `{{ ... }}` sections. These placeholders represent the parts of the page that are variable and will only be known at runtime.

Now that the presentation of the page was offloaded to the HTML template, the view function can be simplified:

Listing 2.3: *app/routes.py*: Use render_template() function

```python
from flask import render_template
from app import app

@app.route('/')
@app.route('/index')
def index():
    user = {'username': 'Miguel'}
    return render_template('index.html', title='Home', user=user)
```

This looks much better, right? Try this new version of the application to see how the template works. Once you have the page loaded in your browser, you may want to view the source HTML and compare it against the original template.

The operation that converts a template into a complete HTML page is called *rendering*. To render the template I had to import a function that comes with the Flask framework called `render_template()`. This function takes a template filename and a variable list of template arguments and returns the same template, but with all the placeholders in it replaced with actual values.

The `render_template()` function invokes the Jinja2[5] template engine that comes bundled with the Flask framework. Jinja2 substitutes `{{ ... }}` blocks with the corresponding values, given by the arguments provided in the `render_template()` call.

2.2 Conditional Statements

You have seen how Jinja2 replaces placeholders with actual values during rendering, but this is just one of many powerful operations Jinja2 supports in template files. For example, templates also support control statements, given inside `{% ... %}` blocks. The next version of the *index.html* template adds a conditional statement:

Listing 2.4: *app/templates/index.html*: Conditional statement in template

```html
<html>
    <head>
        {% if title %}
        <title>{{ title }} - Microblog</title>
        {% else %}
        <title>Welcome to Microblog!</title>
        {% endif %}
    </head>
    <body>
        <h1>Hello, {{ user.username }}!</h1>
    </body>
</html>
```

Now the template is a bit smarter. If the view function forgets to pass a value for the `title` placeholder variable, then instead of showing an empty title the template will provide a default one. You can try how this conditional works by removing the `title` argument in the `render_template()` call of the view function.

2.3 Loops

The logged in user will probably want to see recent posts from connected users in the home page, so what I'm going to do now is extend the application to support that.

Once again, I'm going to rely on the handy fake object trick to create some users and some posts to show:

---

[5]http://jinja.pocoo.org

Listing 2.5: *app/routes.py*: Fake posts in view function

```python
from flask import render_template
from app import app

@app.route('/')
@app.route('/index')
def index():
    user = {'username': 'Miguel'}
    posts = [
        {
            'author': {'username': 'John'},
            'body': 'Beautiful day in Portland!'
        },
        {
            'author': {'username': 'Susan'},
            'body': 'The Avengers movie was so cool!'
        }
    ]
    return render_template('index.html', title='Home', user=user, posts=posts)
```

To represent user posts I'm using a list, where each element is a dictionary that has `author` and `body` fields. When I get to implement users and blog posts for real I'm going to try to preserve these field names as much as possible, so that all the work I'm doing to design and test the home page template using these fake objects will continue to be valid when I introduce real users and posts.

On the template side I have to solve a new problem. The list of posts can have any number of elements, it is up to the view function to decide how many posts are going to be presented in the page. The template cannot make any assumptions about how many posts there are, so it needs to be prepared to render as many posts as the view sends in a generic way.

For this type of problem, Jinja2 offers a `for` control structure:

Listing 2.6: *app/templates/index.html*: for-loop in template

```html
<html>
    <head>
        {% if title %}
        <title>{{ title }} - Microblog</title>
        {% else %}
        <title>Welcome to Microblog</title>
        {% endif %}
    </head>
    <body>
        <h1>Hi, {{ user.username }}!</h1>
        {% for post in posts %}
        <div><p>{{ post.author.username }} says: <b>{{ post.body }}</b></p></div>
        {% endfor %}
    </body>
</html>
```

Simple, right? Give this new version of the application a try, and be sure to play with adding more content to the posts list to see how the template adapts and always renders all the posts the view function sends.

2.4 Template Inheritance

Most web applications these days have a navigation bar at the top of the page with a few frequently used links, such as a link to edit your profile, to login, logout, etc. I can easily add a navigation bar to the `index.html` template with some more HTML, but as the application grows I will be needing this same navigation bar in other pages. I don't really want to have to maintain several copies of the navigation bar in many HTML templates, it is a good practice to not repeat yourself if that is possible.

Jinja2 has a template inheritance feature that specifically addresses this problem. In essence, what you can do is move the parts of the page layout that are common to all templates to a base template, from which all other templates are derived.

So what I'm going to do now is define a base template called `base.html` that includes a simple navigation bar and also the title logic I implemented earlier. You need to write the following template in file *app/templates/base.html*:

Listing 2.7: *app/templates/base.html*: Base template with navigation bar

```
<html>
    <head>
      {% if title %}
      <title>{{ title }} - Microblog</title>
      {% else %}
      <title>Welcome to Microblog</title>
      {% endif %}
    </head>
    <body>
        <div>Microblog: <a href="/index">Home</a></div>
        <hr>
        {% block content %}{% endblock %}
    </body>
</html>
```

In this template I used the `block` control statement to define the place where the derived templates can insert themselves. Blocks are given a unique name, which derived templates can reference when they provide their content.

With the base template in place, I can now simplify *index.html* by making it inherit from *base.html*:

Listing 2.8: *app/templates/index.html*: Inherit from base template

```
{% extends "base.html" %}

{% block content %}
    <h1>Hi, {{ user.username }}!</h1>
    {% for post in posts %}
    <div><p>{{ post.author.username }} says: <b>{{ post.body }}</b></p></div>
    {% endfor %}
{% endblock %}
```

Since the *base.html* template will now take care of the general page structure, I have removed all those elements from *index.html* and left only the content part. The `extends` statement establishes the inheritance link between the two templates, so that Jinja2 knows that when it is asked to render `index.html` it needs to embed it inside `base.html`. The two templates have matching `block` statements with name `content`, and this is how Jinja2 knows how to combine the two templates into one. Now if I need to create additional pages for the application, I can

2.4. TEMPLATE INHERITANCE

create them as derived templates from the same *base.html* template, and that is how I can have all the pages of the application sharing the same look and feel without duplication.

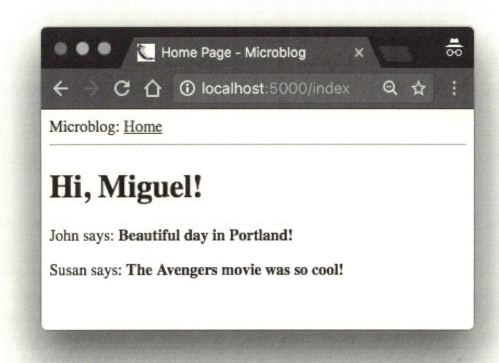

Chapter 3

Web Forms

In Chapter 2 I created a simple template for the home page of the application, and used fake objects as placeholders for things I don't have yet, like users or blog posts. In this chapter I'm going to address one of the many holes I still have in this application, specifically how to accept input from users through web forms.

Web forms are one of the most basic building blocks in any web application. I will be using forms to allow users to submit blog posts, and also for logging in to the application.

Before you proceed with this chapter, make sure you have the *microblog* application as I left it in the previous chapter installed, and that you can run it without any errors.

The GitHub links for this chapter are: Browse[1], Zip[2], Diff[3].

3.1 Introduction to Flask-WTF

To handle the web forms in this application I'm going to use the Flask-WTF[4] extension, which is a thin wrapper around the WTForms[5] package that nicely integrates it with Flask. This is the first Flask extension that I'm presenting to you, but it is not going to be the last. Extensions are a very important part of the Flask ecosystem, as they provide solutions to problems that Flask is intentionally not opinionated about.

---

[1] https://github.com/miguelgrinberg/microblog/tree/v0.3
[2] https://github.com/miguelgrinberg/microblog/archive/v0.3.zip
[3] https://github.com/miguelgrinberg/microblog/compare/v0.2...v0.3
[4] http://packages.python.org/Flask-WTF
[5] https://wtforms.readthedocs.io/

Flask extensions are regular Python packages that are installed with `pip`. You can go ahead and install Flask-WTF in your virtual environment:

```
(venv) $ pip install flask-wtf
```

3.2 Configuration

So far the application is very simple, and for that reason I did not need to worry about its *configuration*. But for any applications except the simplest ones, you are going to find that Flask (and possibly also the Flask extensions that you use) offer some amount of freedom in how to do things, and you need to make some decisions, which you pass to the framework as a list of configuration variables.

There are several formats for the application to specify configuration options. The most basic solution is to define your variables as keys in `app.config`, which uses a dictionary style to work with variables. For example, you could do something like this:

```python
app = Flask(__name__)
app.config['SECRET_KEY'] = 'you-will-never-guess'
# ... add more variables here as needed
```

While the above syntax is sufficient to create configuration options for Flask, I like to enforce the principle of *separation of concerns*, so instead of putting my configuration in the same place where I create my application I will use a slightly more elaborate structure that allows me to keep my configuration in a separate file.

A format that I really like because it is very extensible, is to use a class to store configuration variables. To keep things nicely organized, I'm going to create the configuration class in a separate Python module. Below you can see the new configuration class for this application, stored in a *config.py* module in the top-level directory.

Listing 3.1: *config.py*: Secret key configuration

```python
import os

class Config(object):
    SECRET_KEY = os.environ.get('SECRET_KEY') or 'you-will-never-guess'
```

Pretty simple, right? The configuration settings are defined as class variables inside the `Config` class. As the application needs more configuration items, they can be added to this class, and

3.2. CONFIGURATION

later if I find that I need to have more than one configuration set, I can create subclasses of it. But don't worry about this just yet.

The `SECRET_KEY` configuration variable that I added as the only configuration item is an important part in most Flask applications. Flask and some of its extensions use the value of the secret key as a cryptographic key, useful to generate signatures or tokens. The Flask-WTF extension uses it to protect web forms against a nasty attack called Cross-Site Request Forgery[6] or CSRF (pronounced "seasurf"). As its name implies, the secret key is supposed to be secret, as the strength of the tokens and signatures generated with it depends on no person outside of the trusted maintainers of the application knowing it.

The value of the secret key is set as an expression with two terms, joined by the `or` operator. The first term looks for the value of an environment variable, also called `SECRET_KEY`. The second term, is just a hardcoded string. This is a pattern that you will see me repeat often for configuration variables. The idea is that a value sourced from an environment variable is preferred, but if the environment does not define the variable, then the hardcoded string is used instead. When you are developing this application, the security requirements are low, so you can just ignore this setting and let the hardcoded string be used. But when this application is deployed on a production server, I will be setting a unique and difficult to guess value in the environment, so that the server has a secure key that nobody else knows.

Now that I have a config file, I need to tell Flask to read it and apply it. That can be done right after the Flask application instance is created using the `app.config.from_object()` method:

Listing 3.2: *app/__init__.py*: Flask configuration

```
from flask import Flask
from config import Config

app = Flask(__name__)
app.config.from_object(Config)

from app import routes
```

The way I'm importing the `Config` class may seem confusing at first, but if you look at how the `Flask` class (uppercase "F") is imported from the `flask` package (lowercase "f") you'll notice that I'm doing the same with the configuration. The lowercase "config" is the name of the Python module *config.py*, and obviously the one with the uppercase "C" is the actual class.

As I mentioned above, the configuration items can be accessed with a dictionary syntax from `app.config`. Here you can see a quick session with the Python interpreter where I check

---

[6]http://en.wikipedia.org/wiki/Cross-site_request_forgery

what is the value of the secret key:

```
>>> from microblog import app
>>> app.config['SECRET_KEY']
'you-will-never-guess'
```

3.3 User Login Form

The Flask-WTF extension uses Python classes to represent web forms. A form class simply defines the fields of the form as class variables.

Once again having separation of concerns in mind, I'm going to use a new *app/forms.py* module to store my web form classes. To begin, let's define a user login form, which asks the user to enter a username and a password. The form will also include a "remember me" check box, and a submit button:

Listing 3.3: *app/forms.py*: Login form

```
from flask_wtf import FlaskForm
from wtforms import StringField, PasswordField, BooleanField, SubmitField
from wtforms.validators import DataRequired

class LoginForm(FlaskForm):
    username = StringField('Username', validators=[DataRequired()])
    password = PasswordField('Password', validators=[DataRequired()])
    remember_me = BooleanField('Remember Me')
    submit = SubmitField('Sign In')
```

Most Flask extensions use a `flask_<name>` naming convention for their top-level import symbol. In this case, Flask-WTF has all its symbols under `flask_wtf`. This is where the `FlaskForm` base class is imported from at the top of *app/forms.py*.

The four classes that represent the field types that I'm using for this form are imported directly from the WTForms package, since the Flask-WTF extension does not provide customized versions. For each field, an object is created as a class variable in the `LoginForm` class. Each field is given a description or label as a first argument.

The optional `validators` argument that you see in some of the fields is used to attach validation behaviors to fields. The `DataRequired` validator simply checks that the field is not submitted empty. There are many more validators available, some of which will be used in other forms.

3.4 Form Templates

The next step is to add the form to an HTML template so that it can be rendered on a web page. The good news is that the fields that are defined in the `LoginForm` class know how to render themselves as HTML, so this task is fairly simple. Below you can see the login template, which I'm going to store in file *app/templates/login.html*:

Listing 3.4: *app/templates/login.html*: Login form template

```
{% extends "base.html" %}

{% block content %}
    <h1>Sign In</h1>
    <form action="" method="post">
        {{ form.hidden_tag() }}
        <p>
            {{ form.username.label }}<br>
            {{ form.username(size=32) }}
        </p>
        <p>
            {{ form.password.label }}<br>
            {{ form.password(size=32) }}
        </p>
        <p>{{ form.remember_me() }} {{ form.remember_me.label }}</p>
        <p>{{ form.submit() }}</p>
    </form>
{% endblock %}
```

For this template I'm reusing one more time the `base.html` template as shown in Chapter 2, through the `extends` template inheritance statement. I will actually do this with all the templates, to ensure a consistent layout that includes a top navigation bar across all the pages of the application.

This template expects a form object instantiated from the `LoginForm` class to be given as an argument, which you can see referenced as `form`. This argument will be sent by the login view function, which I still haven't written.

The HTML `<form>` element is used as a container for the web form. The `action` attribute of the form is used to tell the browser the URL that should be used when submitting the information the user entered in the form. When the action is set to an empty string the form is submitted to the URL that is currently in the address bar, which is the URL that rendered the form on the page. The `method` attribute specifies the HTTP request method that should be used when submitting the form to the server. The default is to send it with a `GET` request, but in almost all cases, using a `POST` request makes for a better user experience because requests of this type can submit the form data in the body of the request, while `GET` requests add the form fields to the URL, cluttering the browser address bar.

The `form.hidden_tag()` template argument generates a hidden field that includes a token that is used to protect the form against CSRF attacks. All you need to do to have the form protected is include this hidden field and have the `SECRET_KEY` variable defined in the Flask configuration. If you take care of these two things, Flask-WTF does the rest for you.

If you've written HTML web forms in the past, you may have found it odd that there are no HTML fields in this template. This is because the fields from the form object know how to render themselves as HTML. All I needed to do was to include `{{ form.<field_name>.label }}` where I wanted the field label, and `{{ form.<field_name>() }}` where I wanted the field. For fields that require additional HTML attributes, those can be passed as arguments. The username and password fields in this template take the `size` as an argument that will be added to the `<input>` HTML element as an attribute. This is how you can also attach CSS classes or IDs to form fields.

3.5 Form Views

The final step before you can see this form in the browser is to code a new view function in the application that renders the template from the previous section.

So let's write a new view function mapped to the */login* URL that creates a form, and passes it to the template for rendering. This view function can also go in the *app/routes.py* module with the previous one:

Listing 3.5: *app/routes.py*: Login view function

```python
from flask import render_template
from app import app
from app.forms import LoginForm

# ...

@app.route('/login')
def login():
    form = LoginForm()
    return render_template('login.html', title='Sign In', form=form)
```

What I did here is import the `LoginForm` class from *forms.py*, instantiated an object from it, and sent it down to the template. The `form=form` syntax may look odd, but is simply passing the `form` object created in the line above (and shown on the right side) to the template with the name `form` (shown on the left). This is all that is required to get form fields rendered.

To make it easy to access the login form, the base template can include a link to it in the navigation bar:

3.5. FORM VIEWS

Listing 3.6: *app/templates/base.html*: Login link in navigation bar

```
<div>
    Microblog:
    <a href="/index">Home</a>
    <a href="/login">Login</a>
</div>
```

At this point you can run the application and see the form in your web browser. With the application running, type `http://localhost:5000/` in the browser's address bar, and then click on the "Login" link in the top navigation bar to see the new login form. Pretty cool, right?

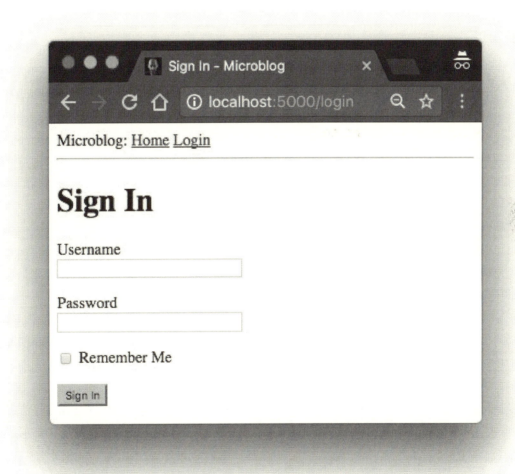

3.6 Receiving Form Data

If you try to press the submit button the browser is going to display a "Method Not Allowed" error. This is because the login view function from the previous section does one half of the job so far. It can display the form on a web page, but it has no logic to process data submitted by the user yet. This is another area where Flask-WTF makes the job really easy. Here is an updated version of the view function that accepts and validates the data submitted by the user:

Listing 3.7: *app/routes.py*: Receiving login credentials

```python
from flask import render_template, flash, redirect

@app.route('/login', methods=['GET', 'POST'])
def login():
    form = LoginForm()
    if form.validate_on_submit():
        flash('Login requested for user {}, remember_me={}'.format(
            form.username.data, form.remember_me.data))
        return redirect('/index')
    return render_template('login.html', title='Sign In', form=form)
```

The first new thing in this version is the `methods` argument in the route decorator. This tells Flask that this view function accepts `GET` and `POST` requests, overriding the default, which is to accept only `GET` requests. The HTTP protocol states that `GET` requests are those that return information to the client (the web browser in this case). All the requests in the application so far are of this type. `POST` requests are typically used when the browser submits form data to the server (in reality `GET` requests can also be used for this purpose, but it is not a recommended practice). The "Method Not Allowed" error that the browser showed you before, appears because the browser tried to send a `POST` request and the application was not configured to accept it. By providing the `methods` argument, you are telling Flask which request methods should be accepted.

The `form.validate_on_submit()` method does all the form processing work. When the browser sends the `GET` request to receive the web page with the form, this method is going to return `False`, so in that case the function skips the if statement and goes directly to render the template in the last line of the function.

When the browser sends the `POST` request as a result of the user pressing the submit button, `form.validate_on_submit()` is going to gather all the data, run all the validators attached to fields, and if everything is all right it will return `True`, indicating that the data is valid and can be processed by the application. But if at least one field fails validation, then the function will return `False`, and that will cause the form to be rendered back to the user, like in the `GET` request case. Later I'm going to add an error message when validation fails.

3.6. RECEIVING FORM DATA

When `form.validate_on_submit()` returns `True`, the login view function calls two new functions, imported from Flask. The `flash()` function is a useful way to show a message to the user. A lot of applications use this technique to let the user know if some action has been successful or not. In this case, I'm going to use this mechanism as a temporary solution, because I don't have all the infrastructure necessary to log users in for real yet. The best I can do for now is show a message that confirms that the application received the credentials.

The second new function used in the login view function is `redirect()`. This function instructs the client web browser to automatically navigate to a different page, given as an argument. This view function uses it to redirect the user to the index page of the application.

When you call the `flash()` function, Flask stores the message, but flashed messages will not magically appear in web pages. The templates of the application need to render these flashed messages in a way that works for the site layout. I'm going to add these messages to the base template, so that all the templates inherit this functionality. This is the updated base template:

Listing 3.8: *app/templates/base.html*: Flashed messages in base template

```
<html>
    <head>
        {% if title %}
        <title>{{ title }} - microblog</title>
        {% else %}
        <title>microblog</title>
        {% endif %}
    </head>
    <body>
        <div>
            Microblog:
            <a href="/index">Home</a>
            <a href="/login">Login</a>
        </div>
        <hr>
        {% with messages = get_flashed_messages() %}
        {% if messages %}
        <ul>
            {% for message in messages %}
            <li>{{ message }}</li>
            {% endfor %}
        </ul>
        {% endif %}
        {% endwith %}
        {% block content %}{% endblock %}
    </body>
</html>
```

Here I'm using a `with` construct to assign the result of calling `get_flashed_messages()` to a `messages` variable, all in the context of the template. The `get_flashed_messages()` function comes from Flask, and returns a list of all the messages that have been registered with `flash()` previously. The conditional that follows checks if `messages` has some content, and in that case, a `<ul>` element is rendered with each message as a `<li>` list item. This style of rendering does not look great, but the topic of styling the web application will come later.

An interesting property of these flashed messages is that once they are requested once through the `get_flashed_messages` function they are removed from the message list, so they appear only once after the `flash()` function is called.

This is a great time to try the application one more time and test how the form works. Make sure you try submitting the form with the username or password fields empty, to see how the `DataRequired` validator halts the submission process.

3.7 Improving Field Validation

The validators that are attached to form fields prevent invalid data from being accepted into the application. The way the application deals with invalid form input is by re-displaying the form, to let the user make the necessary corrections.

If you tried to submit invalid data, I'm sure you noticed that while the validation mechanisms work well, there is no indication given to the user that something is wrong with the form, the user simply gets the form back. The next task is to improve the user experience by adding a meaningful error message next to each field that failed validation.

In fact, the form validators generate these descriptive error messages already, so all that is missing is some additional logic in the template to render them.

Here is the login template with added field validation messages in the username and password fields:

Listing 3.9: *app/templates/login.html*: Validation errors in login form template

```
{% extends "base.html" %}

{% block content %}
    <h1>Sign In</h1>
    <form action="" method="post">
        {{ form.hidden_tag() }}
        <p>
            {{ form.username.label }}<br>
            {{ form.username(size=32) }}<br>
            {% for error in form.username.errors %}
            <span style="color: red;">[{{ error }}]</span>
            {% endfor %}
        </p>
        <p>
```

3.7. IMPROVING FIELD VALIDATION

```
            {{ form.password.label }}<br>
            {{ form.password(size=32) }}<br>
            {% for error in form.password.errors %}
            <span style="color: red;">[{{ error }}]</span>
            {% endfor %}
        </p>
        <p>{{ form.remember_me() }} {{ form.remember_me.label }}</p>
        <p>{{ form.submit() }}</p>
    </form>
{% endblock %}
```

The only change I've made is to add for loops right after the username and password fields that render the error messages added by the validators in red color. As a general rule, any fields that have validators attached will have any error messages that result from validation added under `form.<field_name>.errors`. This is going to be a list, because fields can have multiple validators attached and more than one may be providing error messages to display to the user.

If you try to submit the form with an empty username or password, you will now get a nice error message in red.

3.8 Generating Links

The login form is fairly complete now, but before closing this chapter I wanted to discuss the proper way to include links in templates and redirects. So far you have seen a few instances in which links are defined. For example, this is the current navigation bar in the base template:

```
<div>
    Microblog:
    <a href="/index">Home</a>
```

3.8. GENERATING LINKS

```
        <a href="/login">Login</a>
    </div>
```

The login view function also defines a link that is passed to the `redirect()` function:

```
@app.route('/login', methods=['GET', 'POST'])
def login():
    form = LoginForm()
    if form.validate_on_submit():
        # ...
        return redirect('/index')
    # ...
```

One problem with writing links directly in templates and source files is that if one day you decide to reorganize your links, then you are going to have to search and replace these links in your entire application.

To have better control over these links, Flask provides a function called `url_for()`, which generates URLs using its internal mapping of URLs to view functions. For example, the expression `url_for('login')` returns `/login`, and `url_for('index')` return `'/index`. The argument to `url_for()` is the *endpoint* name, which is the name of the view function.

You may ask why is it better to use the function names instead of URLs. The fact is that URLs are much more likely to change than view function names, which are completely internal. A secondary reason is that as you will learn later, some URLs have dynamic components in them, so generating those URLs by hand would require concatenating multiple elements, which is tedious and error prone. The `url_for()` is also able to generate these complex URLs.

So from now on, I'm going to use `url_for()` every time I need to generate an application URL. The navigation bar in the base template then becomes:

Listing 3.10: *app/templates/base.html*: Use url_for() function for links

```
<div>
    Microblog:
    <a href="{{ url_for('index') }}">Home</a>
    <a href="{{ url_for('login') }}">Login</a>
</div>
```

And here is the updated `login()` view function:

Listing 3.11: *app/routes.py*: Use url_for() function for links

```python
from flask import render_template, flash, redirect, url_for

# ...

@app.route('/login', methods=['GET', 'POST'])
def login():
    form = LoginForm()
    if form.validate_on_submit():
        # ...
        return redirect(url_for('index'))
    # ...
```

Chapter 4

Database

The topic of this chapter is extremely important. For most applications, there is going to be a need to maintain persistent data that can be retrieved efficiently, and this is exactly what *databases* are made for.

The GitHub links for this chapter are: Browse[1], Zip[2], Diff[3].

4.1 Databases in Flask

As I'm sure you have heard already, Flask does not support databases natively. This is one of the many areas in which Flask is intentionally not opinionated, which is great, because you have the freedom to choose the database that best fits your application instead of being forced to adapt to one.

There are great choices for databases in Python, many of them with Flask extensions that make a better integration with the application. The databases can be separated into two big groups, those that follow the *relational* model, and those that do not. The latter group is often called *NoSQL*, indicating that they do not implement the popular relational query language SQL[4]. While there are great database products in both groups, my opinion is that relational databases are a better match for applications that have structured data such as lists of users, blog posts, etc., while NoSQL databases tend to be better for data that has a less defined structure. This application, like most others, can be implemented using either type of database, but for the

---

[1] https://github.com/miguelgrinberg/microblog/tree/v0.4
[2] https://github.com/miguelgrinberg/microblog/archive/v0.4.zip
[3] https://github.com/miguelgrinberg/microblog/compare/v0.3...v0.4
[4] https://en.wikipedia.org/wiki/SQL

reasons stated above, I'm going to go with a relational database.

In Chapter 3 I showed you a first Flask extension. In this chapter I'm going to use two more. The first is Flask-SQLAlchemy[5], an extension that provides a Flask-friendly wrapper to the popular SQLAlchemy[6] package, which is an Object Relational Mapper[7] or ORM. ORMs allow applications to manage a database using high-level entities such as classes, objects and methods instead of tables and SQL. The job of the ORM is to translate the high-level operations into database commands.

The nice thing about SQLAlchemy is that it is an ORM not for one, but for many relational databases. SQLAlchemy supports a long list of database engines, including the popular MySQL[8], PostgreSQL[9] and SQLite[10]. This is extremely powerful, because you can do your development using a simple SQLite database that does not require a server, and then when the time comes to deploy the application on a production server you can choose a more robust MySQL or PostgreSQL server, without having to change your application.

To install Flask-SQLAlchemy in your virtual environment, make sure you have activated it first, and then run:

```
(venv) $ pip install flask-sqlalchemy
```

4.2 Database Migrations

Most database tutorials I've seen cover creation and use of a database, but do not adequately address the problem of making updates to an existing database as the application needs change or grow. This is hard because relational databases are centered around structured data, so when the structure changes the data that is already in the database needs to be *migrated* to the modified structure.

The second extension that I'm going to present in this chapter is Flask-Migrate[11], which is actually one created by yours truly. This extension is a Flask wrapper for Alembic[12], a database migration framework for SQLAlchemy. Working with database migrations adds a bit of work

---

[5]http://packages.python.org/Flask-SQLAlchemy
[6]http://www.sqlalchemy.org
[7]http://en.wikipedia.org/wiki/Object-relational_mapping
[8]https://www.mysql.com/
[9]https://www.postgresql.org/
[10]https://www.sqlite.org/
[11]https://github.com/miguelgrinberg/flask-migrate
[12]https://bitbucket.org/zzzeek/alembic

4.3 Flask-SQLAlchemy Configuration

to get a database started, but that is a small price to pay for a robust way to make changes to your database in the future.

The installation process for Flask-Migrate is similar to other extensions you have seen:

```
(venv) $ pip install flask-migrate
```

4.3 Flask-SQLAlchemy Configuration

During development, I'm going to use a SQLite database. SQLite databases are the most convenient choice for developing small applications, sometimes even not so small ones, as each database is stored in a single file on disk and there is no need to run a database server like MySQL and PostgreSQL.

We have two new configuration items to add to the config file:

Listing 4.1: *config.py*: Flask-SQLAlchemy configuration

```
import os
basedir = os.path.abspath(os.path.dirname(__file__))

class Config(object):
    # ...
    SQLALCHEMY_DATABASE_URI = os.environ.get('DATABASE_URL') or \
        'sqlite:///' + os.path.join(basedir, 'app.db')
    SQLALCHEMY_TRACK_MODIFICATIONS = False
```

The Flask-SQLAlchemy extension takes the location of the application's database from the `SQLALCHEMY_DATABASE_URI` configuration variable. As you recall from Chapter 3, it is in general a good practice to set configuration from environment variables, and provide a fallback value when the environment does not define the variable. In this case I'm taking the database URL from the `DATABASE_URL` environment variable, and if that isn't defined, I'm configuring a database named *app.db* located in the main directory of the application, which is stored in the `basedir` variable.

The `SQLALCHEMY_TRACK_MODIFICATIONS` configuration option is set to `False` to disable a feature of Flask-SQLAlchemy that I do not need, which is to signal the application every time a change is about to be made in the database.

The database is going to be represented in the application by the *database instance*. The database migration engine will also have an instance. These are objects that need to be created after the application, in the *app/__init__.py* file:

Listing 4.2: *app/__init__.py*: Flask-SQLAlchemy and Flask-Migrate initialization

```
from flask import Flask
from config import Config
from flask_sqlalchemy import SQLAlchemy
from flask_migrate import Migrate

app = Flask(__name__)
app.config.from_object(Config)
db = SQLAlchemy(app)
migrate = Migrate(app, db)

from app import routes, models
```

I have made three changes to the init script. First, I have added a `db` object that represents the database. Then I have added another object that represents the migration engine. Hopefully you see a pattern in how to work with Flask extensions. Most extensions are initialized as these two. Finally, I'm importing a new module called `models` at the bottom. This module will define the structure of the database.

4.4 Database Models

The data that will be stored in the database will be represented by a collection of classes, usually called *database models*. The ORM layer within SQLAlchemy will do the translations required to map objects created from these classes into rows in the proper database tables.

Let's start by creating a model that represents users. Using the WWW SQL Designer[13] tool, I have made the following diagram to represent the data that we want to use in the users table:

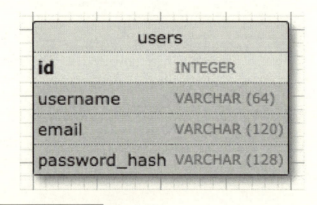

---
[13]http://ondras.zarovi.cz/sql/demo

4.4. DATABASE MODELS

The `id` field is usually in all models, and is used as the *primary key*. Each user in the database will be assigned a unique id value, stored in this field. Primary keys are, in most cases, automatically assigned by the database, so I just need to provide the `id` field marked as a primary key.

The `username`, `email` and `password_hash` fields are defined as strings (or `VARCHAR` in database jargon), and their maximum lengths are specified so that the database can optimize space usage. While the `username` and `email` fields are self-explanatory, the `password_hash` fields deserves some attention. I want to make sure the application that I'm building adopts security best practices, and for that reason I will not be storing user passwords in the database. The problem with storing passwords is that if the database ever becomes compromised, the attackers will have access to the passwords, and that could be devastating for users. Instead of writing the passwords directly, I'm going to write *password hashes*, which greatly improve security. This is going to be the topic of another chapter, so don't worry about it too much for now.

So now that I know what I want for my users table, I can translate that into code in the new *app/models.py* module:

Listing 4.3: *app/models.py*: User database model

```python
from app import db

class User(db.Model):
    id = db.Column(db.Integer, primary_key=True)
    username = db.Column(db.String(64), index=True, unique=True)
    email = db.Column(db.String(120), index=True, unique=True)
    password_hash = db.Column(db.String(128))

    def __repr__(self):
        return '<User {}>'.format(self.username)
```

The `User` class created above inherits from `db.Model`, a base class for all models from Flask-SQLAlchemy. This class defines several fields as class variables. Fields are created as instances of the `db.Column` class, which takes the field type as an argument, plus other optional arguments that, for example, allow me to indicate which fields are unique and indexed, which is important so that database searches are efficient.

The `__repr__` method tells Python how to print objects of this class, which is going to be useful for debugging. You can see the `__repr__()` method in action in the Python interpreter session below:

```
>>> from app.models import User
>>> u = User(username='susan', email='susan@example.com')
>>> u
<User susan>
```

4.5 Creating The Migration Repository

The model class created in the previous section defines the initial database structure (or *schema*) for this application. But as the application continues to grow, it is likely that I will need to make changes to that structure such as adding new things, and sometimes to modify or remove items. Alembic (the migration framework used by Flask-Migrate) will make these schema changes in a way that does not require the database to be recreated from scratch every time a change needs to be made.

To accomplish this seemingly difficult task, Alembic maintains a *migration repository*, which is a directory in which it stores its migration scripts. Each time a change is made to the database schema, a migration script is added to the repository with the details of the change. To apply the migrations to a database, these migration scripts are executed in the sequence they were created.

Flask-Migrate exposes its commands through the `flask` command. You have already seen `flask run`, which is a sub-command that is native to Flask. The `flask db` sub-command is added by Flask-Migrate to manage everything related to database migrations. So let's create the migration repository for microblog by running `flask db init`:

```
(venv) $ flask db init
  Creating directory /home/miguel/microblog/migrations ... done
  Creating directory /home/miguel/microblog/migrations/versions ... done
  Generating /home/miguel/microblog/migrations/alembic.ini ... done
  Generating /home/miguel/microblog/migrations/env.py ... done
  Generating /home/miguel/microblog/migrations/README ... done
  Generating /home/miguel/microblog/migrations/script.py.mako ... done
  Please edit configuration/connection/logging settings in
  '/home/miguel/microblog/migrations/alembic.ini' before proceeding.
```

Remember that the `flask` command relies on the `FLASK_APP` environment variable to know where the Flask application lives. For this application, you want to set `FLASK_APP` to the value `microblog.py`, as discussed in Chapter 1.

After you run this command, you will find a new *migrations* directory, with a few files and a *versions* sub-directory inside. All these files should be treated as part of your project from now on, and in particular, should be added to source control along with your application code.

4.6 The First Database Migration

With the migration repository in place, it is time to create the first database migration, which will include the users table that maps to the `User` database model. There are two ways to create a database migration: manually or automatically. To generate a migration automatically, Alembic compares the database schema as defined by the database models, against the actual database schema currently used in the database. It then populates the migration script with the changes necessary to make the database schema match the application models. In this case, since there is no previous database, the automatic migration will add the entire `User` model to the migration script. The `flask db migrate` sub-command generates these automatic migrations:

```
(venv) $ flask db migrate -m "users table"
INFO  [alembic.runtime.migration] Context impl SQLiteImpl.
INFO  [alembic.runtime.migration] Will assume non-transactional DDL.
INFO  [alembic.autogenerate.compare] Detected added table 'user'
INFO  [alembic.autogenerate.compare] Detected added index 'ix_user_email' on '['email']'
INFO  [alembic.autogenerate.compare] Detected added index 'ix_user_username' on '['username']'
  Generating /home/miguel/microblog/migrations/versions/e517276bb1c2_users_table.py ... done
```

The output of the command gives you an idea of what Alembic included in the migration. The first two lines are informational and can usually be ignored. It then says that it found a user table and two indexes. Then it tells you where it wrote the migration script. The `e517276bb1c2` code is an automatically generated unique code for the migration (it will be different for you). The comment given with the `-m` option is optional, it adds a short descriptive text to the migration.

The generated migration script is now part of your project, and needs to be incorporated to source control. You are welcome to inspect the script if you are curious to see how it looks. You will find that it has two functions called `upgrade()` and `downgrade()`. The `upgrade()` function applies the migration, and the `downgrade()` function removes it. This allows Alembic to migrate the database to any point in the history, even to older versions, by using the downgrade path.

The `flask db migrate` command does not make any changes to the database, it just generates the migration script. To apply the changes to the database, the `flask db upgrade` command must be used.

```
(venv) $ flask db upgrade
INFO  [alembic.runtime.migration] Context impl SQLiteImpl.
INFO  [alembic.runtime.migration] Will assume non-transactional DDL.
INFO  [alembic.runtime.migration] Running upgrade  -> e517276bb1c2, users table
```

Because this application uses SQLite, the `upgrade` command will detect that a database does not exist and will create it (you will notice a file named *app.db* is added after this command finishes, that is the SQLite database). When working with database servers such as MySQL and PostgreSQL, you have to create the database in the database server before running `upgrade`.

Note that Flask-SQLAlchemy uses a "snake case" naming conversion for database tables by default. For the `User` model above, the corresponding table in the database will be named `user`. For a `AddressAndPhone` model class, the table would be named `address_and_phone`. If you prefer to choose your own table names, you can add an attribute named `__tablename__` to the model class, set to the desired name as a string.

4.7 Database Upgrade and Downgrade Workflow

The application is in its infancy at this point, but it does not hurt to discuss what is going to be the database migration strategy going forward. Imagine that you have your application on your development machine, and also have a copy deployed to a production server that is online and in use.

Let's say that for the next release of your app you have to introduce a change to your models, for example a new table needs to be added. Without migrations you would need to figure out how to change the schema of your database, both in your development machine and then again in your server, and this could be a lot of work.

But with database migration support, after you modify the models in your application you generate a new migration script (`flask db migrate`), you probably review it to make sure the automatic generation did the right thing, and then apply the changes to your development database (`flask db upgrade`). You will add the migration script to source control and commit it.

When you are ready to release the new version of the application to your production server, all you need to do is grab the updated version of your application, which will include the new migration script, and run `flask db upgrade`. Alembic will detect that the production database is not updated to the latest revision of the schema, and run all the new migration scripts that were created after the previous release.

As I mentioned earlier, you also have a `flask db downgrade` command, which undoes the last migration. While you will be unlikely to need this option on a production system, you may find it very useful during development. You may have generated a migration script and applied it, only to find that the changes that you made are not exactly what you need. In this case, you can downgrade the database, delete the migration script, and then generate a new one to

4.8 Database Relationships

replace it.

Relational databases are good at storing relations between data items. Consider the case of a user writing a blog post. The user will have a record in the `users` table, and the post will have a record in the `posts` table. The most efficient way to record who wrote a given post is to link the two related records.

Once a link between a user and a post is established, the database can answer queries about this link. The most trivial one is when you have a blog post and need to know what user wrote it. A more complex query is the reverse of this one. If you have a user, you may want to know all the posts that this user wrote. Flask-SQLAlchemy will help with both types of queries.

Let's expand the database to store blog posts to see relationships in action. Here is the schema for a new `posts` table:

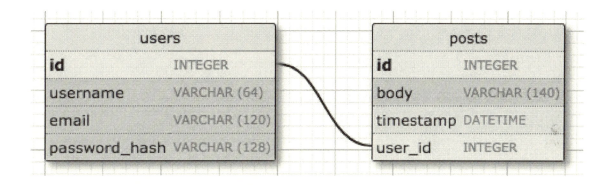

The `posts` table will have the required `id`, the `body` of the post and a `timestamp`. But in addition to these expected fields, I'm adding a `user_id` field, which links the post to its author. You've seen that all users have a `id` primary key, which is unique. The way to link a blog post to the user that authored it is to add a reference to the user's `id`, and that is exactly what the `user_id` field is. This `user_id` field is called a *foreign key*. The database diagram above shows foreign keys as a link between the field and the `id` field of the table it refers to. This kind of relationship is called a *one-to-many*, because "one" user writes "many" posts.

The modified *app/models.py* is shown below:

Listing 4.4: *app/models.py*: Posts database table and relationship

```
from datetime import datetime
from app import db

class User(db.Model):
    id = db.Column(db.Integer, primary_key=True)
    username = db.Column(db.String(64), index=True, unique=True)
    email = db.Column(db.String(120), index=True, unique=True)
    password_hash = db.Column(db.String(128))
    posts = db.relationship('Post', backref='author', lazy='dynamic')

    def __repr__(self):
        return '<User {}>'.format(self.username)

class Post(db.Model):
    id = db.Column(db.Integer, primary_key=True)
    body = db.Column(db.String(140))
    timestamp = db.Column(db.DateTime, index=True, default=datetime.utcnow)
    user_id = db.Column(db.Integer, db.ForeignKey('user.id'))

    def __repr__(self):
        return '<Post {}>'.format(self.body)
```

The new `Post` class will represent blog posts written by users. The `timestamp` field is going to be indexed, which is useful if you want to retrieve posts in chronological order. I have also added a `default` argument, and passed the `datetime.utcnow` function. When you pass a function as a default, SQLAlchemy will set the field to the value of calling that function (note that I did not include the `()` after `utcnow`, so I'm passing the function itself, and not the result of calling it). In general, you will want to work with UTC dates and times in a server application. This ensures that you are using uniform timestamps regardless of where the users are located. These timestamps will be converted to the user's local time when they are displayed.

The `user_id` field was initialized as a foreign key to `user.id`, which means that it references an `id` value from the users table. In this reference the `user` part is the name of the database table for the model. It is an unfortunate inconsistency that in some instances such as in a `db.relationship()` call, the model is referenced by the model class, which typically starts with an uppercase character, while in other cases such as this `db.ForeignKey()` declaration, a model is given by its database table name, for which SQLAlchemy automatically uses lowercase characters and, for multi-word model names, snake case.

The `User` class has a new `posts` field, that is initialized with `db.relationship`. This is not an actual database field, but a high-level view of the relationship between users and posts, and for that reason it isn't in the database diagram. For a one-to-many relationship, a `db.relationship` field is normally defined on the "one" side, and is used as a convenient way to get access to the "many". So for example, if I have a user stored in `u`, the expression `u.posts` will run a database query that returns all the posts written by that user. The first argument to `db.relationship` is the model class that represents the "many" side of the

4.9. PLAY TIME

relationship. This argument can be provided as a string with the class name if the model is defined later in the module. The `backref` argument defines the name of a field that will be added to the objects of the "many" class that points back at the "one" object. This will add a `post.author` expression that will return the user given a post. The `lazy` argument defines how the database query for the relationship will be issued, which is something that I will discuss later. Don't worry if these details don't make much sense just yet, I'll show you examples of this at the end of this article.

Since I have updates to the application models, a new database migration needs to be generated:

```
(venv) $ flask db migrate -m "posts table"
INFO  [alembic.runtime.migration] Context impl SQLiteImpl.
INFO  [alembic.runtime.migration] Will assume non-transactional DDL.
INFO  [alembic.autogenerate.compare] Detected added table 'post'
INFO  [alembic.autogenerate.compare] Detected added index 'ix_post_timestamp' on '['timestamp']'
  Generating /home/miguel/microblog/migrations/versions/780739b227a7_posts_table.py ... done
```

And the migration needs to be applied to the database:

```
(venv) $ flask db upgrade
INFO  [alembic.runtime.migration] Context impl SQLiteImpl.
INFO  [alembic.runtime.migration] Will assume non-transactional DDL.
INFO  [alembic.runtime.migration] Running upgrade e517276bb1c2 -> 780739b227a7, posts table
```

If you are storing your project in source control, also remember to add the new migration script to it.

4.9 Play Time

I have made you suffer through a long process to define the database, but I haven't shown you how everything works yet. Since the application does not have any database logic yet, let's play with the database in the Python interpreter to familiarize with it. So go ahead and fire up Python by running `python`. Make sure your virtual environment is activated before you start the interpreter.

Once in the Python prompt, let's import the database instance and the models:

```
>>> from app import db
>>> from app.models import User, Post
```

Start by creating a new user:

```
>>> u = User(username='john', email='john@example.com')
>>> db.session.add(u)
>>> db.session.commit()
```

Changes to a database are done in the context of a database session, which can be accessed as `db.session`. Multiple changes can be accumulated in a session and once all the changes have been registered you can issue a single `db.session.commit()`, which writes all the changes atomically. If at any time while working on a session there is an error, a call to `db.session.rollback()` will abort the session and remove any changes stored in it. The important thing to remember is that changes are only written to the database when a commit is issued with `db.session.commit()`. Sessions guarantee that the database will never be left in an inconsistent state.

Let's add another user:

```
>>> u = User(username='susan', email='susan@example.com')
>>> db.session.add(u)
>>> db.session.commit()
```

The database can answer a query that returns all the users:

```
>>> users = User.query.all()
>>> users
[<User john>, <User susan>]
>>> for u in users:
...     print(u.id, u.username)
...
1 john
2 susan
```

All models have a `query` attribute that is the entry point to run database queries. The most basic query is that one that returns all elements of that class, which is appropriately named `all()`. Note that the `id` fields were automatically set to 1 and 2 when those users were added.

Here is another way to do queries. If you know the `id` of a user, you can retrieve that user as follows:

```
>>> u = User.query.get(1)
>>> u
<User john>
```

4.9. PLAY TIME

Now let's add a blog post:

```
>>> u = User.query.get(1)
>>> p = Post(body='my first post!', author=u)
>>> db.session.add(p)
>>> db.session.commit()
```

I did not need to set a value for the `timestamp` field because that field has a default, which you can see in the model definition. And what about the `user_id` field? Recall that the `db.relationship` that I created in the `User` class adds a `posts` attribute to users, and also a `author` attribute to posts. I assign an author to a post using the `author` virtual field instead of having to deal with user IDs. SQLAlchemy is great in that respect, as it provides a high-level abstraction over relationships and foreign keys.

To complete this session, let's look at a few more database queries:

```
>>> # get all posts written by a user
>>> u = User.query.get(1)
>>> u
<User john>
>>> posts = u.posts.all()
>>> posts
[<Post my first post!>]

>>> # same, but with a user that has no posts
>>> u = User.query.get(2)
>>> u
<User susan>
>>> u.posts.all()
[]

>>> # print post author and body for all posts
>>> posts = Post.query.all()
>>> for p in posts:
...     print(p.id, p.author.username, p.body)
...
1 john my first post!

# get all users in reverse alphabetical order
>>> User.query.order_by(User.username.desc()).all()
[<User susan>, <User john>]
```

The Flask-SQLAlchemy[14] documentation is the best place to learn about the many options that are available to query the database.

To complete this section, let's erase the test users and posts created above, so that the database is clean and ready for the next chapter:

---
[14] http://packages.python.org/Flask-SQLAlchemy/index.html

```
>>> users = User.query.all()
>>> for u in users:
...     db.session.delete(u)
...
>>> posts = Post.query.all()
>>> for p in posts:
...     db.session.delete(p)
...
>>> db.session.commit()
```

4.10 Shell Context

Remember what you did at the start of the previous section, right after starting a Python interpreter? The first thing you did was to run some imports:

```
>>> from app import db
>>> from app.models import User, Post
```

While you work on your application, you will need to test things out in a Python shell very often, so having to repeat the above imports every time is going to get tedious. The `flask shell` command is another very useful tool in the `flask` umbrella of commands. The `shell` command is the second "core" command implemented by Flask, after `run`. The purpose of this command is to start a Python interpreter in the context of the application. What does that mean? See the following example:

```
(venv) $ python
>>> app
Traceback (most recent call last):
  File "<stdin>", line 1, in <module>
NameError: name 'app' is not defined
>>>

(venv) $ flask shell
>>> app
<Flask 'app'>
```

With a regular interpreter session, the `app` symbol is not known unless it is explicitly imported, but when using `flask shell`, the command pre-imports the application instance. The nice thing about `flask shell` is not that it pre-imports `app`, but that you can configure a "shell context", which is a list of other symbols to pre-import.

The following function in *microblog.py* creates a shell context that adds the database instance and models to the shell session:

4.10. SHELL CONTEXT

```
from app import app, db
from app.models import User, Post

@app.shell_context_processor
def make_shell_context():
    return {'db': db, 'User': User, 'Post': Post}
```

The `app.shell_context_processor` decorator registers the function as a shell context function. When the `flask shell` command runs, it will invoke this function and register the items returned by it in the shell session. The reason the function returns a dictionary and not a list is that for each item you have to also provide a name under which it will be referenced in the shell, which is given by the dictionary keys.

After you add the shell context processor function you can work with database entities without having to import them:

```
(venv) $ flask shell
>>> db
<SQLAlchemy engine=sqlite:////Users/migu7781/Documents/dev/flask/microblog2/app.db>
>>> User
<class 'app.models.User'>
>>> Post
<class 'app.models.Post'>
```

Chapter 5

User Logins

In Chapter 3 you learned how to create the user login form, and in Chapter 4 you learned how to work with a database. This chapter will teach you how to combine the topics from those two chapters to create a simple user login system.

The GitHub links for this chapter are: Browse[1], Zip[2], Diff[3].

5.1 Password Hashing

In Chapter 4 the user model was given a `password_hash` field, that so far is unused. The purpose of this field is to hold a hash of the user password, which will be used to verify the password entered by the user during the log in process. Password hashing is a complicated topic that should be left to security experts, but there are several easy to use libraries that implement all that logic in a way that is simple to be invoked from an application.

One of the packages that implement password hashing is Werkzeug[4], which you may have seen referenced in the output of pip when you install Flask, since it is one of its core dependencies. Since it is a dependency, Werkzeug is already installed in your virtual environment. The following Python shell session demonstrates how to hash a password:

---

[1] https://github.com/miguelgrinberg/microblog/tree/v0.5
[2] https://github.com/miguelgrinberg/microblog/archive/v0.5.zip
[3] https://github.com/miguelgrinberg/microblog/compare/v0.4...v0.5
[4] http://werkzeug.pocoo.org/

```
>>> from werkzeug.security import generate_password_hash
>>> hash = generate_password_hash('foobar')
>>> hash
'pbkdf2:sha256:50000$vT9fkZM8$04dfa35c6476acf7e788a1b5b3c35e217c78dc04539d295f011f01f18cd2175f'
```

In this example, the password `foobar` is transformed into a long encoded string through a series of cryptographic operations that have no known reverse operation, which means that a person that obtains the hashed password will be unable to use it to obtain the original password. As an additional measure, if you hash the same password multiple times, you will get different results, so this makes it impossible to identify if two users have the same password by looking at their hashes.

The verification process is done with a second function from Werkzeug, as follows:

```
>>> from werkzeug.security import check_password_hash
>>> check_password_hash(hash, 'foobar')
True
>>> check_password_hash(hash, 'barfoo')
False
```

The verification function takes a password hash that was previously generated, and a password entered by the user at the time of log in. The function returns `True` if the password provided by the user matches the hash, or `False` otherwise.

The whole password hashing logic can be implemented as two new methods in the user model:

Listing 5.1: *app/models.py*: Password hashing and verification

```python
from werkzeug.security import generate_password_hash, check_password_hash

# ...

class User(db.Model):
    # ...

    def set_password(self, password):
        self.password_hash = generate_password_hash(password)

    def check_password(self, password):
        return check_password_hash(self.password_hash, password)
```

With these two methods in place, a user object is now able to do secure password verification, without the need to ever store original passwords. Here is an example usage of these new methods:

```
>>> u = User(username='susan', email='susan@example.com')
>>> u.set_password('mypassword')
>>> u.check_password('anotherpassword')
False
>>> u.check_password('mypassword')
True
```

5.2 Introduction to Flask-Login

In this chapter I'm going to introduce you to a very popular Flask extension called Flask-Login[5]. This extension manages the user logged-in state, so that for example users can log in to the application and then navigate to different pages while the application "remembers" that the user is logged in. It also provides the "remember me" functionality that allows users to remain logged in even after closing the browser window. To be ready for this chapter, you can start by installing Flask-Login in your virtual environment:

```
(venv) $ pip install flask-login
```

As with other extensions, Flask-Login needs to be created and initialized right after the application instance in *app/__init__.py*. This is how this extension is initialized:

Listing 5.2: *app/__init__.py*: Flask-Login initialization

```python
# ...
from flask_login import LoginManager

app = Flask(__name__)
# ...
login = LoginManager(app)

# ...
```

5.3 Preparing The User Model for Flask-Login

The Flask-Login extension works with the application's user model, and expects certain properties and methods to be implemented in it. This approach is nice, because as long as these

---
[5]https://flask-login.readthedocs.io/

required items are added to the model, Flask-Login does not have any other requirements, so for example, it can work with user models that are based on any database system.

The four required items are listed below:

- `is_authenticated`: a property that is `True` if the user has valid credentials or `False` otherwise.

- `is_active`: a property that is `True` if the user's account is active or `False` otherwise.

- `is_anonymous`: a property that is `False` for regular users, and `True` for a special, anonymous user.

- `get_id()`: a method that returns a unique identifier for the user as a string (unicode, if using Python 2).

I can implement these four easily, but since the implementations are fairly generic, Flask-Login provides a *mixin* class called `UserMixin` that includes generic implementations that are appropriate for most user model classes. Here is how the mixin class is added to the model:

Listing 5.3: *app/models.py*: Flask-Login user mixin class

```python
# ...
from flask_login import UserMixin

class User(UserMixin, db.Model):
    # ...
```

5.4 User Loader Function

Flask-Login keeps track of the logged in user by storing its unique identifier in Flask's *user session*, a storage space assigned to each user who connects to the application. Each time the logged-in user navigates to a new page, Flask-Login retrieves the ID of the user from the session, and then loads that user into memory.

Because Flask-Login knows nothing about databases, it needs the application's help in loading a user. For that reason, the extension expects that the application will configure a user loader function, that can be called to load a user given the ID. This function can be added in the *app/models.py* module:

Listing 5.4: *app/models.py*: Flask-Login user loader function

```python
from app import login
# ...

@login.user_loader
def load_user(id):
    return User.query.get(int(id))
```

The user loader is registered with Flask-Login with the `@login.user_loader` decorator. The `id` that Flask-Login passes to the function as an argument is going to be a string, so databases that use numeric IDs need to convert the string to integer as you see above.

5.5 Logging Users In

Let's revisit the login view function, which as you recall, implemented a fake login that just issued a `flash()` message. Now that the application has access to a user database and knows how to generate and verify password hashes, this view function can be completed.

Listing 5.5: *app/routes.py*: Login view function logic

```python
# ...
from flask_login import current_user, login_user
from app.models import User

# ...
@app.route('/login', methods=['GET', 'POST'])
def login():
    if current_user.is_authenticated:
        return redirect(url_for('index'))
    form = LoginForm()
    if form.validate_on_submit():
        user = User.query.filter_by(username=form.username.data).first()
        if user is None or not user.check_password(form.password.data):
            flash('Invalid username or password')
            return redirect(url_for('login'))
        login_user(user, remember=form.remember_me.data)
        return redirect(url_for('index'))
    return render_template('login.html', title='Sign In', form=form)
```

The top two lines in the `login()` function deal with a weird situation. Imagine you have a user that is logged in, and the user navigates to the */login* URL of your application. Clearly that is a mistake, so I want to not allow that. The `current_user` variable comes from Flask-Login and can be used at any time during the handling to obtain the user object that represents the client of the request. The value of this variable can be a user object from the database (which Flask-Login reads through the user loader callback I provided above), or a special anonymous user object if the user did not log in yet. Remember those properties that Flask-Login required in the user object? One of those was `is_authenticated`, which comes in handy to check if the user is logged in or not. When the user is already logged in, I just redirect to the index page.

In place of the `flash()` call that I used earlier, now I can log the user in for real. The first step is to load the user from the database. The username came with the form submission, so I can query the database with that to find the user. For this purpose I'm using the `filter_by()` method of the SQLAlchemy query object. The result of `filter_by()` is a query that only includes the objects that have a matching username. Since I know there is only going to be one or zero results, I complete the query by calling `first()`, which will return the user object if it exists, or `None` if it does not. In Chapter 4 you have seen that when you call the `all()` method in a query, the query executes and you get a list of all the results that match that query. The `first()` method is another commonly used way to execute a query, when you only need to have one result.

If I got a match for the username that was provided, I can next check if the password that also came with the form is valid. This is done by invoking the `check_password()` method I defined above. This will take the password hash stored with the user and determine if the password entered in the form matches the hash or not. So now I have two possible error conditions: the username can be invalid, or the password can be incorrect for the user. In either of those cases, I flash an message, and redirect back to the login prompt so that the user can try again.

If the username and password are both correct, then I call the `login_user()` function, which comes from Flask-Login. This function will register the user as logged in, so that means that any future pages the user navigates to will have the `current_user` variable set to that user.

To complete the login process, I just redirect the newly logged-in user to the index page.

5.6 Logging Users Out

I know I will also need to offer users the option to log out of the application. This can be done with Flask-Login's `logout_user()` function. Here is the logout view function:

Listing 5.6: *app/routes.py*: Logout view function

```
# ...
from flask_login import logout_user
```

5.7. REQUIRING USERS TO LOGIN

```
# ...

@app.route('/logout')
def logout():
    logout_user()
    return redirect(url_for('index'))
```

To expose this link to users, I can make the Login link in the navigation bar automatically switch to a Logout link after the user logs in. This can be done with a conditional in the *base.html* template:

Listing 5.7: *app/templates/base.html*: Conditional login and logout links

```
<div>
    Microblog:
    <a href="{{ url_for('index') }}">Home</a>
    {% if current_user.is_anonymous %}
    <a href="{{ url_for('login') }}">Login</a>
    {% else %}
    <a href="{{ url_for('logout') }}">Logout</a>
    {% endif %}
</div>
```

The `is_anonymous` property is one of the attributes that Flask-Login adds to user objects through the `UserMixin` class. The `current_user.is_anonymous` expression is going to be `True` only when the user is not logged in.

5.7 Requiring Users To Login

Flask-Login provides a very useful feature that forces users to log in before they can view certain pages of the application. If a user who is not logged in tries to view a protected page, Flask-Login will automatically redirect the user to the login form, and only redirect back to the page the user wanted to view after the login process is complete.

For this feature to be implemented, Flask-Login needs to know what is the view function that handles logins. This can be added in *app/__init__.py*:

```
# ...
login = LoginManager(app)
login.login_view = 'login'
```

The `'login'` value above is the function (or endpoint) name for the login view. In other words, the name you would use in a `url_for()` call to get the URL.

The way Flask-Login protects a view function against anonymous users is with a decorator called `@login_required`. When you add this decorator to a view function below the `@app.route` decorators from Flask, the function becomes protected and will not allow access to users that are not authenticated. Here is how the decorator can be applied to the index view function of the application:

Listing 5.8: *app/routes.py*: @login_required decorator

```python
from flask_login import login_required

@app.route('/')
@app.route('/index')
@login_required
def index():
    # ...
```

What remains is to implement the redirect back from the successful login to the page the user wanted to access. When a user that is not logged in accesses a view function protected with the `@login_required` decorator, the decorator is going to redirect to the login page, but it is going to include some extra information in this redirect so that the application can then return to the first page. If the user navigates to */index*, for example, the `@login_required` decorator will intercept the request and respond with a redirect to */login*, but it will add a query string argument to this URL, making the complete redirect URL */login?next=/index*. The `next` query string argument is set to the original URL, so the application can use that to redirect back after login.

Here is a snippet of code that shows how to read and process the `next` query string argument:

Listing 5.9: *app/routes.py*: Redirect to "next" page

```python
from flask import request
from werkzeug.urls import url_parse

@app.route('/login', methods=['GET', 'POST'])
def login():
    # ...
    if form.validate_on_submit():
        user = User.query.filter_by(username=form.username.data).first()
        if user is None or not user.check_password(form.password.data):
            flash('Invalid username or password')
            return redirect(url_for('login'))
        login_user(user, remember=form.remember_me.data)
        next_page = request.args.get('next')
        if not next_page or url_parse(next_page).netloc != '':
```

5.8. SHOWING THE LOGGED IN USER IN TEMPLATES

```
        next_page = url_for('index')
    return redirect(next_page)
# ...
```

Right after the user is logged in by calling Flask-Login's `login_user()` function, the value of the `next` query string argument is obtained. Flask provides a `request` variable that contains all the information that the client sent with the request. In particular, the `request.args` attribute exposes the contents of the query string in a friendly dictionary format. There are actually three possible cases that need to be considered to determine where to redirect after a successful login:

- If the login URL does not have a `next` argument, then the user is redirected to the index page.

- If the login URL includes a `next` argument that is set to a relative path (or in other words, a URL without the domain portion), then the user is redirected to that URL.

- If the login URL includes a `next` argument that is set to a full URL that includes a domain name, then the user is redirected to the index page.

The first and second cases are self-explanatory. The third case is in place to make the application more secure. An attacker could insert a URL to a malicious site in the `next` argument, so the application only redirects when the URL is relative, which ensures that the redirect stays within the same site as the application. To determine if the URL is relative or absolute, I parse it with Werkzeug's `url_parse()` function and then check if the `netloc` component is set or not.

5.8 Showing The Logged In User in Templates

Do you recall that way back in Chapter 2 I created a fake user to help me design the home page of the application before the user subsystem was in place? Well, the application has real users now, so I can now remove the fake user and start working with real users. Instead of the fake user I can use Flask-Login's `current_user` in the template:

Listing 5.10: *app/templates/index.html*: Pass current user to template

```
{% extends "base.html" %}
```

```
{% block content %}
    <h1>Hi, {{ current_user.username }}!</h1>
    {% for post in posts %}
    <div><p>{{ post.author.username }} says: <b>{{ post.body }}</b></p></div>
    {% endfor %}
{% endblock %}
```

And I can remove the `user` template argument in the view function:

Listing 5.11: *app/routes.py*: Do not pass user to template anymore

```
@app.route('/')
@app.route('/index')
def index():
    # ...
    return render_template("index.html", title='Home Page', posts=posts)
```

This is a good time to test how the login and logout functionality works. Since there is still no user registration, the only way to add a user to the database is to do it via the Python shell, so run `flask shell` and enter the following commands to register a user:

```
>>> u = User(username='susan', email='susan@example.com')
>>> u.set_password('cat')
>>> db.session.add(u)
>>> db.session.commit()
```

If you start the application and go to the application's */* or */index* URLs, you will be immediately redirected to the login page, and after you log in using the credentials of the user that you added to your database, you will be returned to the original page, in which you will see a personalized greeting.

5.9 User Registration

The last piece of functionality that I'm going to build in this chapter is a registration form, so that users can register themselves through a web form. Let's begin by creating the web form class in *app/forms.py*:

Listing 5.12: *app/forms.py*: User registration form

5.9. USER REGISTRATION

```
from flask_wtf import FlaskForm
from wtforms import StringField, PasswordField, BooleanField, SubmitField
from wtforms.validators import ValidationError, DataRequired, Email, EqualTo
from app.models import User

# ...

class RegistrationForm(FlaskForm):
    username = StringField('Username', validators=[DataRequired()])
    email = StringField('Email', validators=[DataRequired(), Email()])
    password = PasswordField('Password', validators=[DataRequired()])
    password2 = PasswordField(
        'Repeat Password', validators=[DataRequired(), EqualTo('password')])
    submit = SubmitField('Register')

    def validate_username(self, username):
        user = User.query.filter_by(username=username.data).first()
        if user is not None:
            raise ValidationError('Please use a different username.')

    def validate_email(self, email):
        user = User.query.filter_by(email=email.data).first()
        if user is not None:
            raise ValidationError('Please use a different email address.')
```

There are a couple of interesting things in this new form related to validation. First, for the `email` field I've added a second validator after `DataRequired`, called `Email`. This is another stock validator that comes with WTForms that will ensure that what the user types in this field matches the structure of an email address.

Since this is a registration form, it is customary to ask the user to type the password two times to reduce the risk of a typo. For that reason I have `password` and `password2` fields. The second password field uses yet another stock validator called `EqualTo`, which will make sure that its value is identical to the one for the first password field.

When you add any methods that match the pattern `validate_<field_name>`, WTForms takes those as custom validators and invokes them in addition to the stock validators. I have added two of those methods to this class for the `username` and `email` fields. In this case I want to make sure that the username and email address entered by the user are not already in the database, so these two methods issue database queries expecting there will be no results. In the event a result exists, a validation error is triggered by raising an exception of type `ValidationError`. The message included as the argument in the exception will be the message that will be displayed next to the field for the user to see.

To display this form on a web page, I need to have an HTML template, which I'm going to store in file *app/templates/register.html*. This template is constructed similarly to the one for the login form:

Listing 5.13: *app/templates/register.html*: Registration template

```
{% extends "base.html" %}

{% block content %}
    <h1>Register</h1>
    <form action="" method="post">
        {{ form.hidden_tag() }}
        <p>
            {{ form.username.label }}<br>
            {{ form.username(size=32) }}<br>
            {% for error in form.username.errors %}
            <span style="color: red;">[{{ error }}]</span>
            {% endfor %}
        </p>
        <p>
            {{ form.email.label }}<br>
            {{ form.email(size=64) }}<br>
            {% for error in form.email.errors %}
            <span style="color: red;">[{{ error }}]</span>
            {% endfor %}
        </p>
        <p>
            {{ form.password.label }}<br>
            {{ form.password(size=32) }}<br>
            {% for error in form.password.errors %}
            <span style="color: red;">[{{ error }}]</span>
            {% endfor %}
        </p>
        <p>
            {{ form.password2.label }}<br>
            {{ form.password2(size=32) }}<br>
            {% for error in form.password2.errors %}
            <span style="color: red;">[{{ error }}]</span>
            {% endfor %}
        </p>
        <p>{{ form.submit() }}</p>
    </form>
{% endblock %}
```

The login form template needs a link that sends new users to the registration form, right below the form:

Listing 5.14: *app/templates/login.html*: Link to registration page

```
<p>New User? <a href="{{ url_for('register') }}">Click to Register!</a></p>
```

And finally, I need to write the view function that is going to handle user registrations in *app/routes.py*:

5.9. USER REGISTRATION

Listing 5.15: *app/routes.py*: User registration view function

```python
from app import db
from app.forms import RegistrationForm

# ...

@app.route('/register', methods=['GET', 'POST'])
def register():
    if current_user.is_authenticated:
        return redirect(url_for('index'))
    form = RegistrationForm()
    if form.validate_on_submit():
        user = User(username=form.username.data, email=form.email.data)
        user.set_password(form.password.data)
        db.session.add(user)
        db.session.commit()
        flash('Congratulations, you are now a registered user!')
        return redirect(url_for('login'))
    return render_template('register.html', title='Register', form=form)
```

And this view function should also be mostly self-explanatory. I first make sure the user that invokes this route is not logged in. The form is handled in the same way as the one for logging in. The logic that is done inside the `if validate_on_submit()` conditional creates a new user with the username, email and password provided, writes it to the database, and then redirects to the login prompt so that the user can log in.

With these changes, users should be able to create accounts on this application, and log in and out. Make sure you try all the validation features I've added in the registration form to better understand how they work. I am going to revisit the user authentication subsystem in a future chapter to add additional functionality such as to allow the user to reset the password if forgotten. But for now, this is enough to continue building other areas of the application.

Chapter 6

Profile Page and Avatars

This chapter is going to be dedicated to adding user profile pages to the application. A user profile page is a page in which information about a user is presented, often with information entered by the users themselves. I will show you how to generate profile pages for all users dynamically, and then I'll add a small profile editor that users can use to enter their information.

The GitHub links for this chapter are: Browse[1], Zip[2], Diff[3].

6.1 User Profile Page

To create a user profile page, let's add a */user/<username>* route to the application.

Listing 6.1: *app/routes.py*: User profile view function

```
@app.route('/user/<username>')
@login_required
def user(username):
    user = User.query.filter_by(username=username).first_or_404()
    posts = [
        {'author': user, 'body': 'Test post #1'},
        {'author': user, 'body': 'Test post #2'}
    ]
    return render_template('user.html', user=user, posts=posts)
```

The `@app.route` decorator that I used to declare this view function looks a little bit different

---

[1] https://github.com/miguelgrinberg/microblog/tree/v0.6
[2] https://github.com/miguelgrinberg/microblog/archive/v0.6.zip
[3] https://github.com/miguelgrinberg/microblog/compare/v0.5...v0.6

than the previous ones. In this case I have a dynamic component in it, which is indicated as the `<username>` URL component that is surrounded by < and >. When a route has a dynamic component, Flask will accept any text in that portion of the URL, and will invoke the view function with the actual text as an argument. For example, if the client browser requests URL */user/susan*, the view function is going to be called with the argument `username` set to `'susan'`. This view function is only going to be accessible to logged in users, so I have added the `@login_required` decorator from Flask-Login.

The implementation of this view function is fairly simple. I first try to load the user from the database using a query by the username. You have seen before that a database query can be executed by calling `all()` if you want to get all results, or `first()` if you want to get just the first result or `None` if there are zero results. In this view function I'm using a variant of `first()` called `first_or_404()`, which works exactly like `first()` when there are results, but in the case that there are no results automatically sends a 404 error[4] back to the client. Executing the query in this way I save myself from checking if the query returned a user, because when the username does not exist in the database the function will not return and instead a 404 exception will be raised.

If the database query does not trigger a 404 error, then that means that a user with the given username was found. Next I initialize a fake list of posts for this user, finally render a new *user.html* template to which I pass the user object and the list of posts.

The *user.html* template is shown below:

Listing 6.2: *app/templates/user.html*: User profile template

```
{% extends "base.html" %}

{% block content %}
    <h1>User: {{ user.username }}</h1>
    <hr>
    {% for post in posts %}
    <p>
    {{ post.author.username }} says: <b>{{ post.body }}</b>
    </p>
    {% endfor %}
{% endblock %}
```

The profile page is now complete, but a link to it does not exist anywhere in the web site. To make it a bit more easy for users to check their own profile, I'm going to add a link to it in the navigation bar at the top:

---

[4]https://en.wikipedia.org/wiki/HTTP_404

6.1. USER PROFILE PAGE

Listing 6.3: *app/templates/base.html*: User profile template

```
<div>
  Microblog:
  <a href="{{ url_for('index') }}">Home</a>
  {% if current_user.is_anonymous %}
  <a href="{{ url_for('login') }}">Login</a>
  {% else %}
  <a href="{{ url_for('user', username=current_user.username) }}">Profile</a>
  <a href="{{ url_for('logout') }}">Logout</a>
  {% endif %}
</div>
```

The only interesting change here is the `url_for()` call that is used to generate the link to the profile page. Since the user profile view function takes a dynamic argument, the `url_for()` function receives a value for it as a keyword argument. Since this is a link that points to the logged in's user profile, I can use Flask-Login's `current_user` to generate the correct URL.

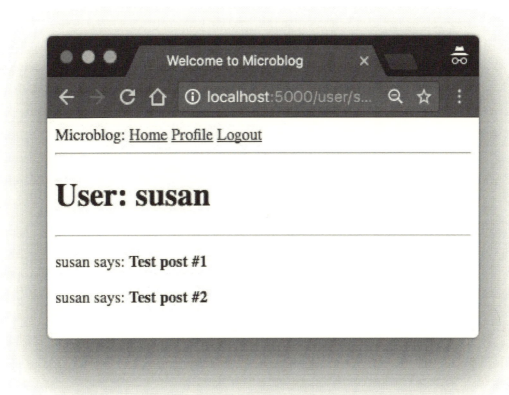

Give the application a try now. Clicking on the `Profile` link at the top should take you to your

own user page. At this point there are no links that will take to the profile page of other users, but if you want to access those pages you can type the URL by hand in the browser's address bar. For example, if you have a user named "john" registered on your application, you can view the corresponding user profile by typing *http://localhost:5000/user/john* in the address bar.

6.2 Avatars

I'm sure you agree that the profile pages that I just built are pretty boring. To make them a bit more interesting, I'm going to add user avatars, but instead of having to deal with a possibly large collection of uploaded images in the server, I'm going to use the Gravatar[5] service to provide images for all users.

The Gravatar service is very simple to use. To request an image for a given user, a URL with the format *https://www.gravatar.com/avatar/<hash>*, where `<hash>` is the MD5 hash of the user's email address. Below you can see how to obtain the Gravatar URL for a user with email `john@example.com`:

```
>>> from hashlib import md5
>>> 'https://www.gravatar.com/avatar/' + md5(b'john@example.com').hexdigest()
'https://www.gravatar.com/avatar/d4c74594d841139328695756648b6bd6'
```

If you want to see an actual example, my own Gravatar URL is:

```
https://www.gravatar.com/avatar/729e26a2a2c7ff24a71958d4aa4e5f35
```

Here is what Gravatar returns for this URL:

By default the image size returned is 80x80 pixels, but a different size can be requested by adding a `s` argument to the URL's query string. For example, to obtain my own avatar as a

---

[5]`http://gravatar.com`

6.2. AVATARS

128x128 pixel image, the URL is *https://www.gravatar.com/avatar/729e26a2a2c7ff24a71958d4aa4e5f35?s=128*.

Another interesting argument that can be passed to Gravatar as a query string argument is `d`, which determines what image Gravatar provides for users that do not have an avatar registered with the service. My favorite is called "identicon", which returns a nice geometric design that is different for every email. For example:

Note that some web browser extensions such as Ghostery block Gravatar images, as they consider that Automattic (the owners of the Gravatar service) can determine what sites you visit based on the requests they get for your avatar. If you don't see avatars in your browser, consider that the problem may be due to an extension that you have installed in your browser.

Since avatars are associated with users, it makes sense to add the logic that generates the avatar URLs to the user model.

Listing 6.4: *app/models.py*: User avatar URLs

```python
from hashlib import md5
# ...

class User(UserMixin, db.Model):
    # ...
    def avatar(self, size):
        digest = md5(self.email.lower().encode('utf-8')).hexdigest()
        return 'https://www.gravatar.com/avatar/{}?d=identicon&s={}'.format(
            digest, size)
```

The new `avatar()` method of the `User` class returns the URL of the user's avatar image, scaled to the requested size in pixels. For users that don't have an avatar registered, an "identicon" image will be generated. To generate the MD5 hash, I first convert the email to lower case, as this is required by the Gravatar service. Then, because the MD5 support in Python works on bytes and not on strings, I encode the string as bytes before passing it on to the hash function.

If you are interested in learning about other options offered by the Gravatar service, visit their documentation website[6].

The next step is to insert the avatar images in the user profile template:

Listing 6.5: *app/templates/user.html*: User avatar in template

```
{% extends "base.html" %}

{% block content %}
    <table>
        <tr valign="top">
            <td><img src="{{ user.avatar(128) }}"></td>
            <td><h1>User: {{ user.username }}</h1></td>
        </tr>
    </table>
    <hr>
    {% for post in posts %}
    <p>
    {{ post.author.username }} says: <b>{{ post.body }}</b>
    </p>
    {% endfor %}
{% endblock %}
```

The nice thing about making the `User` class responsible for returning avatar URLs is that if some day I decide Gravatar avatars are not what I want, I can just rewrite the `avatar()` method to return different URLs, and all the templates will start showing the new avatars automatically.

I have a nice big avatar at the top of the user profile page, but really there is no reason to stop there. I have some posts from the user at the bottom that could each have a little avatar as well. For the user profile page of course all posts will have the same avatar, but then I can implement the same functionality on the main page, and then each post will be decorated with the author's avatar, and that will look really nice.

To show avatars for the individual posts I just need to make one more small change in the template:

Listing 6.6: *app/templates/user.html*: User avatars in posts

```
{% extends "base.html" %}

{% block content %}
    <table>
        <tr valign="top">
            <td><img src="{{ user.avatar(128) }}"></td>
            <td><h1>User: {{ user.username }}</h1></td>
        </tr>
```

---

[6]https://gravatar.com/site/implement/images

```
    </table>
    <hr>
    {% for post in posts %}
    <table>
        <tr valign="top">
            <td><img src="{{ post.author.avatar(36) }}"></td>
            <td>{{ post.author.username }} says:<br>{{ post.body }}</td>
        </tr>
    </table>
    {% endfor %}
{% endblock %}
```

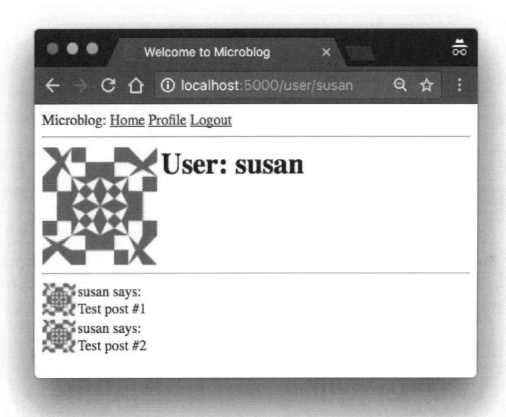

6.3 Using Jinja2 Sub-Templates

I designed the user profile page so that it displays the posts written by the user, along with their avatars. Now I want the index page to also also display posts with a similar layout. I could just copy/paste the portion of the template that deals with the rendering of a post, but that is really not ideal because later if I decide to make changes to this layout I'm going to have to remember to update both templates.

Instead, I'm going to make a sub-template that just renders one post, and then I'm going to reference it from both the *user.html* and *index.html* templates. To begin, I can create the sub-template, with just the HTML markup for a single post. I'm going to name this template *app/templates/_post.html*. The _ prefix is just a naming convention to help me recognize which template files are sub-templates.

Listing 6.7: *app/templates/_post.html*: Post sub-template

```
<table>
    <tr valign="top">
        <td><img src="{{ post.author.avatar(36) }}"></td>
        <td>{{ post.author.username }} says:<br>{{ post.body }}</td>
    </tr>
</table>
```

To invoke this sub-template from the *user.html* template I use Jinja2's `include` statement:

Listing 6.8: *app/templates/user.html*: User avatars in posts

```
{% extends "base.html" %}

{% block content %}
    <table>
        <tr valign="top">
            <td><img src="{{ user.avatar(128) }}"></td>
            <td><h1>User: {{ user.username }}</h1></td>
        </tr>
    </table>
    <hr>
    {% for post in posts %}
        {% include '_post.html' %}
    {% endfor %}
{% endblock %}
```

The index page of the application isn't really fleshed out yet, so I'm not going to add this functionality there yet.

6.4 More Interesting Profiles

One problem the new user profile pages have is that they don't really show much on them. Users like to tell a bit about them on these pages, so I'm going to let them write something

6.4. MORE INTERESTING PROFILES

about themselves to show here. I'm also going to keep track of what was the last time each user accessed the site and also show display it on their profile page.

The first I need to do to support all this extra information is to extend the users table in the database with two new fields:

Listing 6.9: *app/models.py*: New fields in user model

```python
class User(UserMixin, db.Model):
    # ...
    about_me = db.Column(db.String(140))
    last_seen = db.Column(db.DateTime, default=datetime.utcnow)
```

Every time the database is modified it is necessary to generate a database migration. In Chapter 4 I showed you how to set up the application to track database changes through migration scripts. Now I have two new fields that I want to add to the database, so the first step is to generate the migration script:

```
(venv) $ flask db migrate -m "new fields in user model"
INFO  [alembic.runtime.migration] Context impl SQLiteImpl.
INFO  [alembic.runtime.migration] Will assume non-transactional DDL.
INFO  [alembic.autogenerate.compare] Detected added column 'user.about_me'
INFO  [alembic.autogenerate.compare] Detected added column 'user.last_seen'
  Generating migrations/versions/37f06a334dbf_new_fields_in_user_model.py ... done
```

The output of the `migrate` command looks good, as it shows that the two new fields in the `User` class were detected. Now I can apply this change to the database:

```
(venv) $ flask db upgrade
INFO  [alembic.runtime.migration] Context impl SQLiteImpl.
INFO  [alembic.runtime.migration] Will assume non-transactional DDL.
INFO  [alembic.runtime.migration] Running upgrade 780739b227a7 -> 37f06a334dbf, new fields in user model
```

I hope you realize how useful it is to work with a migration framework. Any users that were in the database are still there, the migration framework surgically applies the changes in the migration script without destroying any data.

For the next step, I'm going to add these two new fields to the user profile template:

Listing 6.10: *app/templates/user.html*: Show user information in user profile template

```
{% extends "base.html" %}

{% block content %}
    <table>
        <tr valign="top">
            <td><img src="{{ user.avatar(128) }}"></td>
            <td>
                <h1>User: {{ user.username }}</h1>
                {% if user.about_me %}<p>{{ user.about_me }}</p>{% endif %}
                {% if user.last_seen %}<p>Last seen on: {{ user.last_seen }}</p>{% endif %}
            </td>
        </tr>
    </table>
    ...
{% endblock %}
```

Note that I'm wrapping these two fields in Jinja2's conditionals, because I only want them to be visible if they are set. At this point these two new fields are empty for all users, so you are not going to see these fields if you run the application now.

6.5 Recording The Last Visit Time For a User

Let's start with the `last_seen` field, which is the easier of the two. What I want to do is write the current time on this field for a given user whenever that user sends a request to the server.

Adding the login to set this field on every possible view function that can be requested from the browser is obviously impractical, but executing a bit of generic logic ahead of a request being dispatched to a view function is such a common task in web applications that Flask offers it as a native feature. Take a look at the solution:

Listing 6.11: *app/routes.py*: Record time of last visit

```
from datetime import datetime

@app.before_request
def before_request():
    if current_user.is_authenticated:
        current_user.last_seen = datetime.utcnow()
        db.session.commit()
```

The `@before_request` decorator from Flask register the decorated function to be executed right before the view function. This is extremely useful because now I can insert code that I want to execute before any view function in the application, and I can have it in a single place. The implementation simply checks if the `current_user` is logged in, and in that case sets

6.5. RECORDING THE LAST VISIT TIME FOR A USER

the `last_seen` field to the current time. I mentioned this before, a server application needs to work in consistent time units, and the standard practice is to use the UTC time zone. Using the local time of the system is not a good idea, because then what goes in the database is dependent on your location. The last step is to commit the database session, so that the change made above is written to the database. If you are wondering why there is no `db.session.add()` before the commit, consider that when you reference `current_user`, Flask-Login will invoke the user loader callback function, which will run a database query that will put the target user in the database session. So you can add the user again in this function, but it is not necessary because it is already there.

If you view your profile page after you make this change, you will see the "Last seen on" line with a time that is very close to the current time. And if you navigate away from the profile page and then return, you will see that the time is constantly updated.

The fact that I'm storing these timestamps in the UTC timezone makes the time displayed on the profile page also be in UTC. In addition to that, the format of the time is not what you would expect, since it is actually the internal representation of the Python datetime object. For now, I'm not going to worry about these two issues, since I'm going to address the topic of handling dates and times in a web application in a later chapter.

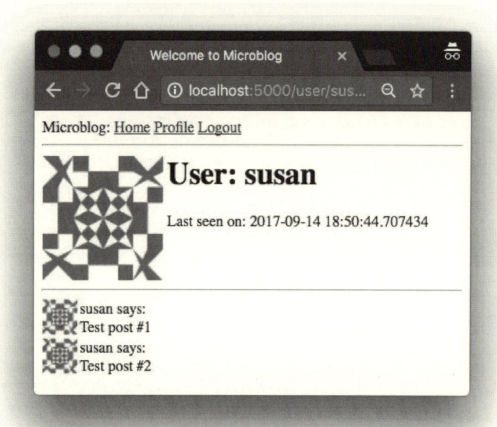

6.6 Profile Editor

I also need to give users a form in which they can enter some information about themselves. The form is going to let users change their username, and also write something about themselves, to be stored in the new `about_me` field. Let's start writing a form class for it:

Listing 6.12: *app/forms.py*: Profile editor form

```
from wtforms import StringField, TextAreaField, SubmitField
from wtforms.validators import DataRequired, Length

# ...
```

6.6. PROFILE EDITOR

```python
class EditProfileForm(FlaskForm):
    username = StringField('Username', validators=[DataRequired()])
    about_me = TextAreaField('About me', validators=[Length(min=0, max=140)])
    submit = SubmitField('Submit')
```

I'm using a new field type and a new validator in this form. For the "About" field I'm using a `TextAreaField`, which is a multi-line box in which the user can enter text. To validate this field I'm using `Length`, which will make sure that the text entered is between 0 and 140 characters, which is the space I have allocated for the corresponding field in the database.

The template that renders this form is shown below:

Listing 6.13: *app/templates/edit_profile.html*: Profile editor form

```html
{% extends "base.html" %}

{% block content %}
    <h1>Edit Profile</h1>
    <form action="" method="post">
        {{ form.hidden_tag() }}
        <p>
            {{ form.username.label }}<br>
            {{ form.username(size=32) }}<br>
            {% for error in form.username.errors %}
            <span style="color: red;">[{{ error }}]</span>
            {% endfor %}
        </p>
        <p>
            {{ form.about_me.label }}<br>
            {{ form.about_me(cols=50, rows=4) }}<br>
            {% for error in form.about_me.errors %}
            <span style="color: red;">[{{ error }}]</span>
            {% endfor %}
        </p>
        <p>{{ form.submit() }}</p>
    </form>
{% endblock %}
```

And finally, here is the view function that ties everything together:

Listing 6.14: *app/routes.py*: Edit profile view function

```python
from app.forms import EditProfileForm

@app.route('/edit_profile', methods=['GET', 'POST'])
@login_required
def edit_profile():
    form = EditProfileForm()
    if form.validate_on_submit():
        current_user.username = form.username.data
```

```
        current_user.about_me = form.about_me.data
        db.session.commit()
        flash('Your changes have been saved.')
        return redirect(url_for('edit_profile'))
    elif request.method == 'GET':
        form.username.data = current_user.username
        form.about_me.data = current_user.about_me
    return render_template('edit_profile.html', title='Edit Profile',
                           form=form)
```

This view function processes the form in a slightly different way. If `validate_on_submit()` returns `True` I copy the data from the form into the user object and then write the object to the database. But when `validate_on_submit()` returns `False` it can be due to two different reasons. First, it can be because the browser just sent a `GET` request, which I need to respond by providing an initial version of the form template. It can also be when the browser sends a `POST` request with form data, but something in that data is invalid. For this form, I need to treat these two cases separately. When the form is being requested for the first time with a `GET` request, I want to pre-populate the fields with the data that is stored in the database, so I need to do the reverse of what I did on the submission case and move the data stored in the user fields to the form, as this will ensure that those form fields have the current data stored for the user. But in the case of a validation error I do not want to write anything to the form fields, because those were already populated by WTForms. To distinguish between these two cases, I check `request.method`, which will be `GET` for the initial request, and `POST` for a submission that failed validation.

6.6. PROFILE EDITOR

To make it easy for users to access the profile editor page, I can add a link in their profile page:

Listing 6.15: *app/templates/user.html*: Edit profile link

```
{% if user == current_user %}
<p><a href="{{ url_for('edit_profile') }}">Edit your profile</a></p>
{% endif %}
```

Pay attention to the clever conditional I'm using to make sure that the Edit link appears when you are viewing your own profile, but not when you are viewing the profile of someone else.

Chapter 7

Error Handling

In this chapter I'm taking a break from coding new features into my microblog application, and instead will discuss a few strategies to deal with bugs, which invariably make an appearance in any software project. To help illustrate this topic, I intentionally let a bug slip in the code that I've added in Chapter 6. Before you continue reading, see if you can find it!

The GitHub links for this chapter are: Browse[1], Zip[2], Diff[3].

7.1 Error Handling in Flask

What happens when an error occurs in a Flask application? The best way to find out is to experience it first hand. Go ahead and start the application, and make sure you have at least two users registered. Log in as one of the users, open the profile page and click the "Edit" link. In the profile editor, try to change the username to the username of another user that is already registered, and boom! This is going to bring a scary looking "Internal Server Error" page:

---

[1] https://github.com/miguelgrinberg/microblog/tree/v0.7
[2] https://github.com/miguelgrinberg/microblog/archive/v0.7.zip
[3] https://github.com/miguelgrinberg/microblog/compare/v0.6...v0.7

If you look in the terminal session where the application is running, you will see a stack trace[4] of the error. Stack traces are extremely useful in debugging errors, because they show the sequence of calls in that stack, all the way to the line that produced the error:

```
(venv) $ flask run
 * Serving Flask app "microblog"
 * Running on http://127.0.0.1:5000/ (Press CTRL+C to quit)
[2017-09-14 22:40:02,027] ERROR in app: Exception on /edit_profile [POST]
Traceback (most recent call last):
  File "venv/lib/python3.6/site-packages/sqlalchemy/engine/base.py", in _execute_context
    context)
  File "venv/lib/python3.6/site-packages/sqlalchemy/engine/default.py", in do_execute
    cursor.execute(statement, parameters)
sqlite3.IntegrityError: UNIQUE constraint failed: user.username
```

The stack trace indicates what is the bug. The application allows a user to change the username, and does not validate that the new username chosen does not collide with another user

---

[4]http://en.wikipedia.org/wiki/Stack_trace

already in the system. The error comes from SQLAlchemy, which tries to write the new username to the database, but the database rejects it because the `username` column is defined with `unique=True`.

It is important to note that the error page that is presented to the user does not provide much information about the error, and that is good. I definitely do not want users to learn that the crash was caused by a database error, or what database I'm using, or what are some of the table and field names in my database. All that information should be kept internal.

There are a few things that are far from ideal. I have an error page that is very ugly and does not match the application layout. I also have important application stack traces being dumped on a terminal that I need to constantly watch to make sure I don't miss any errors. And of course I have a bug to fix. I'm going to address all these issues, but first, let's talk about Flask's *debug mode*.

7.2 Debug Mode

The way you saw that errors are handled above is great for a system that is running on a production server. If there is an error, the user gets a vague error page (though I'm going to make this error page nicer), and the important details of the error are in the server process output or in a log file.

But when you are developing your application, you can enable debug mode, a mode in which Flask outputs a really nice debugger directly on your browser. To activate debug mode, stop the application, and then set the following environment variable:

```
(venv) $ export FLASK_DEBUG=1
```

If you are on Microsoft Windows, remember to use `set` instead of `export`.

After you set `FLASK_DEBUG`, restart the server. The output on your terminal is going to be slightly different than what you are used to see:

```
(venv) microblog2 $ flask run
 * Serving Flask app "microblog"
 * Forcing debug mode on
 * Running on http://127.0.0.1:5000/ (Press CTRL+C to quit)
 * Restarting with stat
 * Debugger is active!
 * Debugger PIN: 177-562-960
```

Now make the application crash one more time to see the interactive debugger in your browser:

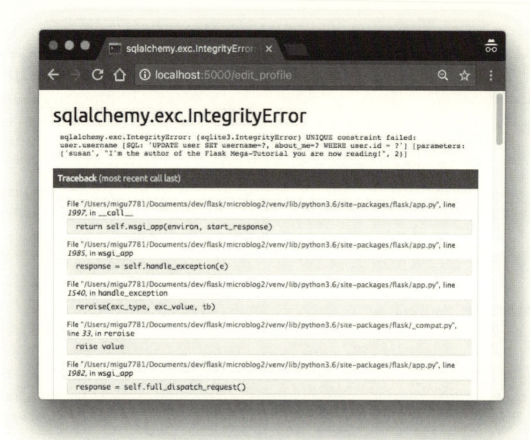

The debugger allows you expand each stack frame and see the corresponding source code. You can also open a Python prompt on any of the frames and execute any valid Python expressions, for example to check the values of variables.

It is extremely important that you never run a Flask application in debug mode on a production server. The debugger allows the user to remotely execute code in the server, so it can be an unexpected gift to a malicious user who wants to infiltrate your application or your server. As an additional security measure, the debugger running in the browser starts locked, and on first use will ask for a PIN number, which you can see in the output of the `flask run` command.

Since I am in the topic of debug mode, I should mention the second important feature that is enabled with debug mode, which is the *reloader*. This is a very useful development feature that automatically restarts the application when a source file is modified. If you run `flask run` while in debug mode, you can then work on your application and any time you save a file, the application will restart to pick up the new code.

7.3 Custom Error Pages

Flask provides a mechanism for an application to install its own error pages, so that your users don't have to see the plain and boring default ones. As an example, let's define custom error pages for the HTTP errors 404 and 500, the two most common ones. Defining pages for other errors works in the same way.

To declare a custom error handler, the `@errorhandler` decorator is used. I'm going to put my error handlers in a new *app/errors.py* module.

Listing 7.1: *app/errors.py*: Custom error handlers

```python
from flask import render_template
from app import app, db

@app.errorhandler(404)
def not_found_error(error):
    return render_template('404.html'), 404

@app.errorhandler(500)
def internal_error(error):
    db.session.rollback()
    return render_template('500.html'), 500
```

The error functions work very similarly to view functions. For these two errors, I'm returning the contents of their respective templates. Note that both functions return a second value after the template, which is the error code number. For all the view functions that I created so far, I did not need to add a second return value because the default of 200 (the status code for a successful response) is what I wanted. In this case these are error pages, so I want the status code of the response to reflect that.

The error handler for the 500 errors could be invoked after a database error, which was actually the case with the username duplicate above. To make sure any failed database sessions do not interfere with any database accesses triggered by the template, I issue a session rollback. This resets the session to a clean state.

Here is the template for the 404 error:

Listing 7.2: *app/templates/404.html*: Not found error template

```
{% extends "base.html" %}

{% block content %}
    <h1>File Not Found</h1>
    <p><a href="{{ url_for('index') }}">Back</a></p>
{% endblock %}
```

And here is the one for the 500 error:

Listing 7.3: *app/templates/500.html*: Internal server error template

```
{% extends "base.html" %}

{% block content %}
    <h1>An unexpected error has occurred</h1>
    <p>The administrator has been notified. Sorry for the inconvenience!</p>
    <p><a href="{{ url_for('index') }}">Back</a></p>
{% endblock %}
```

Both templates inherit from the `base.html` template, so that the error page has the same look and feel as the normal pages of the application.

To get these error handlers registered with Flask, I need to import the new *app/errors.py* module after the application instance is created:

Listing 7.4: *app/__init__.py*: Import error handlers

```
# ...
from app import routes, models, errors
```

If you set `FLASK_DEBUG=0` in your terminal session and then trigger the duplicate username bug one more time, you are going to see a slightly more friendly error page.

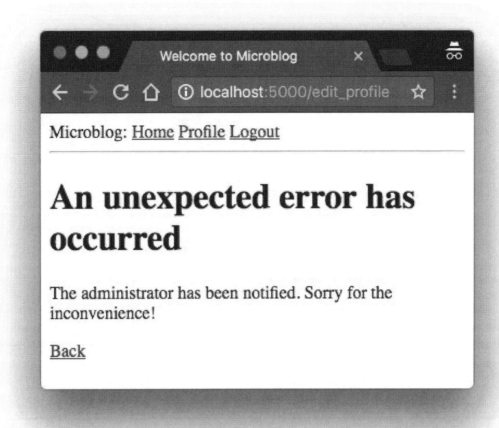

7.4 Sending Errors by Email

The other problem with the default error handling provided by Flask is that there are no notifications, stack trace for errors are printed to the terminal, which means that the output of the server process needs to be monitored to discover errors. When you are running the application during development, this is perfectly fine, but once the application is deployed on a production server, nobody is going to be looking at the output, so a more robust solution needs to be put in place.

I think it is very important that I take a proactive approach regarding errors. If an error occurs on the production version of the application, I want to know right away. So my first solution is going to be to configure Flask to send me an email immediately after an error, with the stack trace of the error in the email body.

The first step is to add the email server details to the configuration file:

Listing 7.5: *config.py*: Email configuration

```
class Config(object):
    # ...
    MAIL_SERVER = os.environ.get('MAIL_SERVER')
    MAIL_PORT = int(os.environ.get('MAIL_PORT') or 25)
    MAIL_USE_TLS = os.environ.get('MAIL_USE_TLS') is not None
    MAIL_USERNAME = os.environ.get('MAIL_USERNAME')
    MAIL_PASSWORD = os.environ.get('MAIL_PASSWORD')
    ADMINS = ['your-email@example.com']
```

The configuration variables for email include the server and port, a boolean flag to enable encrypted connections, and optional username and password. The five configuration variables are sourced from their environment variable counterparts. If the email server is not set in the environment, then I will use that as a sign that emailing errors needs to be disabled. The email server port can also be given in an environment variable, but if not set, the standard port 25 is used. Email server credentials are by default not used, but can be provided if needed. The `ADMINS` configuration variable is a list of the email addresses that will receive error reports, so your own email address should be in that list.

Flask uses Python's `logging` package to write its logs, and this package already has the ability to send logs by email. All I need to do to get emails sent out on errors is to add a SMTPHandler[5] instance to the Flask logger object, which is `app.logger`:

Listing 7.6: *app/__init__.py*: Log errors by email

```
import logging
from logging.handlers import SMTPHandler

# ...

if not app.debug:
    if app.config['MAIL_SERVER']:
        auth = None
        if app.config['MAIL_USERNAME'] or app.config['MAIL_PASSWORD']:
            auth = (app.config['MAIL_USERNAME'], app.config['MAIL_PASSWORD'])
        secure = None
        if app.config['MAIL_USE_TLS']:
            secure = ()
        mail_handler = SMTPHandler(
            mailhost=(app.config['MAIL_SERVER'], app.config['MAIL_PORT']),
            fromaddr='no-reply@' + app.config['MAIL_SERVER'],
            toaddrs=app.config['ADMINS'], subject='Microblog Failure',
```

---

[5]https://docs.python.org/3.6/library/logging.handlers.html#smtphandler

7.4. SENDING ERRORS BY EMAIL

```
                credentials=auth, secure=secure)
    mail_handler.setLevel(logging.ERROR)
    app.logger.addHandler(mail_handler)
```

As you can see, I'm only going to enable the email logger when the application is running without debug mode, which is indicated by `app.debug` being `True`, and also when the email server exists in the configuration.

Setting up the email logger is somewhat tedious due to having to handle optional security options that are present in many email servers. But in essence, the code above creates a `SMTPHandler` instance, sets its level so that it only reports errors and not warnings, informational or debugging messages, and finally attaches it to the `app.logger` object from Flask.

There are two approaches to test this feature. The easiest one is to use the SMTP debugging server from Python. This is a fake email server that accepts emails, but instead of sending them, it prints them to the console. To run this server, open a second terminal session and run the following command on it:

```
(venv) $ python -m smtpd -n -c DebuggingServer localhost:8025
```

To test the application with this server, then you will set `MAIL_SERVER=localhost` and `MAIL_PORT=8025`. If you are on a Linux or Mac OS system, you will likely need to prefix the command with `sudo`, so that it can execute with administration privileges. If you are on a Windows system, you may need to open your terminal window as an administrator. Administrator rights are needed for this command because ports below 1024 are administrator-only ports. Alternatively, you can change the port to a higher port number, say 5025, and set `MAIL_PORT` variable to your chosen port in the environment, and that will not require administration rights.

Leave the debugging SMTP server running and go back to your first terminal and set `export MAIL_SERVER=localhost` and and `MAIL_PORT=8025` in the environment (use `set` instead of `export` if you are using Microsoft Windows). Make sure the `FLASK_DEBUG` variable is set to `0` or not set at all, since the application will not send emails in debug mode. Run the application and trigger the SQLAlchemy error one more time to see how the terminal session running the fake email server shows an email with the full stack trace of the error.

A second testing approach for this feature is to configure a real email server. Below is the configuration to use your Gmail account's email server:

```
export MAIL_SERVER=smtp.googlemail.com
export MAIL_PORT=587
export MAIL_USE_TLS=1
```

```
export MAIL_USERNAME=<your-gmail-username>
export MAIL_PASSWORD=<your-gmail-password>
```

If you are using Microsoft Windows, remember to use `set` instead of `export` in each of the statements above.

The security features in your Gmail account may prevent the application from sending emails through it unless you explicitly allow "less secure apps" access to your Gmail account. You can read about this here[6], and if you are concerned about the security of your account, you can create a secondary account that you configure just for testing emails, or you can enable less secure apps only temporarily to run this test and then revert back to the default.

7.5 Logging to a File

Receiving errors via email is nice, but sometimes this isn't enough. There are some failure conditions that do not end in a Python exception and are not a major problem, but they may still be interesting enough to save for debugging purposes. For this reason, I'm also going to maintain a log file for the application.

To enable a file based log another handler, this time of type RotatingFileHandler[7], needs to be attached to the application logger, in a similar way to the email handler.

Listing 7.7: *app/__init__.py*: Email configuration

```
# ...
from logging.handlers import RotatingFileHandler
import os

# ...

if not app.debug:
    # ...

    if not os.path.exists('logs'):
        os.mkdir('logs')
    file_handler = RotatingFileHandler('logs/microblog.log', maxBytes=10240,
                                       backupCount=10)
    file_handler.setFormatter(logging.Formatter(
        '%(asctime)s %(levelname)s: %(message)s [in %(pathname)s:%(lineno)d]'))
    file_handler.setLevel(logging.INFO)
    app.logger.addHandler(file_handler)
```

[6] https://support.google.com/accounts/answer/6010255?hl=en
[7] https://docs.python.org/3.6/library/logging.handlers.html#rotatingfilehandler

```
app.logger.setLevel(logging.INFO)
app.logger.info('Microblog startup')
```

I'm writing the log file with name `microblog.log` in a *logs* directory, which I create if it doesn't already exist.

The `RotatingFileHandler` class is nice because it rotates the logs, ensuring that the log files do not grow too large when the application runs for a long time. In this case I'm limiting the size of the log file to 10KB, and I'm keeping the last ten log files as backup.

The `logging.Formatter` class provides custom formatting for the log messages. Since these messages are going to a file, I want them to have as much information as possible. So I'm using a format that includes the timestamp, the logging level, the message and the source file and line number from where the log entry originated.

To make the logging more useful, I'm also lowering the logging level to the `INFO` category, both in the application logger and the file logger handler. In case you are not familiar with the logging categories, they are `DEBUG`, `INFO`, `WARNING`, `ERROR` and `CRITICAL` in increasing order of severity.

As a first interesting use of the log file, the server writes a line to the logs each time it starts. When this application runs on a production server, these log entries will tell you when the server was restarted.

7.6 Fixing the Duplicate Username Bug

I have exploited the username duplication bug for too long. Now that I have showed you how to prepare the application to handle this type of errors, I can go ahead and fix it.

If you recall, the `RegistrationForm` already implements validation for usernames, but the requirements of the edit form are slightly different. During registration, I need to make sure the username entered in the form does not exist in the database. On the edit profile form I have to do the same check, but with one exception. If the user leaves the original username untouched, then the validation should allow it, since that username is already assigned to that user. Below you can see how I implemented the username validation for this form:

Listing 7.8: *app/forms.py*: Validate username in edit profile form.

```
class EditProfileForm(FlaskForm):
    username = StringField('Username', validators=[DataRequired()])
```

```python
    about_me = TextAreaField('About me', validators=[Length(min=0, max=140)])
    submit = SubmitField('Submit')

    def __init__(self, original_username, *args, **kwargs):
        super(EditProfileForm, self).__init__(*args, **kwargs)
        self.original_username = original_username

    def validate_username(self, username):
        if username.data != self.original_username:
            user = User.query.filter_by(username=self.username.data).first()
            if user is not None:
                raise ValidationError('Please use a different username.')
```

The implementation is in a custom validation method, but there is an overloaded constructor that accepts the original username as an argument. This username is saved as an instance variable, and checked in the `validate_username()` method. If the username entered in the form is the same as the original username, then there is no reason to check the database for duplicates.

To use this new validation method, I need to add the original username argument in the view function, where the form object is created:

Listing 7.9: *app/routes.py*: Validate username in edit profile form.

```python
@app.route('/edit_profile', methods=['GET', 'POST'])
@login_required
def edit_profile():
    form = EditProfileForm(current_user.username)
    # ...
```

Now the bug is fixed and duplicates in the edit profile form will be prevented in most cases. This is not a perfect solution, because it may not work when two or more processes are accessing the database at the same time. In that situation, a *race condition* could cause the validation to pass, but a moment later when the rename is attempted the database was already changed by another process and cannot rename the user. This is somewhat unlikely except for very busy applications that have a lot of server processes, so I'm not going to worry about it for now.

At this point you can try to reproduce the error one more time to see how the new form validation method prevents it.

Chapter 8

Followers

In this chapter I am going to work on the application's database some more. I want users of the application to be able to easily choose which other users they want to follow. So I'm going to be expanding the database so that it can keep track of who is following whom, which is harder than you may think.

The GitHub links for this chapter are: Browse[1], Zip[2], Diff[3].

8.1 Database Relationships Revisited

I said above that I want to maintain a list of "followed" and "follower" users for each user. Unfortunately, a relational database does not have a list type that I can use for these lists, all there is are tables with records and relationships between these records.

The database has a table that represents users, so what's left is to come up with the proper relationship type that can model the follower/followed link. This is a good time to review the basic database relationship types:

8.1.1 One-to-Many

I have already used a one-to-many relationship in Chapter 4. Here is the diagram for this relationship:

---

[1] https://github.com/miguelgrinberg/microblog/tree/v0.8
[2] https://github.com/miguelgrinberg/microblog/archive/v0.8.zip
[3] https://github.com/miguelgrinberg/microblog/compare/v0.7...v0.8

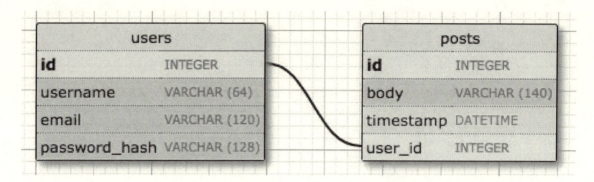

The two entities linked by this relationship are users and posts. I say that a user has *many* posts, and a post has *one* user (or author). The relationship is represented in the database with the use of a *foreign key* on the "many" side. In the relationship above, the foreign key is the `user_id` field added to the `posts` table. This field links each post to the record of its author in the user table.

It is pretty clear that the `user_id` field provides direct access to the author of a given post, but what about the reverse direction? For the relationship to be useful I should be able to get the list of posts written by a given user. The `user_id` field in the `posts` table is also sufficient to answer this question, as databases have indexes that allow for efficient queries such us "retrieve all posts that have a user_id of X".

8.1.2 Many-to-Many

A many-to-many relationship is a bit more complex. As an example, consider a database that has `students` and `teachers`. I can say that a student has *many* teachers, and a teacher has *many* students. It's like two overlapped one-to-many relationships from both ends.

For a relationship of this type I should be able to query the database and obtain the list of teachers that teach a given student, and the list of students in a teacher's class. This is actually non-trivial to represent in a relational database, as it cannot be done by adding foreign keys to the existing tables.

The representation of a many-to-many relationship requires the use of an auxiliary table called an *association table*. Here is how the database would look for the students and teachers example:

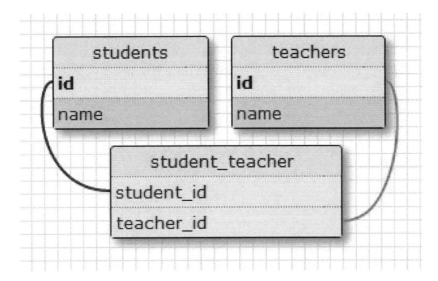

While it may not seem obvious at first, the association table with its two foreign keys is able to efficiently answer all the queries about the relationship.

8.1.3 Many-to-One and One-to-One

A many-to-one is similar to a one-to-many relationship. The difference is that this relationship is looked at from the "many" side.

A one-to-one relationship is a special case of a one-to-many. The representation is similar, but a constrain is added to the database to prevent the "many" side to have more than one link. While there are cases in which this type of relationship is useful, it isn't as common as the other types.

8.2 Representing Followers

Looking at the summary of all the relationship types, it is easy to determine that the proper data model to track followers is the many-to-many relationship, because a user follows *many* users, and a user has *many* followers. But there is a twist. In the students and teachers example I had two entities that were related through the many-to-many relationship. But in the case of followers, I have users following other users, so there is just users. So what is the second entity of the many-to-many relationship?

The second entity of the relationship is also the users. A relationship in which instances of a class are linked to other instances of the same class is called a *self-referential relationship*, and that is exactly what I have here.

Here is a diagram of the self-referential many-to-many relationship that keeps track of followers:

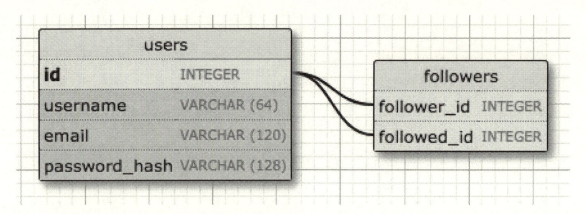

The `followers` table is the association table of the relationship. The foreign keys in this table are both pointing at entries in the user table, since it is linking users to users. Each record in this table represents one link between a follower user and a followed user. Like the students and teachers example, a setup like this one allows the database to answer all the questions about followed and follower users that I will ever need. Pretty neat.

8.3 Database Model Representation

Let's add followers to the database first. Here is the `followers` association table:

Listing 8.1: *app/models.py*: Followers association table

```
followers = db.Table('followers',
    db.Column('follower_id', db.Integer, db.ForeignKey('user.id')),
    db.Column('followed_id', db.Integer, db.ForeignKey('user.id'))
)
```

This is a direct translation of the association table from my diagram above. Note that I am not declaring this table as a model, like I did for the users and posts tables. Since this is an auxiliary table that has no data other than the foreign keys, I created it without an associated model class.

Now I can declare the many-to-many relationship in the users table:

8.3. DATABASE MODEL REPRESENTATION

Listing 8.2: *app/models.py*: Many-to-many followers relationship

```
class User(UserMixin, db.Model):
    # ...
    followed = db.relationship(
        'User', secondary=followers,
        primaryjoin=(followers.c.follower_id == id),
        secondaryjoin=(followers.c.followed_id == id),
        backref=db.backref('followers', lazy='dynamic'), lazy='dynamic')
```

The setup of the relationship is non-trivial. Like I did for the `posts` one-to-many relationship, I'm using the `db.relationship` function to define the relationship in the model class. This relationship links `User` instances to other `User` instances, so as a convention let's say that for a pair of users linked by this relationship, the left side user is following the right side user. I'm defining the relationship as seen from the left side user with the name `followed`, because when I query this relationship from the left side I will get the list of followed users (i.e those on the right side). Let's examine all the arguments to the `db.relationship()` call one by one:

- `'User'` is the right side entity of the relationship (the left side entity is the parent class). Since this is a self-referential relationship, I have to use the same class on both sides.

- `secondary` configures the association table that is used for this relationship, which I defined right above this class.

- `primaryjoin` indicates the condition that links the left side entity (the follower user) with the association table. The join condition for the left side of the relationship is the user ID matching the `follower_id` field of the association table. The value of this argument is `followers.c.follower_id`, which qreferences the `follower_id` column of the association table.

- `secondaryjoin` indicates the condition that links the right side entity (the followed user) with the association table. This condition is similar to the one for `primaryjoin`, with the only difference that now I'm using `followed_id`, which is the other foreign key in the association table.

- `backref` defines how this relationship will be accessed from the right side entity. From the left side, the relationship is named `followed`, so from the right side I am going to use the name `followers` to represent all the left side users that are linked to the target user in the right side. The additional `lazy` argument indicates the execution mode for this query. A mode of `dynamic` sets up the query to not run until specifically requested, which is also how I set up the posts one-to-many relationship.

- `lazy` is similar to the parameter of the same name in the `backref`, but this one applies to the left side query instead of the right side.

Don't worry if this is hard to understand. I will show you how to work with these queries in a moment, and then everything will become clearer.

The changes to the database need to be recorded in a new database migration:

```
(venv) $ flask db migrate -m "followers"
INFO  [alembic.runtime.migration] Context impl SQLiteImpl.
INFO  [alembic.runtime.migration] Will assume non-transactional DDL.
INFO  [alembic.autogenerate.compare] Detected added table 'followers'
  Generating /home/miguel/microblog/migrations/versions/ae346256b650_followers.py ... done

(venv) $ flask db upgrade
INFO  [alembic.runtime.migration] Context impl SQLiteImpl.
INFO  [alembic.runtime.migration] Will assume non-transactional DDL.
INFO  [alembic.runtime.migration] Running upgrade 37f06a334dbf -> ae346256b650, followers
```

8.4 Adding and Removing "follows"

Thanks to the SQLAlchemy ORM, a user following another user can be recorded in the database working with the `followed` relationship as if it was a list. For example, if I had two users stored in `user1` and `user2` variables, I can make the first follow the second with this simple statement:

```
user1.followed.append(user2)
```

To stop following the user, then I could do:

```
user1.followed.remove(user2)
```

Even though adding and removing followers is fairly easy, I want to promote reusability in my code, so I'm not going to sprinkle "appends" and "removes" through the code. Instead, I'm going to implement the "follow" and "unfollow" functionality as methods in the `User` model. It is always best to move the application logic away from view functions and into models or other auxiliary classes or modules, because as you will see later in this chapter, that makes unit testing much easier.

Below are the changes in the user model to add and remove relationships:

Listing 8.3: *app/models.py*: Add and remove followers

```python
class User(UserMixin, db.Model):
    #...

    def follow(self, user):
        if not self.is_following(user):
            self.followed.append(user)

    def unfollow(self, user):
        if self.is_following(user):
            self.followed.remove(user)

    def is_following(self, user):
        return self.followed.filter(
            followers.c.followed_id == user.id).count() > 0
```

The `follow()` and `unfollow()` methods use the `append()` and `remove()` methods of the relationship object as I have shown above, but before they touch the relationship they use the `is_following()` supporting method to make sure the requested action makes sense. For example, if I ask `user1` to follow `user2`, but it turns out that this following relationship already exists in the database, I do not want to add a duplicate. The same logic can be applied to unfollowing.

The `is_following()` method issues a query on the `followed` relationship to check if a link between two users already exists. You have seen me use the `filter_by()` method of the SQLAlchemy query object before, for example to find a user given its username. The `filter()` method that I'm using here is similar, but lower level, as it can include arbitrary filtering conditions, unlike `filter_by()` which can only check for equality to a constant value. The condition that I'm using in `is_following()` looks for items in the association table that have the left side foreign key set to the `self` user, and the right side set to the `user` argument. The query is terminated with a `count()` method, which returns the number of results. The result of this query is going to be `0` or `1`, so checking for the count being 1 or greater than 0 is actually equivalent. Other query terminators you have seen me use in the past are `all()` and `first()`.

8.5 Obtaining the Posts from Followed Users

Support for followers in the database is almost complete, but I'm actually missing one important feature. In the index page of the application I'm going to show blog posts written by all the people that are followed by the logged in user, so I need to come up with a database query that returns these posts.

The most obvious solution is to run a query that returns the list of followed users, which as you already know, it would be `user.followed.all()`. Then for each of these returned users I can run a query to get the posts. Once I have all the posts I can merge them into a single list and sort them by date. Sounds good? Well, not really.

This approach has a couple of problems. What happens if a user is following a thousand people? I would need to execute a thousand database queries just to collect all the posts. And then I will need to merge and sort the thousand lists in memory. As a secondary problem, consider that the application's home page will eventually have *pagination* implemented, so it will not display all the available posts but just the first few, with a link to get more if desired. If I'm going to display posts sorted by their date, how can I know which posts are the most recent of all followed users combined, unless I get all the posts and sort them first? This is actually an awful solution that does not scale well.

There is really no way to avoid this merging and sorting of blog posts, but doing it in the application results in a very inefficient process. This kind of work is what relational databases excel at. The database has indexes that allow it to perform the queries and the sorting in a much more efficient way that I can possibly do from my side. So what I really want is to come up with a single database query that defines the information that I want to get, and then let the database figure out how to extract that information in the most efficient way.

Below you can see this query:

Listing 8.4: *app/models.py*: Followed posts query

```
class User(db.Model):
    #...
    def followed_posts(self):
        return Post.query.join(
            followers, (followers.c.followed_id == Post.user_id)).filter(
                followers.c.follower_id == self.id).order_by(
                    Post.timestamp.desc())
```

This is by far the most complex query I have used on this application. I'm going to try to decipher this query one piece at a time. If you look at the structure of this query, you are going to notice that there are three main sections designed by the `join()`, `filter()` and `order_by()` methods of the SQLAlchemy query object:

```
Post.query.join(...).filter(...).order_by(...)
```

8.5.1 Joins

To understand what a join operation does, let's look at an example. Let's assume that I have a `User` table with the following contents:

id	username
1	john
2	susan
3	mary
4	david

To keep things simple I am not showing all the fields in the user model, just the ones that are important for this query.

Let's say that the `followers` association table says that user `john` is following users `susan` and `david`, user `susan` is following `mary` and user `mary` is following `david`. The data that represents the above is this:

follower_id	followed_id
1	2
1	4
2	3
3	4

Finally, the posts table contains one post from each user:

id	text	user_id
1	post from susan	2
2	post from mary	3
3	post from david	4
4	post from john	1

This table also omits some fields that are not part of this discussion.

Here is the `join()` call that I defined for this query once again:

```
Post.query.join(followers, (followers.c.followed_id == Post.user_id))
```

I'm invoking the join operation on the posts table. The first argument is the followers association table, and the second argument is the join *condition*. What I'm saying with this call is that

I want the database to create a temporary table that combines data from posts and followers tables. The data is going to be merged according to the condition that I passed as argument.

The condition that I used says that the `followed_id` field of the followers table must be equal to the `user_id` of the posts table. To perform this merge, the database will take each record from the posts table (the left side of the join) and append any records from the `followers` table (the right side of the join) that match the condition. If multiple records in `followers` match the condition, then the post entry will be repeated for each. If for a given post there is no match in followers, then that post record is not part of the join.

With the example data I defined above, the result of the join operation is:

id	text	user_id	follower_id	followed_id
1	post from susan	2	1	2
2	post from mary	3	2	3
3	post from david	4	1	4
3	post from david	4	3	4

Note how the `user_id` and `followed_id` columns are equal in all cases, as this was the join condition. The post from user `john` does not appear in the joined table because there are no entries in followers that have `john` as a followed user, or in other words, nobody is following john. And the post from `david` appears twice, because that user is followed by two different users.

It may not be immediately clear what do I gain by creating this join, but keep reading, as this is just one part of the bigger query.

8.5.2 Filters

The join operation gave me a list of all the posts that are followed by some user, which is a lot more data that I really want. I'm only interested in a subset of this list, the posts followed by a single user, so I need trim all the entries I don't need, which I can do with a `filter()` call.

Here is the filter portion of the query:

```
filter(followers.c.follower_id == self.id)
```

Since this query is in a method of class `User`, the `self.id` expression refers to the user ID of the user I'm interested in. The `filter()` call selects the items in the joined table that have the `follower_id` column set to this user, which in other words means that I'm keeping only the entries that have this user as a follower.

Let's say the user I'm interested in is `john`, which has its `id` field set to 1. Here is how the joined table looks after the filtering:

id	text	user_id	follower_id	followed_id
1	post from susan	2	1	2
3	post from david	4	1	4

And these are exactly the posts that I wanted!

Remember that the query was issued on the `Post` class, so even though I ended up with a temporary table that was created by the database as part of this query, the result will be the posts that are included in this temporary table, without the extra columns added by the join operation.

8.5.3 Sorting

The final step of the process is to sort the results. The part of the query that does that says:

```
order_by(Post.timestamp.desc())
```

Here I'm saying that I want the results sorted by the timestamp field of the post in descending order. With this ordering, the first result will be the most recent blog post.

8.6 Combining Own and Followed Posts

The query that I'm using in the `followed_posts()` function is extremely useful, but has one limitation. People expect to see their own posts included in their timeline of followed users, and the query as it is does not have that capability.

There are two possible ways to expand this query to include the user's own posts. The most straightforward way is to leave the query as it is, but make sure all users are following themselves. If you are your own follower, then the query as shown above will find your own posts along with those of all the people you follow. The disadvantage of this method is that it affects the stats regarding followers. All follower counts are going to be inflated by one, so they'll have to be adjusted before they are shown. The second way to do this is by create a second query that returns the user's own posts, and then use the "union" operator to combine the two queries into a single one.

After considering both options I decided to go with the second one. Below you can see the `followed_posts()` function after it has been expanded to include the user's posts through a union:

Listing 8.5: *app/models.py*: Followed posts query with user's own posts.

```
def followed_posts(self):
    followed = Post.query.join(
        followers, (followers.c.followed_id == Post.user_id)).filter(
            followers.c.follower_id == self.id)
    own = Post.query.filter_by(user_id=self.id)
    return followed.union(own).order_by(Post.timestamp.desc())
```

Note how the `followed` and `own` queries are combined into one, before the sorting is applied.

8.7 Unit Testing the User Model

While I don't consider the followers implementation I have built a "complex" feature, I think it is also not trivial. My concern when I write non-trivial code, is to ensure that this code will continue to work in the future, as I make modifications on different parts of the application. The best way to ensure that code you have already written continues to work in the future is to create a suite of automated tests that you can re-run each time changes are made.

Python includes a very useful `unittest` package that makes it easy to write and execute unit tests. Let's write some unit tests for the existing methods in the `User` class in a *tests.py* module:

Listing 8.6: *tests.py*: User model unit tests.

```
from datetime import datetime, timedelta
import unittest
from app import app, db
from app.models import User, Post

class UserModelCase(unittest.TestCase):
    def setUp(self):
        app.config['SQLALCHEMY_DATABASE_URI'] = 'sqlite://'
        db.create_all()

    def tearDown(self):
        db.session.remove()
        db.drop_all()
```

8.7. UNIT TESTING THE USER MODEL

```python
    def test_password_hashing(self):
        u = User(username='susan')
        u.set_password('cat')
        self.assertFalse(u.check_password('dog'))
        self.assertTrue(u.check_password('cat'))

    def test_avatar(self):
        u = User(username='john', email='john@example.com')
        self.assertEqual(u.avatar(128), ('https://www.gravatar.com/avatar/'
                                        'd4c74594d841139328695756648b6bd6'
                                        '?d=identicon&s=128'))

    def test_follow(self):
        u1 = User(username='john', email='john@example.com')
        u2 = User(username='susan', email='susan@example.com')
        db.session.add(u1)
        db.session.add(u2)
        db.session.commit()
        self.assertEqual(u1.followed.all(), [])
        self.assertEqual(u1.followers.all(), [])

        u1.follow(u2)
        db.session.commit()
        self.assertTrue(u1.is_following(u2))
        self.assertEqual(u1.followed.count(), 1)
        self.assertEqual(u1.followed.first().username, 'susan')
        self.assertEqual(u2.followers.count(), 1)
        self.assertEqual(u2.followers.first().username, 'john')

        u1.unfollow(u2)
        db.session.commit()
        self.assertFalse(u1.is_following(u2))
        self.assertEqual(u1.followed.count(), 0)
        self.assertEqual(u2.followers.count(), 0)

    def test_follow_posts(self):
        # create four users
        u1 = User(username='john', email='john@example.com')
        u2 = User(username='susan', email='susan@example.com')
        u3 = User(username='mary', email='mary@example.com')
        u4 = User(username='david', email='david@example.com')
        db.session.add_all([u1, u2, u3, u4])

        # create four posts
        now = datetime.utcnow()
        p1 = Post(body="post from john", author=u1,
                  timestamp=now + timedelta(seconds=1))
        p2 = Post(body="post from susan", author=u2,
                  timestamp=now + timedelta(seconds=4))
        p3 = Post(body="post from mary", author=u3,
                  timestamp=now + timedelta(seconds=3))
        p4 = Post(body="post from david", author=u4,
                  timestamp=now + timedelta(seconds=2))
        db.session.add_all([p1, p2, p3, p4])
        db.session.commit()

        # setup the followers
        u1.follow(u2)  # john follows susan
        u1.follow(u4)  # john follows david
```

```
        u2.follow(u3)    # susan follows mary
        u3.follow(u4)    # mary follows david
        db.session.commit()

        # check the followed posts of each user
        f1 = u1.followed_posts().all()
        f2 = u2.followed_posts().all()
        f3 = u3.followed_posts().all()
        f4 = u4.followed_posts().all()
        self.assertEqual(f1, [p2, p4, p1])
        self.assertEqual(f2, [p2, p3])
        self.assertEqual(f3, [p3, p4])
        self.assertEqual(f4, [p4])

if __name__ == '__main__':
    unittest.main(verbosity=2)
```

I have added four tests that exercise the password hashing, user avatar and followers functionality in the user model. The `setUp()` and `tearDown()` methods are special methods that the unit testing framework executes before and after each test respectively. I have implemented a little hack in `setUp()`, to prevent the unit tests from using the regular database that I use for development. By changing the application configuration to `sqlite://` I get SQLAlchemy to use an in-memory SQLite database during the tests. The `db.create_all()` call creates all the database tables. This is a quick way to create a database from scratch that is useful for testing. For development and production use I have already shown you how to create database tables through database migrations.

You can run the entire test suite with the following command:

```
(venv) $ python tests.py
test_avatar (__main__.UserModelCase) ... ok
test_follow (__main__.UserModelCase) ... ok
test_follow_posts (__main__.UserModelCase) ... ok
test_password_hashing (__main__.UserModelCase) ... ok

----------------------------------------------------------------------
Ran 4 tests in 0.494s

OK
```

From now on, every time a change is made to the application, you can re-run the tests to make sure the features that are being tested have not been affected. Also, each time another feature is added to the application, a unit test should be written for it.

8.8 Integrating Followers with the Application

The support of followers in the database and models is now complete, but I don't have any of this functionality incorporated into the application, so I'm going to add that now. The good news is that there are no big challenges in doing this, it's all based on concepts you have already learned.

Let's add two new routes in the application to follow and unfollow a user:

Listing 8.7: *app/routes.py*: Follow and unfollow routes.

```python
@app.route('/follow/<username>')
@login_required
def follow(username):
    user = User.query.filter_by(username=username).first()
    if user is None:
        flash('User {} not found.'.format(username))
        return redirect(url_for('index'))
    if user == current_user:
        flash('You cannot follow yourself!')
        return redirect(url_for('user', username=username))
    current_user.follow(user)
    db.session.commit()
    flash('You are following {}!'.format(username))
    return redirect(url_for('user', username=username))

@app.route('/unfollow/<username>')
@login_required
def unfollow(username):
    user = User.query.filter_by(username=username).first()
    if user is None:
        flash('User {} not found.'.format(username))
        return redirect(url_for('index'))
    if user == current_user:
        flash('You cannot unfollow yourself!')
        return redirect(url_for('user', username=username))
    current_user.unfollow(user)
    db.session.commit()
    flash('You are not following {}.'.format(username))
    return redirect(url_for('user', username=username))
```

These should be self-explanatory, but pay attention to all the error checking that I'm doing to prevent unexpected issues and try to provide a useful message to the user when a problem has occurred.

With the view functions now in place, I can link to them from pages in the application. I'm going to add links to follow and unfollow a user in the profile page of each user:

Listing 8.8: *app/templates/user.html*: Follow and unfollow links in user profile page.

```
...
<h1>User: {{ user.username }}</h1>
{% if user.about_me %}<p>{{ user.about_me }}</p>{% endif %}
{% if user.last_seen %}<p>Last seen on: {{ user.last_seen }}</p>{% endif %}
<p>{{ user.followers.count() }} followers, {{ user.followed.count() }} following.</p>
{% if user == current_user %}
<p><a href="{{ url_for('edit_profile') }}">Edit your profile</a></p>
{% elif not current_user.is_following(user) %}
<p><a href="{{ url_for('follow', username=user.username) }}">Follow</a></p>
{% else %}
<p><a href="{{ url_for('unfollow', username=user.username) }}">Unfollow</a></p>
{% endif %}
...
```

The changes to the user profile template add a line below the last seen timestamp that shows how many followers and followed users this user has. And the line that has the "Edit" link when you are viewing your own profile now can have one of three possible links:

- If the user is viewing his or her own profile, the "Edit" link shows as before.
- If the user is viewing a user that is not currently followed, the "Follow" link shows.
- If the user is viewing a user that is currently followed, the "Unfollow" link shows.

At this point you can run the application, create a few users and play with following and unfollowing users. The only thing you need to remember is to type the profile page URL of the user you want to follow or unfollow, since there is currently no way to see a list of users. For example, if you want to follow a user with the `susan` username, you will need to type *http://localhost:5000/user/susan* in the browser's address bar to access the profile page for that user. Make sure you check how the followed and follower user counts change as you issue follows or unfollows.

I should be showing the list of followed posts in the index page of the application, but I don't have all the pieces in place to do that yet, since users cannot write blog posts yet. So I'm going to delay this change until that functionality is in place.

Chapter 9

Pagination

In Chapter 8 I have made several database changes that were necessary to support the "follower" paradigm that is so popular with social networks. With that functionality in place, I'm ready to remove the last piece of scaffolding that I have put in place in the beginning, the fake posts. In this chapter the application will start accepting blog posts from users, and also deliver them in the home and profile pages.

The GitHub links for this chapter are: Browse[1], Zip[2], Diff[3].

9.1 Submission of Blog Posts

Let's start with something simple. The home page needs to have a form in which users can type new posts. First I create a form class:

Listing 9.1: *app/forms.py*: Blog submission form.

```
class PostForm(FlaskForm):
    post = TextAreaField('Say something', validators=[
        DataRequired(), Length(min=1, max=140)])
    submit = SubmitField('Submit')
```

Next, I can add this form to the template for the main page of the application:

---

[1] https://github.com/miguelgrinberg/microblog/tree/v0.9
[2] https://github.com/miguelgrinberg/microblog/archive/v0.9.zip
[3] https://github.com/miguelgrinberg/microblog/compare/v0.8...v0.9

Listing 9.2: *app/templates/index.html*: Post submission form in index template

```
{% extends "base.html" %}

{% block content %}
    <h1>Hi, {{ current_user.username }}!</h1>
    <form action="" method="post">
        {{ form.hidden_tag() }}
        <p>
            {{ form.post.label }}<br>
            {{ form.post(cols=32, rows=4) }}<br>
            {% for error in form.post.errors %}
            <span style="color: red;">[{{ error }}]</span>
            {% endfor %}
        </p>
        <p>{{ form.submit() }}</p>
    </form>
    {% for post in posts %}
    <p>
    {{ post.author.username }} says: <b>{{ post.body }}</b>
    </p>
    {% endfor %}
{% endblock %}
```

The changes in this template are similar to how previous forms were handled. The final part is to add the form creation and handling in the view function:

Listing 9.3: *app/routes.py*: Post submission form in index view function.

```
from app.forms import PostForm
from app.models import Post

@app.route('/', methods=['GET', 'POST'])
@app.route('/index', methods=['GET', 'POST'])
@login_required
def index():
    form = PostForm()
    if form.validate_on_submit():
        post = Post(body=form.post.data, author=current_user)
        db.session.add(post)
        db.session.commit()
        flash('Your post is now live!')
        return redirect(url_for('index'))
    posts = [
        {
            'author': {'username': 'John'},
            'body': 'Beautiful day in Portland!'
        },
        {
            'author': {'username': 'Susan'},
            'body': 'The Avengers movie was so cool!'
        }
    ]
    return render_template("index.html", title='Home Page', form=form,
                            posts=posts)
```

Let's review the changes in this view function one by one:

- I'm now importing the `Post` and `PostForm` classes

- I accept `POST` requests in both routes associated with the `index` view function in addition to `GET` requests, since this view function will now receive form data.

- The form processing logic inserts a new `Post` record into the database.

- The template receives the `form` object as an additional argument, so that it can render the text field.

Before I continue, I wanted to mention something important related to processing of web forms. Notice how after I process the form data, I end the request by issuing a redirect to the home page. I could have easily skipped the redirect and allowed the function to continue down into the template rendering part, since this is already the index view function.

So, why the redirect? It is a standard practice to respond to a `POST` request generated by a web form submission with a redirect. This helps mitigate an annoyance with how the refresh command is implemented in web browsers. All the web browser does when you hit the refresh key is to re-issue the last request. If a `POST` request with a form submission returns a regular response, then a refresh will re-submit the form. Because this is unexpected, the browser is going to ask the user to confirm the duplicate submission, but most users will not understand what the browser is asking them. But if a `POST` request is answered with a redirect, the browser is now instructed to send a `GET` request to grab the page indicated in the redirect, so now the last request is not a `POST` request anymore, and the refresh command works in a more predictable way.

This simple trick is called the Post/Redirect/Get[4] pattern. It avoids inserting duplicate posts when a user inadvertently refreshes the page after submitting a web form.

9.2 Displaying Blog Posts

If you recall, I created a couple of fake blog posts that I've been displaying in the home page for a long time. These fake objects are created explicitly in the `index` view function as a simple Python list:

---

[4]`https://en.wikipedia.org/wiki/Post/Redirect/Get`

```
posts = [
    {
        'author': {'username': 'John'},
        'body': 'Beautiful day in Portland!'
    },
    {
        'author': {'username': 'Susan'},
        'body': 'The Avengers movie was so cool!'
    }
]
```

But now I have the `followed_posts()` method in the `User` model that returns a query for the posts that a given user wants to see. So now I can replace the fake posts with real posts:

Listing 9.4: *app/routes.py*: Display real posts in home page.

```
@app.route('/', methods=['GET', 'POST'])
@app.route('/index', methods=['GET', 'POST'])
@login_required
def index():
    # ...
    posts = current_user.followed_posts().all()
    return render_template("index.html", title='Home Page', form=form,
                           posts=posts)
```

The `followed_posts` method of the `User` class returns a SQLAlchemy query object that is configured to grab the posts the user is interested in from the database. Calling `all()` on this query triggers its execution, with the return value being a list with all the results. So I end up with a structure that is very much alike the one with fake posts that I have been using until now. It's so close that the template does not even need to change.

9.3 Making It Easier to Find Users to Follow

As I'm sure you noticed, the application as it is does not do a great job at letting users find other users to follow. In fact, there is actually no way to see what other users are there at all. I'm going to address that with a few simple changes.

I'm going to create a new page that I'm going to call the "Explore" page. This page will work like the home page, but instead of only showing posts from followed users, it will show a global post stream from all users. Here is the new explore view function:

9.3. MAKING IT EASIER TO FIND USERS TO FOLLOW

Listing 9.5: *app/routes.py*: Explore view function.

```python
@app.route('/explore')
@login_required
def explore():
    posts = Post.query.order_by(Post.timestamp.desc()).all()
    return render_template('index.html', title='Explore', posts=posts)
```

Did you notice something odd in this view function? The `render_template()` call references the *index.html* template, which I'm using in the main page of the application. Since this page is going to be very similar to the main page, I decided to reuse the template. But one difference with the main page is that in the explore page I do not want to have a form to write blog posts, so in this view function I did not include the `form` argument in the template call.

To prevent the *index.html* template from crashing when it tries to render a web form that does not exist, I'm going to add a conditional that only renders the form if it is defined:

Listing 9.6: *app/templates/index.html*: Make the blog post submission form optional.

```html
{% extends "base.html" %}

{% block content %}
    <h1>Hi, {{ current_user.username }}!</h1>
    {% if form %}
    <form action="" method="post">
        ...
    </form>
    {% endif %}
    ...
{% endblock %}
```

I'm also going to add a link to this new page in the navigation bar:

Listing 9.7: *app/templates/base.html*: Link to explore page in navigation bar.

```html
            <a href="{{ url_for('explore') }}">Explore</a>
```

Remember the *_post.html* sub-template that I have introduced in Chapter 6 to render blog posts in the user profile page? This was a small template that was included from the user profile page template, and was separate so that it can also be used from other templates. I'm now going to make a small improvement to it, which is to show the username of the blog post author as a link:

Listing 9.8: *app/templates/_post.html*: Show link to author in blog posts.

```
<table>
    <tr valign="top">
        <td><img src="{{ post.author.avatar(36) }}"></td>
        <td>
            <a href="{{ url_for('user', username=post.author.username) }}">
                {{ post.author.username }}
            </a>
            says:<br>{{ post.body }}
        </td>
    </tr>
</table>
```

I can now use this sub-template to render blog posts in the home and explore pages:

Listing 9.9: *app/templates/index.html*: Use blog post sub-template.

```
...
{% for post in posts %}
    {% include '_post.html' %}
{% endfor %}
...
```

The sub-template expects a variable named `post` to exist, and that is how the loop variable in the index template is named, so that works perfectly.

With these small changes, the usability of the application has improved considerably. Now a user can visit the explore page to read blog posts from unknown users and based on those posts find new users to follow, which can be done by simply clicking on a username to access the profile page. Amazing, right?

At this point I suggest you try the application once again, so that you experience these last user interface improvements.

9.4 Pagination of Blog Posts

The application is looking better than ever, but showing all of the followed posts in the home page is going to become a problem sooner rather than later. What happens if a user has a thousand followed posts? Or a million? As you can imagine, managing such a large list of posts will be extremely slow and inefficient.

To address that problem, I'm going to *paginate* the post list. This means that initially I'm going to show just a limited number of posts at a time, and include links to navigate through the entire list of posts. Flask-SQLAlchemy supports pagination natively with the `paginate()` query method. If for example, I want to get the first twenty followed posts of the user, I can replace the `all()` call that terminates the query with:

```
>>> user.followed_posts().paginate(1, 20, False).items
```

The `paginate` method can be called on any query object from Flask-SQLAlchemy. It takes three arguments:

- the page number, starting from 1

- the number of items per page

- an error flag. If `True`, when an out of range page is requested a 404 error will be automatically returned to the client. If `False`, an empty list will be returned for out of range pages.

The return value from `paginate` is a `Pagination` object. The `items` attribute of this object contains the list of items in the requested page. There are other useful things in the `Pagination` object that I will discuss later.

Now let's think about how I can implement pagination in the `index()` view function. I can start by adding a configuration item to the application that determines how many items will be displayed per page.

Listing 9.10: *config.py*: Posts per page configuration.

```
class Config(object):
    # ...
    POSTS_PER_PAGE = 3
```

It is a good idea to have these application-wide "knobs" that can change behaviors in the configuration file, because then I can go to a single place to make adjustments. In the final application I will of course use a larger number than three items per page, but for testing it is useful to work with small numbers.

Next, I need to decide how the page number is going to be incorporated into application URLs. A fairly common way is to use a *query string* argument to specify an optional page number, defaulting to page 1 if it is not given. Here are some example URLs that show how I'm going to be implement this:

- Page 1, implicit: *http://localhost:5000/index*

- Page 1, explicit: *http://localhost:5000/index?page=1*

9.4. PAGINATION OF BLOG POSTS

- Page 3: *http://localhost:5000/index?page=3*

To access arguments given in the query string, I can use the Flask's `request.args` object. You have seen this already in Chapter 5, where I implemented user login URLs from Flask-Login that can include a `next` query string argument.

Below you can see how I added pagination to the home and explore view functions:

Listing 9.11: *app/routes.py*: Followers association table

```python
@app.route('/', methods=['GET', 'POST'])
@app.route('/index', methods=['GET', 'POST'])
@login_required
def index():
    # ...
    page = request.args.get('page', 1, type=int)
    posts = current_user.followed_posts().paginate(
        page, app.config['POSTS_PER_PAGE'], False)
    return render_template('index.html', title='Home', form=form,
                           posts=posts.items)

@app.route('/explore')
@login_required
def explore():
    page = request.args.get('page', 1, type=int)
    posts = Post.query.order_by(Post.timestamp.desc()).paginate(
        page, app.config['POSTS_PER_PAGE'], False)
    return render_template("index.html", title='Explore', posts=posts.items)
```

With these changes, the two routes determine the page number to display, either from the `page` query string argument or a default of 1, and then use the `paginate()` method to retrieve only the desired page of results. The `POSTS_PER_PAGE` configuration item that determines the page size is accessed through the `app.config` object.

Note how easy these changes are, and how little code is affected each time a change is made. I am trying to write each part of the application without making any assumptions about how the other parts work, and this enables me to write modular and robust applications that are easier to extend and to test, and are less likely to fail or have bugs.

Go ahead and try the pagination support. First make sure you have more than three blog posts. This is easier to see in the explore page, which shows posts from all users. You are now going to see just the three most recent posts. If you want to see the next three, type *http://localhost:5000/explore?page=2* in your browser's address bar.

9.5 Page Navigation

The next change is to add links at the bottom of the blog post list that allow users to navigate to the next and/or previous pages. Remember that I mentioned that the return value from a `paginate()` call is an object of a `Pagination` class from Flask-SQLAlchemy? So far, I have used the `items` attribute of this object, which contains the list of items retrieved for the selected page. But this object has a few other attributes that are useful when building pagination links:

- `has_next`: True if there is at least one more page after the current one
- `has_prev`: True if there is at least one more page before the current one
- `next_num`: page number for the next page
- `prev_num`: page number for the previous page

With these four elements, I can generate next and previous page links and pass them down to the templates for rendering:

Listing 9.12: *app/routes.py*: Next and previous page links.

```python
@app.route('/', methods=['GET', 'POST'])
@app.route('/index', methods=['GET', 'POST'])
@login_required
def index():
    # ...
    page = request.args.get('page', 1, type=int)
    posts = current_user.followed_posts().paginate(
        page, app.config['POSTS_PER_PAGE'], False)
    next_url = url_for('index', page=posts.next_num) \
        if posts.has_next else None
    prev_url = url_for('index', page=posts.prev_num) \
        if posts.has_prev else None
    return render_template('index.html', title='Home', form=form,
                           posts=posts.items, next_url=next_url,
                           prev_url=prev_url)

@app.route('/explore')
@login_required
def explore():
    page = request.args.get('page', 1, type=int)
    posts = Post.query.order_by(Post.timestamp.desc()).paginate(
        page, app.config['POSTS_PER_PAGE'], False)
    next_url = url_for('explore', page=posts.next_num) \
        if posts.has_next else None
    prev_url = url_for('explore', page=posts.prev_num) \
        if posts.has_prev else None
    return render_template("index.html", title='Explore', posts=posts.items,
                           next_url=next_url, prev_url=prev_url)
```

9.5. PAGE NAVIGATION

The `next_url` and `prev_url` in these two view functions are going to be set to a URL returned by `url_for()` only if there is a page in that direction. If the current page is at one of the ends of the collection of posts, then the `has_next` or `has_prev` attributes of the `Pagination` object will be `False`, and in that case the link in that direction will be set to `None`.

One interesting aspect of the `url_for()` function that I haven't discussed before is that you can add any keyword arguments to it, and if the names of those arguments are not referenced in the URL directly, then Flask will include them in the URL as query arguments.

The pagination links are being set to the *index.html* template, so now let's render them on the page, right below the post list:

Listing 9.13: *app/templates/index.html*: Render pagination links on the template.

```
...
{% for post in posts %}
    {% include '_post.html' %}
{% endfor %}
{% if prev_url %}
<a href="{{ prev_url }}">Newer posts</a>
{% endif %}
{% if next_url %}
<a href="{{ next_url }}">Older posts</a>
{% endif %}
...
```

This change adds to link below the post list on both the index and explore pages. The first link is labeled "Newer posts", and it points to the previous page (keep in mind I'm showing posts sorted by newest first, so the first page is the one with the newest content). The second link is labeled "Older posts" and points to the next page of posts. If any of these two links is `None`, then it is omitted from the page, through a conditional.

9.6 Pagination in the User Profile Page

The changes for the index page are sufficient for now. However, there is also a list of posts in the user profile page, which shows only posts from the owner of the profile. To be consistent, the user profile page should be changed to match the pagination style of the index page.

I begin by updating the user profile view function, which still had a list of fake post objects in it.

Listing 9.14: *app/routes.py*: Pagination in the user profile view function.

```
@app.route('/user/<username>')
@login_required
```

9.6. PAGINATION IN THE USER PROFILE PAGE

```
def user(username):
    user = User.query.filter_by(username=username).first_or_404()
    page = request.args.get('page', 1, type=int)
    posts = user.posts.order_by(Post.timestamp.desc()).paginate(
        page, app.config['POSTS_PER_PAGE'], False)
    next_url = url_for('user', username=user.username, page=posts.next_num) \
        if posts.has_next else None
    prev_url = url_for('user', username=user.username, page=posts.prev_num) \
        if posts.has_prev else None
    return render_template('user.html', user=user, posts=posts.items,
                           next_url=next_url, prev_url=prev_url)
```

To get the list of posts from the user, I take advantage of the fact that the `user.posts` relationship is a query that is already set up by SQLAlchemy as a result of the `db.relationship()` definition in the `User` model. I take this query and add a `order_by()` clause so that I get the newest posts first, and then do the pagination exactly like I did for the posts in the index and explore pages. Note that the pagination links that are generated by the `url_for()` function need the extra `username` argument, because they are pointing back at the user profile page, which has this username as a dynamic component of the URL.

Finally, the changes to the *user.html* template are identical to those I made on the index page:

Listing 9.15: *app/templates/user.html*: Pagination links in the user profile template.

```
...
{% for post in posts %}
    {% include '_post.html' %}
{% endfor %}
{% if prev_url %}
<a href="{{ prev_url }}">Newer posts</a>
{% endif %}
{% if next_url %}
<a href="{{ next_url }}">Older posts</a>
{% endif %}
```

After you are done experiment with the pagination feature, you can set the `POSTS_PER_PAGE` configuration item to a more reasonable value:

Listing 9.16: *config.py*: Posts per page configuration.

```
class Config(object):
    # ...
    POSTS_PER_PAGE = 25
```

Chapter 10

Email Support

The application is doing pretty well on the database front now, so in this chapter I want to depart from that topic and add another important piece that most web applications need, which is the sending of emails.

Why does an application need to email its users? There are many reasons, but one common one is to solve authentication related problems. In this chapter I'm going to add a password reset feature for users that forget their password. When a user requests a password reset, the application will send an email with a specially crafted link. The user then needs to click that link to have access to a form in which to set a new password.

The GitHub links for this chapter are: Browse[1], Zip[2], Diff[3].

10.1 Introduction to Flask-Mail

As far as the actual sending of emails, Flask has a popular extension called Flask-Mail[4] that can make the task very easy. As always, this extension is installed with pip:

```
(venv) $ pip install flask-mail
```

The password reset links will have a secure token in them. To generate these tokens, I'm going

---

[1] https://github.com/miguelgrinberg/microblog/tree/v0.10
[2] https://github.com/miguelgrinberg/microblog/archive/v0.10.zip
[3] https://github.com/miguelgrinberg/microblog/compare/v0.9...v0.10
[4] https://pythonhosted.org/Flask-Mail/

to use JSON Web Tokens[5], which also have a popular Python package:

```
(venv) $ pip install pyjwt
```

The Flask-Mail extension is configured from the `app.config` object. Remember when in Chapter 7 I added the email configuration for sending yourself an email whenever an error occurred in production? I did not tell you this then, but my choice of configuration variables was modeled after Flask-Mail's requirements, so there isn't really any additional work that is needed, the configuration variables are already in the application.

Like most Flask extensions, you need to create an instance right after the Flask application is created. In this case this is an object of class `Mail`:

Listing 10.1: *app/__init__.py*: Flask-Mail instance.

```python
# ...
from flask_mail import Mail

app = Flask(__name__)
# ...
mail = Mail(app)
```

If you are planning to test sending of emails you have the same two options I mentioned in Chapter 7. If you want to use an emulated email server, Python provides one that is very handy that you can start in a second terminal with the following command:

```
(venv) $ python -m smtpd -n -c DebuggingServer localhost:8025
```

To configure for this server you will need to set two environment variables:

```
(venv) $ export MAIL_SERVER=localhost
(venv) $ export MAIL_PORT=8025
```

If you prefer to have emails sent for real, you need to use a real email server. If you have one, then you just need to set the `MAIL_SERVER`, `MAIL_PORT`, `MAIL_USE_TLS`, `MAIL_USERNAME` and `MAIL_PASSWORD` environment variables for it. If you want a quick solution, you can use a Gmail account to send email, with the following settings:

---

[5] https://jwt.io

```
(venv) $ export MAIL_SERVER=smtp.googlemail.com
(venv) $ export MAIL_PORT=587
(venv) $ export MAIL_USE_TLS=1
(venv) $ export MAIL_USERNAME=<your-gmail-username>
(venv) $ export MAIL_PASSWORD=<your-gmail-password>
```

If you are using Microsoft Windows, you need to replace `export` with `set` in each of the `export` statements above.

Remember that the security features in your Gmail account may prevent the application from sending emails through it unless you explicitly allow "less secure apps" access to your Gmail account. You can read about this here[6], and if you are concerned about the security of your account, you can create a secondary account that you configure just for testing emails, or you can enable less secure apps only temporarily to run your tests and then revert back to the more secure default.

10.2 Flask-Mail Usage

To learn how Flask-Mail works, I'll show you how to send an email from a Python shell. So fire up Python with `flask shell`, and then run the following commands:

```
>>> from flask_mail import Message
>>> from app import mail
>>> msg = Message('test subject', sender=app.config['ADMINS'][0],
...     recipients=['your-email@example.com'])
>>> msg.body = 'text body'
>>> msg.html = '<h1>HTML body</h1>'
>>> mail.send(msg)
```

The snippet of code above will send an email to a list of email addresses that you put in the `recipients` argument. I put the sender as the first configured admin (I've added the `ADMINS` configuration variable in Chapter 7). The email will have plain text and HTML versions, so depending on how your email client is configured you may see one or the other.

So as you see, this is pretty simple. Now let's integrate emails into the application.

---

[6]https://support.google.com/accounts/answer/6010255?hl=en

10.3 A Simple Email Framework

I will begin by writing a helper function that sends an email, which is basically a generic version of the shell exercise from the previous section. I will put this function in a new module called `app/email.py`:

Listing 10.2: *app/email.py*: Email sending wrapper function.

```
from flask_mail import Message
from app import mail

def send_email(subject, sender, recipients, text_body, html_body):
    msg = Message(subject, sender=sender, recipients=recipients)
    msg.body = text_body
    msg.html = html_body
    mail.send(msg)
```

Flask-Mail supports some features that I'm not utilizing here such as Cc and Bcc lists. Be sure to check the Flask-Mail Documentation[7] if you are interested in those options.

10.4 Requesting a Password Reset

As I mentioned above, I want users to have the option to request their password to be reset. For this purpose I'm going to add a link in the login page:

Listing 10.3: *app/templates/login.html*: Password reset link in login form.

```
<p>
    Forgot Your Password?
    <a href="{{ url_for('reset_password_request') }}">Click to Reset It</a>
</p>
```

When the user clicks the link, a new web form will appear that requests the user's email address as a way to initiate the password reset process. Here is the form class:

Listing 10.4: *app/forms.py*: Reset password request form.

```
class ResetPasswordRequestForm(FlaskForm):
    email = StringField('Email', validators=[DataRequired(), Email()])
    submit = SubmitField('Request Password Reset')
```

---

[7]https://pythonhosted.org/Flask-Mail/

10.4. REQUESTING A PASSWORD RESET

And here is the corresponding HTML template:

Listing 10.5: *app/templates/reset_password_request.html*: Reset password request template.

```html
{% extends "base.html" %}

{% block content %}
    <h1>Reset Password</h1>
    <form action="" method="post">
        {{ form.hidden_tag() }}
        <p>
            {{ form.email.label }}<br>
            {{ form.email(size=64) }}<br>
            {% for error in form.email.errors %}
            <span style="color: red;">[{{ error }}]</span>
            {% endfor %}
        </p>
        <p>{{ form.submit() }}</p>
    </form>
{% endblock %}
```

I also need a view function to handle this form:

Listing 10.6: *app/routes.py*: Reset password request view function.

```python
from app.forms import ResetPasswordRequestForm
from app.email import send_password_reset_email

@app.route('/reset_password_request', methods=['GET', 'POST'])
def reset_password_request():
    if current_user.is_authenticated:
        return redirect(url_for('index'))
    form = ResetPasswordRequestForm()
    if form.validate_on_submit():
        user = User.query.filter_by(email=form.email.data).first()
        if user:
            send_password_reset_email(user)
        flash('Check your email for the instructions to reset your password')
        return redirect(url_for('login'))
    return render_template('reset_password_request.html',
                           title='Reset Password', form=form)
```

This is view function is fairly similar to others that process a form. I start by making sure the user is not logged in. If the user is logged in, then there is no point in using the password reset functionality, so I redirect to the index page.

When the form is submitted and valid, I look up the user by the email provided by the user in the form. If I find the user, I send a password reset email. The `send_password_reset_email()` helper function performs this task. I will show you this function below.

After the email is sent, I flash a message directing the user to look for the email for further instructions, and then redirect back to the login page. You may notice that the flashed message is displayed even if the email provided by the user is unknown. This is so that clients cannot use this form to figure out if a given user is a member or not.

10.5 Password Reset Tokens

Before I implement the `send_password_reset_email()` function, I need to have a way to generate a password request link. This is going to be the link that is sent to the user via email. When the link is clicked, a page where a new password can be set is presented to the user. The tricky part of this plan is to make sure that only valid reset links can be used to reset an account's password.

The links are going to be provisioned with a *token*, and this token will be validated before allowing the password change, as proof that the user that requested the email has access to the email address on the account. A very popular token standard for this type of process is the JSON Web Token, or JWT. The nice thing about JWTs is that they are self contained. You can send a token to a user in an email, and when the user clicks the link that feeds the token back into the application, it can be verified on its own.

How do JWTs work? Nothing better than a quick Python shell session to understand them:

```
>>> import jwt
>>> token = jwt.encode({'a': 'b'}, 'my-secret', algorithm='HS256')
>>> token
b'eyJ0eXAiOiJKV1QiLCJhbGciOiJIUzI1NiJ9.eyJhIjoiYiJ9.dvOo58OBDHiuSHD4uW88nfJik_sfUHq1mDi4G0'
>>> jwt.decode(token, 'my-secret', algorithms=['HS256'])
{'a': 'b'}
```

The `{'a': 'b'}` dictionary is an example payload that is going to be written into the token. To make the token secure, a secret key needs to be provided to be used in creating a cryptographic signature. For this example I have used the string `'my-secret'`, but with the application I'm going to use the `SECRET_KEY` from the configuration. The `algorithm` argument specifies how the token is to be generated. The `HS256` algorithm is the most widely used.

As you can see the resulting token is a long sequence of characters. But do not think that this is an encrypted token. The contents of the token, including the payload, can be decoded easily by anyone (don't believe me? Copy the above token and then enter it in the JWT debugger[8] to

---

[8]https://jwt.io/#debugger-io

10.5. PASSWORD RESET TOKENS

see its contents). What makes the token secure is that the payload is *signed*. If somebody tried to forge or tamper with the payload in a token, then the signature would be invalidated, and to generate a new signature the secret key is needed. When a token is verified, the contents of the payload are decoded and returned back to the caller. If the token's signature was validated, then the payload can be trusted as authentic.

The payload that I'm going to use for the password reset tokens is going to have the format `{'reset_password': user_id, 'exp': token_expiration}`. The `exp` field is standard for JWTs and if present it indicates an expiration time for the token. If a token has a valid signature, but it is past its expiration timestamp, then it will also be considered invalid. For the password reset feature, I'm going to give these tokens 10 minutes of life.

When the user clicks on the emailed link, the token is going to be sent back to the application as part of the URL, and the first thing the view function that handles this URL will do is to verify it. If the signature is valid, then the user can be identified by the ID stored in the payload. Once the user's identity is known, the application can ask for a new password and set it on the user's account.

Since these tokens belong to users, I'm going to write the token generation and verification functions as methods in the `User` model:

Listing 10.7: *app/models.py*: Reset password token methods.

```python
from time import time
import jwt
from app import app

class User(UserMixin, db.Model):
    # ...

    def get_reset_password_token(self, expires_in=600):
        return jwt.encode(
            {'reset_password': self.id, 'exp': time() + expires_in},
            app.config['SECRET_KEY'], algorithm='HS256').decode('utf-8')

    @staticmethod
    def verify_reset_password_token(token):
        try:
            id = jwt.decode(token, app.config['SECRET_KEY'],
                            algorithms=['HS256'])['reset_password']
        except:
            return
        return User.query.get(id)
```

The `get_reset_password_token()` function generates a JWT token as a string. Note that the `decode('utf-8')` is necessary because the `jwt.encode()` function returns the token as a byte sequence, but in the application it is more convenient to have the token as a string.

The `verify_reset_password_token()` is a static method, which means that it can be invoked directly from the class. A static method is similar to a class method, with the only difference that static methods do not receive the class as a first argument. This method takes a token and attempts to decode it by invoking PyJWT's `jwt.decode()` function. If the token cannot be validated or is expired, an exception will be raised, and in that case I catch it to prevent the error, and then return `None` to the caller. If the token is valid, then the value of the `reset_password` key from the token's payload is the ID of the user, so I can load the user and return it.

10.6 Sending a Password Reset Email

The `send_password_reset_email()` function relies on the `send_email()` function I wrote above to generate the password reset emails.

Listing 10.8: *app/email.py*: Send password reset email function.

```python
from flask import render_template
from app import app

# ...

def send_password_reset_email(user):
    token = user.get_reset_password_token()
    send_email('[Microblog] Reset Your Password',
               sender=app.config['ADMINS'][0],
               recipients=[user.email],
               text_body=render_template('email/reset_password.txt',
                                         user=user, token=token),
               html_body=render_template('email/reset_password.html',
                                         user=user, token=token))
```

The interesting part in this function is that the text and HTML content for the emails is generated from templates using the familiar `render_template()` function. The templates receive the user and the token as arguments, so that a personalized email message can be generated. Here is the text template for the reset password email:

Listing 10.9: *app/templates/email/reset_password.txt*: Text for password reset email.

```
Dear {{ user.username }},

To reset your password click on the following link:

{{ url_for('reset_password', token=token, _external=True) }}
```

10.7. RESETTING A USER PASSWORD

```
If you have not requested a password reset simply ignore this message.
Sincerely,
The Microblog Team
```

And here is the nicer HTML version of the same email:

Listing 10.10: *app/templates/email/reset_password.html*: HTML for password reset email.

```html
<p>Dear {{ user.username }},</p>
<p>
    To reset your password
    <a href="{{ url_for('reset_password', token=token, _external=True) }}">
        click here
    </a>.
</p>
<p>Alternatively, you can paste the following link in your browser's address bar:</p>
<p>{{ url_for('reset_password', token=token, _external=True) }}</p>
<p>If you have not requested a password reset simply ignore this message.</p>
<p>Sincerely,</p>
<p>The Microblog Team</p>
```

The `reset_password` route that is referenced in the `url_for()` call in these two email templates does not exist yet, this will be added in the next section. The `_external=True` argument that I included in the `url_for()` calls in both templates is also new. The URLs that are generated by `url_for()` by default are relative URLs that only include the path portion of the URL. This is normally sufficient for links that are generated in web pages, because the web browser completes the URL by taking the missing parts from the URL in the address bar. When sending a URL by email however, that context does not exist, so fully qualified URLs need to be used. When `_external=True` is passed as an argument, complete URLs are generated, so the previous example would return *http://localhost:5000/user/susan*, or the appropriate URL when the application is deployed on a domain name.

10.7 Resetting a User Password

When the user clicks on the email link, a second route associated with this feature is triggered. Here is the password request view function:

Listing 10.11: *app/routes.py*: Password reset view function.

```
from app.forms import ResetPasswordForm

@app.route('/reset_password/<token>', methods=['GET', 'POST'])
def reset_password(token):
    if current_user.is_authenticated:
        return redirect(url_for('index'))
    user = User.verify_reset_password_token(token)
    if not user:
        return redirect(url_for('index'))
    form = ResetPasswordForm()
    if form.validate_on_submit():
        user.set_password(form.password.data)
        db.session.commit()
        flash('Your password has been reset.')
        return redirect(url_for('login'))
    return render_template('reset_password.html', form=form)
```

In this view function I first make sure the user is not logged in, and then I determine who the user is by invoking the token verification method in the `User` class. This method returns the user if the token is valid, or `None` if not. If the token is invalid I redirect to the home page.

If the token is valid, then I present the user with a second form, in which the new password is requested. This form is processed in a way similar to previous forms, and as a result of a valid form submission, I invoke the `set_password()` method of `User` to change the password, and then redirect to the login page, where the user can now login.

Here is the `ResetPasswordForm` class:

Listing 10.12: *app/forms.py*: Password reset form.

```
class ResetPasswordForm(FlaskForm):
    password = PasswordField('Password', validators=[DataRequired()])
    password2 = PasswordField(
        'Repeat Password', validators=[DataRequired(), EqualTo('password')])
    submit = SubmitField('Request Password Reset')
```

And here is the corresponding HTML template:

Listing 10.13: *app/templates/reset_password.html*: Password reset form template.

```
{% extends "base.html" %}

{% block content %}
    <h1>Reset Your Password</h1>
    <form action="" method="post">
        {{ form.hidden_tag() }}
        <p>
            {{ form.password.label }}<br>
```

10.8. ASYNCHRONOUS EMAILS

```
            {{ form.password(size=32) }}<br>
            {% for error in form.password.errors %}
            <span style="color: red;">[{{ error }}]</span>
            {% endfor %}
        </p>
        <p>
            {{ form.password2.label }}<br>
            {{ form.password2(size=32) }}<br>
            {% for error in form.password2.errors %}
            <span style="color: red;">[{{ error }}]</span>
            {% endfor %}
        </p>
        <p>{{ form.submit() }}</p>
    </form>
{% endblock %}
```

The password reset feature is now complete, so make sure you try it.

10.8 Asynchronous Emails

If you are using the simulated email server that Python provides you may not have noticed this, but sending an email slows the application down considerably. All the interactions that need to happen when sending an email make the task slow, it usually takes a few seconds to get an email out, and maybe more if the email server of the addressee is slow, or if there are multiple addressees.

What I really want is for the `send_email()` function to be *asynchronous*. What does that mean? It means that when this function is called, the task of sending the email is scheduled to happen in the background, freeing the `send_email()` to return immediately so that the application can continue running concurrently with the email being sent.

Python has support for running asynchronous tasks, actually in more than one way. The `threading` and `multiprocessing` modules can both do this. Starting a background thread for email being sent is much less resource intensive than starting a brand new process, so I'm going to go with that approach:

Listing 10.14: *app/email.py*: Send emails asynchronously.

```
from threading import Thread
# ...

def send_async_email(app, msg):
    with app.app_context():
        mail.send(msg)
```

```
def send_email(subject, sender, recipients, text_body, html_body):
    msg = Message(subject, sender=sender, recipients=recipients)
    msg.body = text_body
    msg.html = html_body
    Thread(target=send_async_email, args=(app, msg)).start()
```

The `send_async_email` function now runs in a background thread, invoked via the `Thread` class in the last line of `send_email()`. With this change, the sending of the email will run in the thread, and when process completes the thread will end and clean itself up. If you have configured a real email server, you will definitely notice a speed improvement when you press the submit button on the password reset request form.

You probably expected that only the `msg` argument would be sent to the thread, but as you can see in the code, I'm also sending the application instance. When working with threads there is an important design aspect of Flask that needs to be kept in mind. Flask uses *contexts* to avoid having to pass arguments across functions. I'm not going to go into a lot of detail on this, but know that there are two types of contexts, the *application context* and the *request context*. In most cases, these contexts are automatically managed by the framework, but when the application starts custom threads, contexts for those threads may need to be manually created.

There are many extensions that require an application context to be in place to work, because that allows them to find the Flask application instance without it being passed as an argument. The reason many extensions need to know the application instance is because they have their configuration stored in the `app.config` object. This is exactly the situation with Flask-Mail. The `mail.send()` method needs to access the configuration values for the email server, and that can only be done by knowing what the application is. The application context that is created with the `with app.app_context()` call makes the application instance accessible via the `current_app` variable from Flask.

Chapter 11

Facelift

You have been playing with my Microblog application for a while now, so I'm sure you noticed that I haven't spent too much time making it look good, or better said, I haven't spent any time on that. The templates that I put together are pretty basic, with absolutely no custom styling. It was useful for me to concentrate on the actual logic of the application without having the distraction of also writing good looking HTML and CSS.

But I've focused on the backend part of this application for a while now. So in this chapter I'm taking a break from that and will spend some time showing you what can be done to make the application look a bit more polished and professional.

This chapter is going to be a bit different than previous ones, because I'm not going to be as detailed as I normally am with the Python side, which after all, is the main topic of this tutorial. Creating good looking web pages is a vast topic that is largely unrelated to Python web development, but I will discuss some basic guidelines and ideas on how to approach the task, and you will also have the application with the redesigned looks to study and learn from.

The GitHub links for this chapter are: Browse[1], Zip[2], Diff[3].

11.1 CSS Frameworks

While we can argue that coding is hard, our pains are nothing compared to those of web designers, who have to write templates that have a nice and consistent look on a list of web

---

[1]https://github.com/miguelgrinberg/microblog/tree/v0.11
[2]https://github.com/miguelgrinberg/microblog/archive/v0.11.zip
[3]https://github.com/miguelgrinberg/microblog/compare/v0.10...v0.11

browsers. It has gotten better in recent years, but there are still obscure bugs or quirks in some browsers that make the task of designing web pages that look nice everywhere very hard. This is even harder if you also need to target resource and screen limited browsers of tablets and smartphones.

If you, like me, are a developer who just wants to create decent looking web pages, but do not have the time or interest to learn the low level mechanisms to achieve this effectively by writing raw HTML and CSS, then the only practical solution is to use a *CSS framework* to simplify the task. You will be losing some creative freedom by taking this path, but on the other side, your web pages will look good in all browsers without a lot of effort. A CSS framework provides a collection of high-level CSS classes with pre-made styles for common types of user interface elements. Most of these frameworks also provide JavaScript add-ons for things that cannot be done strictly with HTML and CSS.

11.2 Introducing Bootstrap

One of the most popular CSS frameworks is Bootstrap[4], created by Twitter. If you want to see the kind of pages that can be designed with this framework, the documentation has some examples[5].

These are some of the benefits of using Bootstrap to style your web pages:

- Similar look in all major web browsers
- Handling of desktop, tablet and phone screen sizes
- Customizable layouts
- Nicely styled navigation bars, forms, buttons, alerts, popups, etc.

The most direct way to use Bootstrap is to simply import the *bootstrap.min.css* file in your base template. You can either download a copy of this file and add it to your project, or import it directly from a CDN[6]. Then you can start using the general purpose CSS classes it provides, according to the documentation[7], which is pretty good. You may also want to import the *bootstrap.min.js* file containing the framework's JavaScript code, so that you can also use the most advanced features.

---

[4] http://getbootstrap.com/
[5] https://getbootstrap.com/docs/3.3/getting-started/#examples
[6] https://en.wikipedia.org/wiki/Content_delivery_network
[7] https://getbootstrap.com/docs/3.3/getting-started/

11.3 Using Flask-Bootstrap

Fortunately, there is a Flask extension called Flask-Bootstrap[8] that provides a ready to use base template that has the Bootstrap framework installed. Let's install this extension:

```
(venv) $ pip install flask-bootstrap
```

11.3 Using Flask-Bootstrap

Flask-Bootstrap needs to be initialized like most other Flask extensions:

Listing 11.1: *app/__init__.py*: Flask-Bootstrap instance.

```python
# ...
from flask_bootstrap import Bootstrap

app = Flask(__name__)
# ...
bootstrap = Bootstrap(app)
```

With the extension initialized, a *bootstrap/base.html* template becomes available, and can be referenced from application templates with the `extends` clause.

But as you recall, I'm already using the `extends` clause with my own base template, which allows me to have the common parts of the page in a single place. My *base.html* template defined the navigation bar, which included a few links, and also exported a `content` block. All other templates in my application inherit from the base template and provide the `content` block with the main content of the page.

So how can I fit the Bootstrap base template? The idea is to use a three-level hierarchy instead of just two. The *bootstrap/base.html* template provides the basic structure of the page, which includes the Bootstrap framework files. This template exports a few blocks for derived templates such as `title`, `navbar` and `content` (see the complete list of blocks here[9]). I'm going to change my *base.html* template to derive from *bootstrap/base.html* and provide implementations for the `title`, `navbar` and `content` blocks. In turn, *base.html* will export its own `app_content` block for its derived templates to define the page content.

Below you can see how the *base.html* looks after I modified it to inherit from the Bootstrap base template. Note that this listing does not include the entire HTML for the navigation bar, but you can see the full implementation on GitHub or by downloading the code for this chapter.

---

[8]https://pythonhosted.org/Flask-Bootstrap/
[9]https://pythonhosted.org/Flask-Bootstrap/basic-usage.html#available-blocks

Listing 11.2: *app/templates/base.html*: Redesigned base template.

```
{% extends 'bootstrap/base.html' %}

{% block title %}
    {% if title %}{{ title }} - Microblog{% else %}Welcome to Microblog{% endif %}
{% endblock %}

{% block navbar %}
    <nav class="navbar navbar-default">
        ... navigation bar here (see complete code on GitHub) ...
    </nav>
{% endblock %}

{% block content %}
    <div class="container">
        {% with messages = get_flashed_messages() %}
        {% if messages %}
            {% for message in messages %}
            <div class="alert alert-info" role="alert">{{ message }}</div>
            {% endfor %}
        {% endif %}
        {% endwith %}

        {# application content needs to be provided in the app_content block #}
        {% block app_content %}{% endblock %}
    </div>
{% endblock %}
```

Here you can see how I make this template derive from *bootstrap/base.html*, followed by the three blocks that implement the page title, navigation bar and page content respectively.

The `title` block needs to define the text that will be used for the page title, with the `<title>` tags. For this block I simply moved the logic that was inside the `<title>` tag in the original base template.

The `navbar` block is an optional block that can be used to define a navigation bar. For this block, I adapted the example in the Bootstrap navigation bar documentation so that it includes a site branding on the left end, followed by the Home and Explore links. I then added the Profile and Login or Logout links aligned with the right border of the page. As I mentioned above, I omitted the HTML in the example above, but you can obtain the full *base.html* template from the download package for this chapter.

Finally, in the `content` block I'm defining a top-level container, and inside it I have the logic that renders flashed messages, which are now going to appear styled as Bootstrap alerts. That is followed with a new `app_content` block that is defined just so that derived templates can define their own content.

The original version of all the page templates defined their content in a block named `content`. As you saw above, the block named `content` is used by Flask-Bootstrap, so I renamed my

11.4. RENDERING BOOTSTRAP FORMS

content block as `app_content`. So all my templates have to be renamed to use `app_content` as their content block. As an example, here how the modified version of the *404.html* template looks like:

Listing 11.3: *app/templates/404.html*: Redesigned 404 error template.

```
{% extends "base.html" %}

{% block app_content %}
    <h1>File Not Found</h1>
    <p><a href="{{ url_for('index') }}">Back</a></p>
{% endblock %}
```

11.4 Rendering Bootstrap Forms

An area where Flask-Bootstrap does a fantastic job is in rendering of forms. Instead of having to style the form fields one by one, Flask-Bootstrap comes with a macro that accepts a Flask-WTF form object as an argument and renders the complete form using Bootstrap styles.

Below you can see the redesigned *register.html* template as an example:

Listing 11.4: *app/templates/register.html*: User registration template.

```
{% extends "base.html" %}
{% import 'bootstrap/wtf.html' as wtf %}

{% block app_content %}
    <h1>Register</h1>
    <div class="row">
        <div class="col-md-4">
            {{ wtf.quick_form(form) }}
        </div>
    </div>
{% endblock %}
```

Isn't this great? The `import` statement near the top works similarly to a Python import on the template side. That adds a `wtf.quick_form()` macro that in a single line of code renders the complete form, including support for display validation errors, and all styled as appropriate for the Bootstrap framework.

Once again, I'm not going to show you all the changes that I've done for the other forms in the application, but these changes are all made in the code that you can download or inspect on GitHub.

11.5 Rendering of Blog Posts

The presentation logic that renders a single blog posts was abstracted into a sub-template called *_post.html*. All I need to do with this template is make some minor adjustments so that it looks good under Bootstrap.

Listing 11.5: *app/templates/_post.html*: Redesigned post sub-template.

```
<table class="table table-hover">
    <tr>
        <td width="70px">
            <a href="{{ url_for('user', username=post.author.username) }}">
                <img src="{{ post.author.avatar(70) }}" />
            </a>
        </td>
        <td>
            <a href="{{ url_for('user', username=post.author.username) }}">
                {{ post.author.username }}
            </a>
            says:
            <br>
            {{ post.body }}
        </td>
    </tr>
</table>
```

11.6 Rendering Pagination Links

Pagination links is another area where Bootstrap provides direct support. For this I just went one more time to the Bootstrap documentation[10] and adapted one of their examples. Here is how these look in the *index.html* page:

Listing 11.6: *app/templates/index.html*: Redesigned pagination links.

```
...
<nav aria-label="...">
    <ul class="pager">
        <li class="previous{% if not prev_url %} disabled{% endif %}">
            <a href="{{ prev_url or '#' }}">
                <span aria-hidden="true">&larr;</span> Newer posts
            </a>
        </li>
        <li class="next{% if not next_url %} disabled{% endif %}">
            <a href="{{ next_url or '#' }}">
                Older posts <span aria-hidden="true">&rarr;</span>
            </a>
```

---

[10]https://getbootstrap.com/docs/3.3/components/#optional-disabled-state

11.7. BEFORE AND AFTER

```
            </a>
        </li>
    </ul>
</nav>
```

Note that in this implementation, instead of hiding the next or previous link when that direction does not have any more content, I'm applying a disabled state, which will make the link appear grayed out.

I'm not going to show it here, but a similar change needs to be applied to *user.html*. The download package for this chapter includes these changes.

11.7 Before And After

To update your application with these changes, please download the zip file for this chapter and update your templates accordingly.

Below you can see a few before and after pictures to see the transformation. Keep in mind that this change was achieved without changing a single line of application logic!

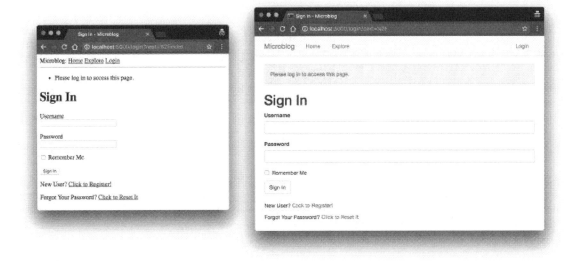

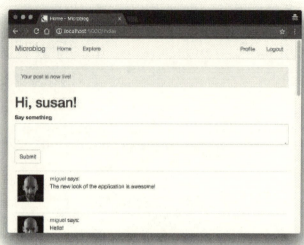

Chapter 12

Dates and Times

One of the aspects of my Microblog application that I have ignored for a long time is the display of dates and times. Until now, I've just let Python render the `datetime` object in the `User` model, and have completely ignored the one in the `Post` model.

The GitHub links for this chapter are: Browse[1], Zip[2], Diff[3].

12.1 Timezone Hell

Using Python on the server to render dates and times that are presented to users on their web browsers is really not a good idea. Consider the following example. I'm writing this at 4:06PM on September 28th, 2017. My timezone at the time I'm writing this is PDT (or UTC-7 if you prefer). Running in a Python interpreter I get the following:

```
>>> from datetime import datetime
>>> str(datetime.now())
'2017-09-28 16:06:30.439388'
>>> str(datetime.utcnow())
'2017-09-28 23:06:51.406499'
```

The `now()` call returns the correct time for my location, while the `utcnow()` call returns the time in the UTC time zone. If I could ask many people living in different parts of the world to run the above code all at that same time with me, the `now()` function will return different

---

[1] https://github.com/miguelgrinberg/microblog/tree/v0.12
[2] https://github.com/miguelgrinberg/microblog/archive/v0.12.zip
[3] https://github.com/miguelgrinberg/microblog/compare/v0.11...v0.12

results for each person, but `utcnow()` will always return the same time, regardless of location. So which one do you think is better to use in a web application that will very likely have users located all over the world?

It is pretty clear that the server must manage times that are consistent and independent of location. If this application grows to the point of needing several production servers in different regions around the world, I would not want each server to write timestamps to the database in different timezones, because that would make working with these times impossible. Since UTC is the most used uniform timezone and is supported in the `datetime` class, that is what I'm going to use.

But there is an important problem with this approach. For users in different timezones, it will be awfully difficult to figure out when a post was made if they see times in the UTC timezone. They would need to know in advance that the times are in UTC so that they can mentally adjust the times to their own timezone. Imagine a user in the PDT timezone that posts something at 3:00pm, and immediately sees that the post appears with a 10:00pm UTC time, or to be more exact 22:00. That is going to be very confusing.

While standardizing the timestamps to UTC makes a lot of sense from the server's perspective, this creates a usability problem for users. The goal of this chapter is to address this problem while keeping all the timestamps managed in the server in UTC.

12.2 Timezone Conversions

The obvious solution to the problem is to convert all timestamps from the stored UTC units to the local time of each user. This allows the server to continue using UTC for consistency, while an on-the-fly conversion tailored to each user solves the usability problem. The tricky part of this solution is to know the location of each user.

Many websites have a configuration page where users can specify their timezone. This would require me to add a new page with a form in which I present users with a dropdown with the list of timezones. Users can be asked to enter their timezone when they access the site for the first time, as part of their registration.

While this is a decent solution that solves the problem, it is a bit odd to ask users to enter a piece of information that they have already configured in their operating system. It seems it would be more efficient if I could just grab the timezone setting from their computers.

As it turns out, the web browser knows the user's timezone, and exposes it through the standard date and time JavaScript APIs. There are actually two ways to take advantage of the timezone information available via JavaScript:

- The "old school" approach would be to have the web browser somehow send the timezone information to the server when the user first logs on to the application. This could be done with an Ajax[4] call, or much more simply with a meta refresh tag[5]. Once the server knows the timezone it can keep it in the user's session or write it to the user's entry in the database, and from then on adjust all timestamps with it at the time templates are rendered.

- The "new school" approach would be to not change a thing in the server, and let the conversion from UTC to local timezone happen in the client, using JavaScript.

Both options are valid, but the second one has a big advantage. Knowing the timezone of the user isn't always enough to present dates and times in the format expected by the user. The browser has also access to the system locale configuration, which specifies things like AM/PM vs. 24 hour clock, DD/MM/YYYY vs. MM/DD/YYYY and many other cultural or regional styles.

And if that isn't enough, there is yet one more advantage for the new school approach. There is an open-source library that does all this work!

12.3 Introducing Moment.js and Flask-Moment

Moment.js[6] is a small open-source JavaScript library that takes date and time rendering to another level, as it provides every imaginable formatting option, and then some. And a while ago I created Flask-Moment, a small Flask extension that makes it very easy to incorporate moment.js into your application.

So let's start by installing Flask-Moment:

```
(venv) $ pip install flask-moment
```

This extension is added to a Flask application in the usual way:

Listing 12.1: *app/__init__.py*: Flask-Moment instance.

---

[4]http://en.wikipedia.org/wiki/Ajax_(programming)
[5]http://en.wikipedia.org/wiki/Meta_refresh
[6]http://momentjs.com

```
# ...
from flask_moment import Moment

app = Flask(__name__)
# ...
moment = Moment(app)
```

Unlike other extensions, Flask-Moment works together with *moment.js*, so all templates of the application must include this library. To ensure that this library is always available, I'm going to add it in the base template. This can be done in two ways. The most direct way is to explicitly add a `<script>` tag that imports the library, but Flask-Moment makes it easier, by exposing a `moment.include_moment()` function that generates the `<script>` tag:

Listing 12.2: *app/templates/base.html*: Including moment.js in the base template.

```
...

{% block scripts %}
    {{ super() }}
    {{ moment.include_moment() }}
{% endblock %}
```

The `scripts` block that I added here is another block exported by Flask-Bootstrap's base template. This is the place where JavaScript imports are to be included. This block is different from previous ones in that it already comes with some content defined in the base template. All I want to do is add the moment.js library, without losing the base contents. And this is achieved with the `super()` statement, which preserves the content from the base template. If you define a block in your template without using `super()`, then any content defined for this block in the base template will be lost.

12.4 Using Moment.js

Moment.js makes a `moment` class available to the browser. The first step to render a timestamp is to create an object of this class, passing the desired timestamp in ISO 8601[7] format. Here is an example:

```
t = moment('2017-09-28T21:45:23Z')
```

---
[7]http://en.wikipedia.org/wiki/ISO_8601

12.4. USING MOMENT.JS

If you are not familiar with the ISO 8601 standard format for dates and times, the format is as follows:

```
{{ year }}-{{ month }}-{{ day }}T{{ hour }}:{{ minute }}:{{ second }}{{ timezone }}
```

I already decided that I was only going to work with UTC timezones, so the last part is always going to be `Z`, which represents UTC in the ISO 8601 standard.

The `moment` object provides several methods for different rendering options. Below are some of the most common options:

```
moment('2017-09-28T21:45:23Z').format('L')
"09/28/2017"
moment('2017-09-28T21:45:23Z').format('LL')
"September 28, 2017"
moment('2017-09-28T21:45:23Z').format('LLL')
"September 28, 2017 2:45 PM"
moment('2017-09-28T21:45:23Z').format('LLLL')
"Thursday, September 28, 2017 2:45 PM"
moment('2017-09-28T21:45:23Z').format('dddd')
"Thursday"
moment('2017-09-28T21:45:23Z').fromNow()
"7 hours ago"
moment('2017-09-28T21:45:23Z').calendar()
"Today at 2:45 PM"
```

This example creates a moment object initialized to September 28th 2017 at 9:45pm UTC. You can see that all the options I tried above are rendered in UTC-7, which is the timezone configured on my computer. You can enter the above commands in your browser's console, making sure the page on which you open the console has moment.js included. You can do it in microblog, as long as you made the changes above to include moment.js, or also on *https://momentjs.com/*.

Note how the different methods create different representations. With `format()` you control the format of the output with a format string, similar to the strftime[8] function from Python. The `fromNow()` and `calendar()` methods are interesting because they render the timestamp in relation to the current time, so you get output such as "a minute ago" or "in two hours", etc.

If you were working directly in JavaScript, the above calls return a string that has the rendered timestamp. Then it is up to you to insert this text in the proper place on the page, which unfortunately requires some JavaScript to work with the DOM[9]. The Flask-Moment extension greatly simplifies the use of moment.js by enabling a `moment` object similar to the JavaScript

---
[8]https://docs.python.org/3.6/library/time.html#time.strftime
[9]https://en.wikipedia.org/wiki/Document_Object_Model

one your templates, incorporating the required JavaScript magic to make the rendered times appear on the page.

Let's look at the timestamp that appears in the profile page. The current *user.html* template lets Python generate a string representation of the time. I can now render this timestamp using Flask-Moment as follows:

Listing 12.3: *app/templates/user.html*: Render timestamp with moment.js.

```
{% if user.last_seen %}
<p>Last seen on: {{ moment(user.last_seen).format('LLL') }}</p>
{% endif %}
```

So as you can see, Flask-Moment uses a syntax that is similar to that of the JavaScript library, with one difference being that the argument to `moment()` is now a Python `datetime` object and not an ISO 8601 string. The `moment()` call issued from a template also automatically generates the required JavaScript code to insert the rendered timestamp in the proper place of the DOM.

The second place where I can take advantage of Flask-Moment is in the *_post.html* sub-template, which is invoked from the index and user pages. In the current version of the template, each post preceded with a "username says:" line. Now I can add a timestamp rendered with `fromNow()`:

Listing 12.4: *app/templates/_post.html*: Render timestamp in post sub-template.

```
<a href="{{ url_for('user', username=post.author.username) }}">
    {{ post.author.username }}
</a>
said {{ moment(post.timestamp).fromNow() }}:
<br>
{{ post.body }}
```

Below you can see how both these timestamps look when rendered with Flask-Moment and moment.js:

12.4. USING MOMENT.JS

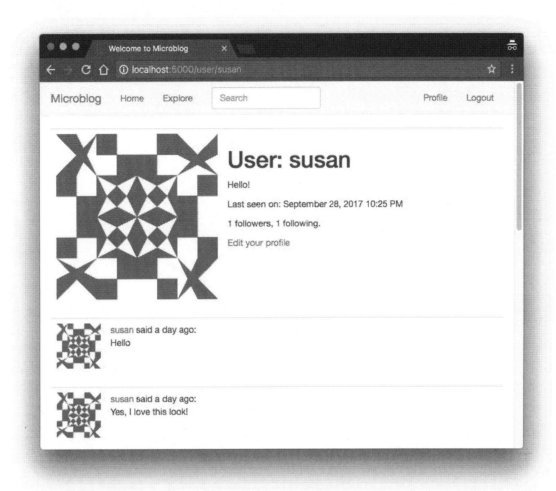

Chapter 13

I18n and L10n

The topics of this chapter are Internationalization and Localization, commonly abbreviated I18n and L10n. To make my application friendly to people who do not speak English, I'm going to implement a translation workflow that, with the help of language translators, will allow me to offer the application to users in a choice of languages.

The GitHub links for this chapter are: Browse[1], Zip[2], Diff[3].

13.1 Introduction to Flask-Babel

As you can probably guess, there is a Flask extension that makes working with translations very easy. The extension is called Flask-Babel[4] and is installed with pip:

```
(venv) $ pip install flask-babel
```

Flask-Babel is initialized like most other Flask extensions:

Listing 13.1: *app/__init__.py*: Flask-Babel instance.

```
# ...
from flask_babel import Babel
```

---

[1]https://github.com/miguelgrinberg/microblog/tree/v0.13
[2]https://github.com/miguelgrinberg/microblog/archive/v0.13.zip
[3]https://github.com/miguelgrinberg/microblog/compare/v0.12...v0.13
[4]https://pythonhosted.org/Flask-Babel/

```
app = Flask(__name__)
# ...
babel = Babel(app)
```

As part of this chapter, I'm going to show you how to translate the application into Spanish, as I happen to speak that language. I could also work with translators that know other languages and support those as well. To keep track of the list of supported languages, I'm going to add a configuration variable:

Listing 13.2: *config.py*: Supported languages list.

```
class Config(object):
    # ...
    LANGUAGES = ['en', 'es']
```

I'm using two-letter language codes for this application, but if you need to be more specific, a country code can be added as well. For example, you could use `en-US`, `en-GB` and `en-CA` to support American, British and Canadian English as different languages.

The `Babel` instance provides a `localeselector` decorator. The decorated function is invoked for each request to select a language translation to use for that request:

Listing 13.3: *app/__init__.py*: Select best language.

```
from flask import request

# ...

@babel.localeselector
def get_locale():
    return request.accept_languages.best_match(app.config['LANGUAGES'])
```

Here I'm using an attribute of Flask's `request` object called `accept_languages`. This object provides a high-level interface to work with the Accept-Language[5] header that clients send with a request. This header specifies the client language and locale preferences as a weighted list. The contents of this header can be configured in the browser's preferences page, with the default being usually imported from the language settings in the computer's operating system. Most people don't even know such a setting exists, but this is useful as users can provide a list of preferred languages, each with a weight. In case you are curious, here is an example of a complex `Accept-Languages` header:

---

[5]https://developer.mozilla.org/en-US/docs/Web/HTTP/Headers/Accept-Language

```
Accept-Language: da, en-gb;q=0.8, en;q=0.7
```

This says that Danish (`da`) is the preferred language (with default weight = 1.0), followed by British English (`en-GB`) with a 0.8 weight, and as a last option generic English (`en`) with a 0.7 weight.

To select the best language, you need to compare the list of languages requested by the client against the languages the application supports, and using the client provided weights, find the best language. The logic to do this is somewhat complicated, but it is all encapsulated in the `best_match()` method, which takes the list of languages offered by the application as an argument and returns the best choice.

13.2 Marking Texts to Translate In Python Source Code

Okay, so now comes the bad news. The normal workflow when making an application available in multiple languages is to mark all the texts that need translations in the source code. After the texts are marked, Flask-Babel will scan all the files and extract those texts into a separate translation file using the gettext[6] tool. Unfortunately this is a tedious task that needs to be done to enable translations.

I'm going to show you a few examples of this marking here, but you can get the complete set of changes from the download package[7] for this chapter or the GitHub repository.

The way texts are marked for translation is by wrapping them in a function call that as a convention is called `_()`, just an underscore. The simplest cases are those where literal strings appear in the source code. Here is an example `flash()` statement:

```
from flask_babel import _
# ...
flash(_('Your post is now live!'))
```

The idea is that the `_()` function wraps the text in the base language (English in this case). This function will use the language selected by the `get_locale()` function to find the correct translation for a given client. The `_()` function then returns the translated text, which in this case will become the argument to `flash()`.

---

[6]https://www.gnu.org/software/gettext/
[7]https://github.com/miguelgrinberg/microblog/tree/v0.13

Unfortunately not all cases are that simple. Consider this other `flash()` call from the application:

```
flash('User {} not found.'.format(username))
```

This text has a dynamic component that is inserted in the middle of the static text. The `_()` function has a syntax that supports this type of texts, but it is based on the older string substitution syntax:

```
flash(_('User %(username)s not found.', username=username))
```

There is an even harder case to handle. Some string literals are assigned outside of a request, usually when the application is starting up, so at the time these texts are evaluated there is no way to know what language to use. An example of this is the labels associated with form fields. The only solution to handle those texts is to find a way to delay the evaluation of the string until it is used, which is going to be under an actual request. Flask-Babel provides a *lazy evaluation* version of `_()` that is called `lazy_gettext()`:

```
from flask_babel import lazy_gettext as _l

class LoginForm(FlaskForm):
    username = StringField(_l('Username'), validators=[DataRequired()])
    # ...
```

Here I'm importing this alternative translation function and renaming to to `_l()` so that it looks similar to the original `_()`. This new function wraps the text in a special object that triggers the translation to be performed later, when the string is used.

The Flask-Login extension flashes a message any time it redirects the user to the login page. This message is in English and comes from the extension itself. To make sure this message also gets translated, I'm going to override the default message and provide my own, wrapper with the `_l()` function for lazy processing:

```
login = LoginManager(app)
login.login_view = 'login'
login.login_message = _l('Please log in to access this page.')
```

13.3 Marking Texts to Translate In Templates

In the previous section you've seen how to mark translatable texts in Python source code, but that is only a part of this process, as template files also have text. The `_()` function is also available in templates, so the process is fairly similar. For example, consider this snippet of HTML from *404.html*:

```
<h1>File Not Found</h1>
```

The translation enabled version becomes:

```
<h1>{{ _('File Not Found') }}</h1>
```

Note that here in addition to wrapping the text with `_()`, the `{{ ... }}` needs to be added, to force the `_()` to be evaluated instead of being considered a literal in the template.

For more complex phrases that have dynamic components, arguments can also be used:

```
<h1>{{ _('Hi, %(username)s!', username=current_user.username) }}</h1>
```

There is a particularly tricky case in *_post.html* that took me a while to figure out:

```
{% set user_link %}
    <a href="{{ url_for('user', username=post.author.username) }}">
        {{ post.author.username }}
    </a>
{% endset %}
{{ _('%(username)s said %(when)s',
    username=user_link, when=moment(post.timestamp).fromNow()) }}
```

The problem here is that I wanted the `username` to be a link that points to the profile page of the user, not just the name, so I had to create an intermediate variable called `user_link` using the `set` and `endset` template directives, and then pass that as an argument to the translation function.

As I mentioned above, you can download[8] a version of the application with all the translatable texts in Python source code and templates marked.

---
[8]https://github.com/miguelgrinberg/microblog/tree/v0.13

13.4 Extracting Text to Translate

Once you have the application with all the `_()` and `_l()` in place, you can use the `pybabel` command to extract them to a *.pot* file, which stands for *portable object template*. This is a text file that includes all the texts that were marked as needing translation. The purpose of this file is to serve as a template to create translation files for each language.

The extraction process needs a small configuration file that tells pybabel what files should be scanned for translatable texts. Below you can see the *babel.cfg* that I created for this application:

Listing 13.4: *babel.cfg*: PyBabel configuration file.

```
[python: app/**.py]
[jinja2: app/templates/**.html]
extensions=jinja2.ext.autoescape,jinja2.ext.with_
```

The first two lines define the filename patterns for Python and Jinja2 template files respectively. The third line defines two extensions provided by the Jinja2 template engine that help Flask-Babel properly parse template files.

To extract all the texts to the *.pot* file, you can use the following command:

```
(venv) $ pybabel extract -F babel.cfg -k _l -o messages.pot .
```

The `pybabel extract` command reads the configuration file given in the `-F` option, then scans all the code and template files in the directories that match the configured sources, starting from the directory given in the command (the current directory or . in this case). By default, `pybabel` will look for `_()` as a text marker, but I have also used the lazy version, which I imported as `_l()`, so I need to tell the tool to look for those too with the `-k _l`. The `-o` option provides the name of the output file.

I should note that the *messages.pot* file is not a file that needs to be incorporated into the project. This is a file that can be easily regenerated any time it is needed, simply by running the command above again. So there is no need to commit this file to source control.

13.5 Generating a Language Catalog

The next step in the process is to create a translation for each language that will be supported in addition to the base one, which in this case is English. I said I was going to start by adding

13.5. GENERATING A LANGUAGE CATALOG

Spanish (language code `es`), so this is the command that does that:

```
(venv) $ pybabel init -i messages.pot -d app/translations -l es
creating catalog app/translations/es/LC_MESSAGES/messages.po based on messages.pot
```

The `pybabel init` command takes the *messages.pot* file as input and writes a new language catalog to the directory given in the `-d` option for the language specified in the `-l` option. I'm going to be installing all the translations in the *app/translations* directory, because that is where Flask-Babel will expect translation files to be by default. The command will create a *es* subdirectory inside this directory for the Spanish data files. In particular, there will be a new file named *app/translations/es/LC_MESSAGES/messages.po*, that is where the translations need to be made.

If you want to support other languages, just repeat the above command with each of the language codes you want, so that each language gets its own repository with a *messages.po* file.

This `messages.po` file that created in each language repository uses a format that is the de facto standard for language translations, the format used by the gettext[9] utility. Here are a few lines from the beginning of the Spanish *messages.po*:

```
# Spanish translations for PROJECT.
# Copyright (C) 2017 ORGANIZATION
# This file is distributed under the same license as the PROJECT project.
# FIRST AUTHOR <EMAIL@ADDRESS>, 2017.
#
msgid ""
msgstr ""
"Project-Id-Version: PROJECT VERSION\n"
"Report-Msgid-Bugs-To: EMAIL@ADDRESS\n"
"POT-Creation-Date: 2017-09-29 23:23-0700\n"
"PO-Revision-Date: 2017-09-29 23:25-0700\n"
"Last-Translator: FULL NAME <EMAIL@ADDRESS>\n"
"Language: es\n"
"Language-Team: es <LL@li.org>\n"
"Plural-Forms: nplurals=2; plural=(n != 1)\n"
"MIME-Version: 1.0\n"
"Content-Type: text/plain; charset=utf-8\n"
"Content-Transfer-Encoding: 8bit\n"
"Generated-By: Babel 2.5.1\n"

#: app/email.py:21
msgid "[Microblog] Reset Your Password"
msgstr ""

#: app/forms.py:12 app/forms.py:19 app/forms.py:50
msgid "Username"
msgstr ""
```

[9]http://www.gnu.org/software/gettext/

```
#: app/forms.py:13 app/forms.py:21 app/forms.py:43
msgid "Password"
msgstr ""
```

If you skip the header, you can see that what follows is a list of strings that were extracted from the `_()` and `_l()` calls. For each text, you get a reference to the location of the text in your application. Then the `msgid` line contains the text in the base language, and the `msgstr` line that follows contains an empty string. Those empty strings need to be edited to have the version of the text in the target language.

There are many translation applications that work with `.po` files. If you feel comfortable editing the text file, then that's sufficient, but if you are working with a large project it may be recommended to work with a specialized editor. The most popular translation application is the open-source poedit[10], which is available for all major operating systems. If you are familiar with vim, then the po.vim[11] plugin gives some key mappings that make working with these files easier.

Below you can see a portion of the Spanish *messages.po* after I added the translations:

```
#: app/email.py:21
msgid "[Microblog] Reset Your Password"
msgstr "[Microblog] Nueva Contraseña"

#: app/forms.py:12 app/forms.py:19 app/forms.py:50
msgid "Username"
msgstr "Nombre de usuario"

#: app/forms.py:13 app/forms.py:21 app/forms.py:43
msgid "Password"
msgstr "Contraseña"
```

The download package[12] for this chapter also contains this file with all the translations in place, so that you don't have to worry about that part for this application.

The *messages.po* file is a sort of source file for translations. When you want to start using these translated texts, this file needs to be *compiled* into a format that is efficient to be used by the application at run-time. To compile all the translations for the application, you can use the `pybabel compile` command as follows:

---

[10]http://www.poedit.net/
[11]https://vim.sourceforge.io/scripts/script.php?script_id=695
[12]https://github.com/miguelgrinberg/microblog/tree/v0.13

13.5. GENERATING A LANGUAGE CATALOG

```
(venv) $ pybabel compile -d app/translations
compiling catalog app/translations/es/LC_MESSAGES/messages.po to
app/translations/es/LC_MESSAGES/messages.mo
```

This operation adds a *messages.mo* file next to *messages.po* in each language repository. The *.mo* file is the file that Flask-Babel will use to load translations for the application.

After you create the *messages.mo* file for Spanish or any other languages you added to the project, these languages are ready to be used in the application. If you want to see how the application looks in Spanish, you can edit the language configuration in your web browser to have Spanish as the preferred language. For Chrome, this is the Advanced part of the Settings page:

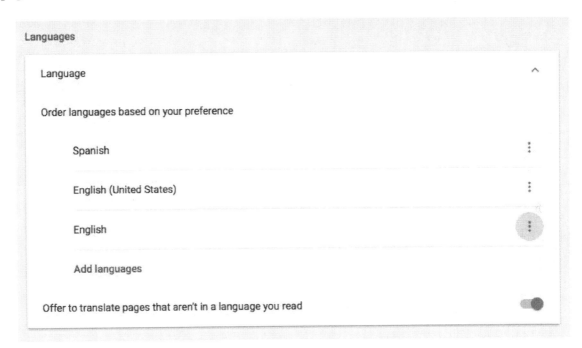

If you prefer not to change your browser settings, the other alternative is to force a language by making the `localeselector` function always return it. For Spanish, this would be how you would do it:

Listing 13.5: *app/__init__.py*: Select best language.

```
@babel.localeselector
def get_locale():
    # return request.accept_languages.best_match(app.config['LANGUAGES'])
    return 'es'
```

Running the application with the browser configured for Spanish, or the `localeselector` function returning `es` will make all the texts appear in Spanish when you use the application.

13.6 Updating the Translations

One common situation when working with translations is that you may want to start using a translation file even if it is incomplete. That is totally fine, you can compile an incomplete *messages.po* file and any translations that are available will be used, while any missing ones will use the base language. You can then continue working on the translations and compile again to update the *messages.mo* file as you make progress.

Another common scenario occurs if you missed some texts when you added the `_()` wrappers. In this case you are going to see that those texts that you missed are going to remain in English, because Flask-Babel knows nothing about them. In this situation you'll want to add the `_()` or `_l()` wrappers when you detect texts that don't have them, and then do an update procedure, which involves two steps:

```
(venv) $ pybabel extract -f babel.cfg -k _l -o messages.pot .
(venv) $ pybabel update -i messages.pot -d app/translations
```

The `extract` command is identical to the one I issued earlier, but now it will generate a new version of *messages.pot* with all the previous texts plus anything new that you recently wrapped with `_()` or `_l()`. The `update` call takes the new `messages.pot` file and merges it into all the *messages.po* files associated with the project. This is going to be an intelligent merge, in which any existing texts will be left alone, while only entries that were added or removed in *messages.pot* will be affected.

After the *messages.po* are updated, you can go ahead and translate any new tests, then compile the messages one more time to make them available to the application.

13.7 Translating Dates and Times

Now I have a complete Spanish translation for all the texts in Python code and templates, but if you run the application in Spanish and are a good observer, you will notice that there are still a few things that appear in English. I'm referring to the timestamps generated by Flask-Moment and moment.js, which obviously have not been included in the translation effort

13.7. TRANSLATING DATES AND TIMES

because none of the texts generated by these packages are part of the source code or templates of the application.

The moment.js library does support localization and internationalization, so all I need to do is configure the proper language. Flask-Babel returns the selected language and locale for a given request via the `get_locale()` function, so what I'm going to do is add the locale to the `g` object, so that I can then access it from the base template:

Listing 13.6: *app/routes.py*: Store selected language in flask.g.

```python
# ...
from flask import g
from flask_babel import get_locale

# ...

@app.before_request
def before_request():
    # ...
    g.locale = str(get_locale())
```

The `get_locale()` function from Flask-Babel returns a locale object, but I just want to have the language code, which can be obtained by converting the object to a string. Now that I have `g.locale`, I can access it from the base template to configure moment.js with the correct language:

Listing 13.7: *app/templates/base.html*: Set locale for moment.js.

```
...
{% block scripts %}
    {{ super() }}
    {{ moment.include_moment() }}
    {{ moment.lang(g.locale) }}
{% endblock %}
```

And now all dates and times should appear in the same language as the text. Below you can see how the application looks in Spanish:

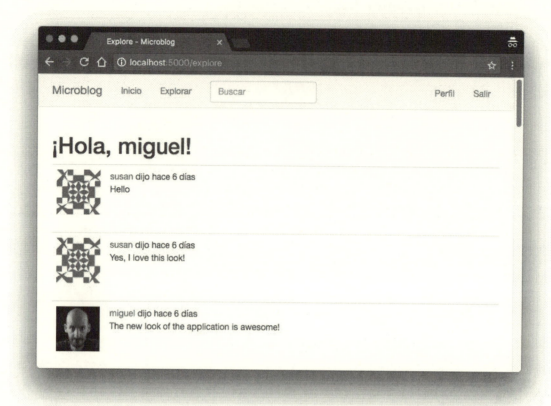

At this point, all texts except those that were provided by the user in blog posts or profile descriptions should be translatable into other languages.

13.8 Command-Line Enhancements

You will probably agree with me that the `pybabel` commands are a bit long and difficult to remember. I'm going to use this opportunity to show you how you can create custom commands that are integrated with the `flask` command. So far, you've seen me use `flask run`, `flask shell`, and several `flask db` sub-commands provided by the Flask-Migrate extension. It is actually easy to add application-specific commands to `flask` as well. So what I'm going to do now is create a few simple commands that trigger the `pybabel` commands with all the arguments that are specific to this application. The commands that I'm going to add are:

- `flask translate init LANG` to add a new language
- `flask translate update` to update all language repositories

13.8. COMMAND-LINE ENHANCEMENTS

- `flask translate compile` to compile all language repositories

The `babel export` step is not going to be a command, because generating the *messages.pot* file is always a pre-requisite to running either the `init` or the `update` commands, so the implementation of these commands will generate the translation template file as a temporary file.

Flask relies on Click[13] for all its command-line operations. Commands like `translate`, which are a root for several sub-commands are created via the `app.cli.group()` decorator. I'm going to put these commands in a new module called *app/cli.py*:

Listing 13.8: *app/cli.py*: Translate command group.

```
from app import app

@app.cli.group()
def translate():
    """Translation and localization commands."""
    pass
```

The name of the command comes from the name of the decorated function, and the help message comes from the docstring. Since this is a parent command that only exists to provide a base for the sub-commands, the function itself does not need to do anything.

The `update` and `compile` are easy to implement, because they do not take any arguments:

Listing 13.9: *app/cli.py*: Update and compile sub-commands.

```
import os

# ...

@translate.command()
def update():
    """Update all languages."""
    if os.system('pybabel extract -F babel.cfg -k _l -o messages.pot .'):
        raise RuntimeError('extract command failed')
    if os.system('pybabel update -i messages.pot -d app/translations'):
        raise RuntimeError('update command failed')
    os.remove('messages.pot')

@translate.command()
def compile():
    """Compile all languages."""
    if os.system('pybabel compile -d app/translations'):
        raise RuntimeError('compile command failed')
```

---
[13] http://click.pocoo.org/5/

Note how the decorator from these functions is derived from the `translate` parent function. This may seem confusing, since `translate()` is a function, but it is the standard way in which Click builds groups of commands. Same as with the `translate()` function, the docstrings for these functions are used as help message in the `-help` output.

You can see that for all commands, I run them and make sure that the return value is zero, which implies that the command did not return any error. If the command errors, then I raise a `RuntimeError`, which will cause the script to stop. The `update()` function combines the `extract` and `update` steps in the same command, and if everything is successful, it deletes the *messages.pot* file after the update is complete, since this file can be easily regenerated when needed again.

The `init` command takes the new language code as an argument. Here is the implementation:

Listing 13.10: *app/cli.py*: Init sub-command.

```
import click

@translate.command()
@click.argument('lang')
def init(lang):
    """Initialize a new language."""
    if os.system('pybabel extract -F babel.cfg -k _l -o messages.pot .'):
        raise RuntimeError('extract command failed')
    if os.system(
            'pybabel init -i messages.pot -d app/translations -l ' + lang):
        raise RuntimeError('init command failed')
    os.remove('messages.pot')
```

This command uses the `@click.argument` decorator to define the language code. Click passes the value provided in the command to the handler function as an argument, and then I incorporate the argument into the `init` command.

The final step to enable these commands to work is to import them, so that the commands get registered. I decided to do this in the *microblog.py* file in the top-level directory:

Listing 13.11: *microblog.py*: Register command-line commands.

```
from app import cli
```

Here the only thing I need to do is import the new *cli.py* module, there is no need to do anything with it, as the import causes the command decorators to run and register the command.

At this point, running `flask -help` will list the `translate` command as an option. And `flask translate -help` will show the three sub-commands that I defined:

13.8. COMMAND-LINE ENHANCEMENTS

```
(venv) $ flask translate --help
Usage: flask translate [OPTIONS] COMMAND [ARGS]...

  Translation and localization commands.

Options:
  --help  Show this message and exit.

Commands:
  compile  Compile all languages.
  init     Initialize a new language.
  update   Update all languages.
```

So now, the workflow is much simpler and there is no need to remember long and complicated commands. To add a new language, you use:

```
(venv) $ flask translate init <language-code>
```

To update all the languages after making changes to the _() and _l() language markers:

```
(venv) $ flask translate update
```

And to compile all languages after updating the translation files:

```
(venv) $ flask translate compile
```

Chapter 14

Ajax

In this article I'm going to take a departure from the "safe zone" of server-side development and to work on a feature that has equally important server and client-side components. Have you seen the "Translate" links that some sites show next to user generated content? These are links that trigger a real time automated translation of content that is not in the user's native language. The translated content is typically inserted below the original version. Google shows it for search results in foreign languages. Facebook does it for posts. Twitter does it for tweets. Today I'm going to show you how to add the very same feature to Microblog!

The GitHub links for this chapter are: Browse[1], Zip[2], Diff[3].

14.1 Server-side vs. Client-side

In the traditional server-side model that I've followed so far there is a client (a web browser commanded by a user) making HTTP requests to the application server. A request can simply ask for an HTML page, like when you click the "Profile" link, or it can trigger an action, like when you click the Submit button after editing your profile information. In both types of requests the server completes the request by sending a new web page to the client, either directly or by issuing a redirect. The client then replaces the current page with the new one. This cycle repeats for as long as the user stays on the application's web site. In this model the server does all the work, while the client just displays the web pages and accepts user input.

There is a different model in which the client takes a more active role. In this model, the client

---

[1] https://github.com/miguelgrinberg/microblog/tree/v0.14
[2] https://github.com/miguelgrinberg/microblog/archive/v0.14.zip
[3] https://github.com/miguelgrinberg/microblog/compare/v0.13...v0.14

issues a request to the server and the server responds with a web page, but unlike the previous case, not all the page data is HTML, there is also sections of the page with code, typically written in Javascript. Once the client receives the page it displays the HTML portions, and executes the code. From then on you have an active client that can do work on its own without little or no contact with the server. In a strict client-side application the entire application is downloaded to the client with the initial page request, and then the application runs entirely on the client, only contacting the server to retrieve or store data and making dynamic changes to the appearance of that first and only web page. This type of applications are called Single Page Applications[4] or SPAs.

Most applications are a hybrid between the two models and combine techniques of both. My Microblog application is mostly a server-side application, but today I will be adding a little bit of client-side action to it. To do real time translations of user posts, the client browser will send *asynchronous requests* to the server, to which the server will respond without causing a page refresh. The client will then insert the translations into the current page dynamically. This technique is known as Ajax[5], which is short for Asynchronous JavaScript and XML (even though these days XML is often replaced with JSON).

14.2 Live Translation Workflow

The application has good support for foreign languages thanks to Flask-Babel, which would make it possible to support as many languages as I can find translators for. But of course, there is one element missing. Users are going to write blog posts in their own languages, so it is quite possible that a user will come across posts that are written in unknown languages. The quality of automated translations isn't always great, but in most cases it is good enough if all you want is to have a basic idea of what a text in another language means.

This is an ideal feature to implement as an Ajax service. Consider that the index or explore pages could be showing several posts, some of which might be in foreign languages. If I implement the translation using traditional server-side techniques, a request for a translation would cause the original page to get replaced with a new page. The fact is that requesting a translation for one out of many displayed blogs posts isn't a big enough action to require a full page update, this feature works much better if the translated text is dynamically inserted below the original text while leaving the rest of the page untouched.

Implementing live automated translations requires a few steps. First, I need a way to identify the source language of the text to translate. I also need to know the preferred language for each

---

[4]http://en.wikipedia.org/wiki/Single-page_application
[5]http://en.wikipedia.org/wiki/Ajax_(programming)

user, because I want to show a "translate" link only for posts written in other languages. When a translation link is offered and the user clicks on it, I will need to send the Ajax request to the server, and the server will contact a third-party translation API. Once the server sends back a response with the translated text, the client-side javascript code will dynamically insert this text into the page. As you can surely notice, there are a few non-trivial problems here. I'm going to look at these one by one.

14.3 Language Identification

The first problem is identifying what language a post was written in. This isn't an exact science, as it is not always possible to unequivocally detect a language, but for most cases, automated detection works fairly well. In Python, there is a good language detection library called `guess_language`. The original version of this package is fairly old and was never ported to Python 3, so I'm going to install a derived version that supports Python 2 and 3:

```
(venv) $ pip install guess-language_spirit
```

The plan is to feed each blog post to this package, to try to determine the language. Since doing this analysis is somewhat time consuming, I don't want to repeating this work every time a post is rendered to a page. What I'm going to do is set the source language for a post at the time it is submitted. The detected language is then going to be stored in the posts table.

The first step is to add a `language` field to the `Post` model:

Listing 14.1: *app/models.py*: Add detected language to Post model.

```python
class Post(db.Model):
    # ...
    language = db.Column(db.String(5))
```

As you recall, each time there is a change made to the database models, a database migration needs to be issued:

```
(venv) $ flask db migrate -m "add language to posts"
INFO  [alembic.runtime.migration] Context impl SQLiteImpl.
INFO  [alembic.runtime.migration] Will assume non-transactional DDL.
INFO  [alembic.autogenerate.compare] Detected added column 'post.language'
  Generating migrations/versions/2b017edaa91f_add_language_to_posts.py ... done
```

And then the migration needs to be applied to the database:

```
(venv) $ flask db upgrade
INFO  [alembic.runtime.migration] Context impl SQLiteImpl.
INFO  [alembic.runtime.migration] Will assume non-transactional DDL.
INFO  [alembic.runtime.migration] Upgrade ae346256b650 -> 2b017edaa91f, add language to posts
```

I can now detect and store the language when a post is submitted:

Listing 14.2: *app/routes.py*: Save language for new posts.

```python
from guess_language import guess_language

@app.route('/', methods=['GET', 'POST'])
@app.route('/index', methods=['GET', 'POST'])
@login_required
def index():
    form = PostForm()
    if form.validate_on_submit():
        language = guess_language(form.post.data)
        if language == 'UNKNOWN' or len(language) > 5:
            language = ''
        post = Post(body=form.post.data, author=current_user,
                    language=language)
        # ...
```

With this change, each time a post is submitted, I run the text through the `guess_language` function to try to determine the language. If the language comes back as unknown or if I get an unexpectedly long result, I play it safe and save an empty string to the database. I'm going to adopt the convention that any post that have the language set to an empty string is assumed to have an unknown language.

14.4 Displaying a "Translate" Link

The second step is easy. What I'm going to do now is add a "Translate" link next to any posts that are not in the language the is active for the current user.

Listing 14.3: *app/templates/_post.html*: Add a translate link to posts.

```
{% if post.language and post.language != g.locale %}
<br><br>
<a href="#">{{ _('Translate') }}</a>
{% endif %}
```

I'm doing this in the `_post.html` sub-template, so that this functionality appears on any page that displays blog posts. The translate link will only appear on posts for which the language was detected, and this language does not match the language selected by the function decorated with Flask-Babel's `localeselector` decorator. Recall from Chapter 13 that the selected locale is stored as `g.locale`. The text of the link needs to be added in a way that it can be translated by Flask-Babel, so I used the `_()` function when I defined it.

Note that I have no associated an action with this link yet. First I want to figure out how to carry out the actual translations.

14.5 Using a Third-Party Translation Service

The two major translation services are Google Cloud Translation API[6] and Microsoft Translator Text API[7]. Both are paid services, but the Microsoft offering has an entry level option for low volume of translations that is free. Google offered a free translation service in the past but today, even the lowest service tier is paid. Because I want to be able to experiment with translations without incurring in expenses, I'm going to implement the Microsoft solution.

Before you can use the Microsoft Translator API, you will need to get an account with Azure[8], Microsoft's cloud service. You can select the free tier, while you will be asked to provide a credit card number during the signup process, your card is not going to be charged while you stay on that level of service.

Once you have the Azure account, go to the Azure Portal and click on the "New" button on the top left, and then type or select the "Translator Text API". When you click the "Create" button, you will be presented with a form in which you define a new translator resource that will be added to your account. You can see below how I completed the form:

---

[6] https://developers.google.com/translate/
[7] http://www.microsofttranslator.com/dev/
[8] https://azure.com

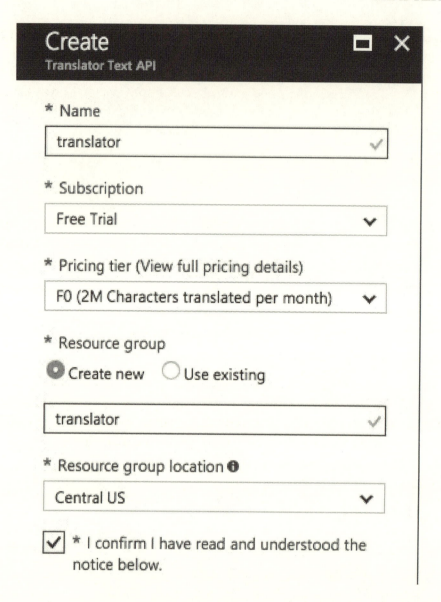

When you click the "Create" button once again, the translator API resource will be added to your account. If you want a few seconds, you will receive a notification in the top bar that the translator resource was deployed. Click the "Go to resource" button in the notification and then on the "Keys" option on the left sidebar. You will now see two keys, labeled "Key 1" and "Key 2". Copy either one of the keys to the clipboard and then enter it into an environment variable in your terminal (if you are using Microsoft Windows, replace `export` with `set`):

```
(venv) $ export MS_TRANSLATOR_KEY=<paste-your-key-here>
```

14.5. USING A THIRD-PARTY TRANSLATION SERVICE

This key is used to authenticate with the translation service, so it needs to be added to the application configuration:

Listing 14.4: *config.py*: Add Microsoft Translator API key to the configuration.

```
class Config(object):
    # ...
    MS_TRANSLATOR_KEY = os.environ.get('MS_TRANSLATOR_KEY')
```

As always with configuration values, I prefer to install them in environment variables and import them into the Flask configuration from there. This is particularly important with sensitive information such as keys or passwords that enable access to third-party services. You definitely do not want to write those explicitly in the code.

The Microsoft Translator API is a web service that accepts HTTP requests. There are a few HTTP clients in Python, but the most popular and simple to use is the `requests` package. So let's install that into the virtual environment:

```
(venv) $ pip install requests
```

Below you can see the function that I coded to translate text using the Microsoft Translator API. I am putting in a new *app/translate.py* module:

Listing 14.5: *app/translate.py*: Text translation function.

```
import json
import requests
from flask_babel import _
from app import app

def translate(text, source_language, dest_language):
    if 'MS_TRANSLATOR_KEY' not in app.config or \
            not app.config['MS_TRANSLATOR_KEY']:
        return _('Error: the translation service is not configured.')
    auth = {'Ocp-Apim-Subscription-Key': app.config['MS_TRANSLATOR_KEY']}
    r = requests.get('https://api.microsofttranslator.com/v2/Ajax.svc'
                     '/Translate?text={}&from={}&to={}'.format(
                         text, source_language, dest_language),
                     headers=auth)
    if r.status_code != 200:
        return _('Error: the translation service failed.')
    return json.loads(r.content.decode('utf-8-sig'))
```

The function takes the text to translate and the source and destination language codes as arguments, and it returns a string with the translated text. It starts by checking that there is a key for the translation service in the configuration, and if it isn't there it returns an error. The error is also a string, so from the outside, this is going to look like the translated text. This ensures that in the case of an error, the user will see a meaningful error message.

The `get()` method from the `requests` package sends an HTTP request with a `GET` method to the URL given as the first argument. I'm using the */v2/Ajax.svc/Translate* URL, which is an endpoint from the translation service that returns translations as a JSON payload. The text, source and destination languages need to be given as query string arguments in the URL, named `text`, `from` and `to` respectively. To authenticate with the service, I need to pass the key that I added to the configuration. This key needs to be given in a custom HTTP header with the name `Ocp-Apim-Subscription-Key`. I created the `auth` dictionary with this header and then pass it to `requests` in the `headers` argument.

The `requests.get()` method returns a response object, which contains all the details provided by the service. I first need to check that the status code is 200, which is the code for a successful request. If I get any other codes, I know that there was an error, so in that case I return an error string. If the status code is 200, then the body of the response has a JSON encoded string with the translation, so all I need to do is use the `json.loads()` function from the Python standard library to decode the JSON into a Python string that I can use. The `content` attribute of the response object contains the raw body of the response as a bytes object, which is converted to a UTF-8 string and sent to `json.loads()`.

Below you can see a Python console session in which I use the new `translate()` function:

```
>>> from app.translate import translate
>>> translate('Hi, how are you today?', 'en', 'es')   # English to Spanish
'Hola, ¿cómo estás hoy?'
>>> translate('Hi, how are you today?', 'en', 'de')   # English to German
'Are Hallo, how you heute?'
>>> translate('Hi, how are you today?', 'en', 'it')   # English to Italian
'Ciao, come stai oggi?'
>>> translate('Hi, how are you today?', 'en', 'fr')   # English to French
"Salut, comment allez-vous aujourd'hui ?"
```

Pretty cool, right? Now it's time to integrate this functionality with the application.

14.6 Ajax From The Server

I'm going to start by implementing the server-side part. When the user clicks the Translate link that appears below a post, an asynchronous HTTP request will be issued to the server. I'll show you how to do this in the next session, so for now I'm going to concentrate on implementing the handling of this request by the server.

14.6. AJAX FROM THE SERVER

An asynchronous (or Ajax) request is similar to the routes and view functions that I have created in the application, with the only difference that instead of returning HTML or a redirect, it just returns data, formatted as XML[9] or more commonly JSON[10]. Below you can see the translation view function, which invokes the Microsoft Translator API and then returns the translated text in JSON format:

Listing 14.6: *app/routes.py*: Text translation view function.

```python
from flask import jsonify
from app.translate import translate

@app.route('/translate', methods=['POST'])
@login_required
def translate_text():
    return jsonify({'text': translate(request.form['text'],
                                      request.form['source_language'],
                                      request.form['dest_language'])})
```

As you can see, this is simple. I implemented this route as a `POST` request. There is really no absolute rule as to when t use `GET` or `POST` (or other request methods that you haven't seen yet). Since the client will be sending data, I decided to use a `POST` request, as that is similar to the requests that submit form data. The `request.form` attribute is a dictionary that Flask exposes with all the data that has included in the submission. When I worked with web forms, I did not need to look at `request.form` because Flask-WTF does all that work for me, but in this case, there is really no web form, so I have to access the data directly.

So what I'm doing in this function is to invoke the `translate()` function from the previous section passing the three arguments directly from the data that was submitted with the request. The result is incorporated into a single-key dictionary, under the key `text`, and the dictionary is passed as an argument to Flask's `jsonify()` function, which converts the dictionary to a JSON formatted payload. The return value from `jsonify()` is the HTTP response that is going to be sent back to the client.

For example, if the client wanted to translate the string `Hello, World!` to Spanish, the response from this request would have the follow payload:

```
{ "text": "Hola, Mundo!" }
```

---

[9] http://en.wikipedia.org/wiki/XML
[10] http://en.wikipedia.org/wiki/JSON

14.7 Ajax From The Client

So now that the server is able to provide translations through the */translate* URL, I need to invoke this URL when the user clicks the "Translate" link I added above, passing the text to translate and the source and destination languages. If you are not familiar with working with JavaScript in the browser this is going to be a good learning experience.

When working with JavaScript in the browser, the page currently being displayed is internally represented in as the Document Object Model or just the DOM. This is a hierarchical structure that references all the elements that exist in the page. The JavaScript code running in this context can make changes to the DOM to trigger changes in the page.

Let's first discuss how my JavaScript code running in the browser can obtain the three arguments that I need to send to the translate function that runs in the server. To obtain the text, I need to locate the node within the DOM that contains the blog post body and read its contents. To make it easy to identify the DOM nodes that contain blog posts, I'm going to attach a unique ID to them. If you look at the *_post.html* template, the line that renders the post body just reads `{{ post.body }}`. What I'm going to do is wrap this content in a `<span>` element. This is not going to change anything visually, but it gives me a place where I can insert an identifier:

Listing 14.7: *app/templates/_post.html*: Add an ID to each blog post.

```
<span id="post{{ post.id }}">{{ post.body }}</span>
```

This is going to assign a unique identifier to each blog post, with the format `post1`, `post2`, and so on, where the number matches the database identifier of each post. Now that each blog post has a unique identifier, given a ID value I can use jQuery to locate the `<span>` element for that post and extract the text in it. For example, if I wanted to get the text for a post with ID 123 this is what I would do:

```
$('#post123').text()
```

Here the `$` sign is the name of a function provided by the jQuery library. This library is used by Bootstrap, so it was already included by Flask-Bootstrap. The `#` is part of the "selector" syntax used by jQuery, which means that what follows is the ID of an element.

I will also want to have a place where I will be inserting the translated text once I receive it from the server. What I'm going to do, is replace the "Translate" link with the translated text, so I also need to have a unique identifier for that node:

14.7. AJAX FROM THE CLIENT

> **Listing 14.8:** *app/templates/_post.html*: Add an ID to the translate link.
>
> ```
> <span id="translation{{ post.id }}">
>     <a href="#">{{ _('Translate') }}</a>
> </span>
> ```

So now for a given post ID, I have a `post<ID>` node for the blog post, and a corresponding `translation<ID>` node where I will need to replace the Translate link with the translated text once I have it.

The next step is to write a function that can do all the translation work. This function will take the input and output DOM nodes, and the source and destination languages, issue the asynchronous request to the server with the three arguments needed, and finally replace the Translate link with the translated text once the server responds. This sounds like a lot of work, but the implementation is fairly simple:

> **Listing 14.9:** *app/templates/base.html*: Client-side translate function.
>
> ```
> {% block scripts %}
>     ...
>     <script>
>         function translate(sourceElem, destElem, sourceLang, destLang) {
>             $(destElem).html('<img src="{{ url_for('static', filename='loading.gif') }}">');
>             $.post('/translate', {
>                 text: $(sourceElem).text(),
>                 source_language: sourceLang,
>                 dest_language: destLang
>             }).done(function(response) {
>                 $(destElem).text(response['text'])
>             }).fail(function() {
>                 $(destElem).text("{{ _('Error: Could not contact server.') }}");
>             });
>         }
>     </script>
> {% endblock %}
> ```

The first two arguments are the unique IDs for the post and the translate link nodes. The last two argument are the source and destination language codes.

The function begins with a nice touch: it adds a *spinner* replacing the Translate link so that the user knows that the translation is in progress. This is done with jQuery, using the `$(destElem).html()` function to replace the original HTML that defined the translate link with new HTML content based on the `<img>` link. For the spinner, I'm going to use a small animated GIF that I have added to the *app/static/loading.gif* directory, which Flask reserves for static files. To generate the URL that references this image, I'm using the `url_for()`

function, passing the special route name `static` and giving the filename of the image as an argument. You can find the *loading.gif* image in the download package[11] for this chapter.

So now I have a nice spinner that took the place of the Translate link, so the user knows to wait for the translation to appear. The next step is to send the `POST` request to the */translate* URL that I defined in the previous section. For this I'm also going to use jQuery, in this case the `$.post()` function. This function submits data to the server in a format that is similar to how the browser submits a web form, which is convenient because that allows Flask to incorporate this data into the `request.form` dictionary. The arguments to `$.post()` are two, first the URL to send the request to, and then a dictionary (or object, as these are called in JavaScript) with the three data items the server expects.

You probably know that JavaScript works a lot with callback functions, or a more advanced form of callbacks called *promises*. What I want to do now is indicate what I want done once this request completes and the browser receives the response. In JavaScript there is no such thing as waiting for something, everything is *asynchronous*. What I need to do instead is to provide a callback function that the browser will invoke when the response is received. And also as a way to make everything as robust as possible, I want to indicate what to do in the case an error has ocurred, so that would be a second callback function to handle errors. There are a few ways to specify these callbacks, but for this case, using promises makes the code fairly clear. The syntax is as follows:

```
$.post(<url>, <data>).done(function(response) {
    // success callback
}).fail(function() {
    // error callback
})
```

The promise syntax allows you to basically "chain" the callbacks to the return value of the `$.post()` call. In the success callback, all I need to do is call `$(destElem).text()` with the translated text, which comes in a dictionary under the `text` key. In the case of an error, I do the same, but the text that I display is a generic error message, which I make sure is entered in the base template as a translatable text.

So now the only thing that is left is to trigger the `translate()` function with the correct arguments as a result of the user clicking a Translate link. There are also a few ways to do this, what I'm going to do is just embed the call to the function in the `href` attribute of the link:

Listing 14.10: *app/templates/_post.html*: Translate link handler.

---

[11]https://github.com/miguelgrinberg/microblog/tree/v0.14

14.7. AJAX FROM THE CLIENT

```
<span id="translation{{ post.id }}">
    <a href="javascript:translate(
                '#post{{ post.id }}',
                '#translation{{ post.id }}',
                '{{ post.language }}',
                '{{ g.locale }}');">{{ _('Translate') }}</a>
</span>
```

The `href` element of a link can accept any JavaScript code if it is prefixed with `javascript:`, so that is a convenient way to make the call to the translation function. Because this link is going to be rendered in the server when the client requests the page, I can use `{{ }}` expressions to generate the four arguments to the function. Each post will have its own translate link, with its uniquely generated arguments. The `#` that you see as a prefix to the `post<ID>` and `translation<ID>` elements indicates that what follows is an element ID.

Now the live translation feature is complete! If you have set a valid Microsoft Translator API key in your environment, you should now be able to trigger translations. Assuming you have your browser set to prefer English, you will need to write a post in another language to see the "Translate" link. Below you can see an example:

In this chapter I introduced a few new texts that need to be translated into all the languages supported by the application, so it is necessary to update the translation catalogs:

```
(venv) $ flask translate update
```

For your own projects you will then need to edit the *messages.po* files in each language repository to include the translations for these new tests, but I have already created the Spanish translations in the download package for this chapter or the GitHub repository.

To publish the new translations, they need to be compiled:

```
(venv) $ flask translate compile
```

Chapter 15

A Better Application Structure

Microblog is already an application of a decent size, so I thought this is a good opportunity to discuss how a Flask application can grow without becoming messy or too difficult to manage. Flask is a framework that is designed to give you the option to organize your project in any way you want, and as part of that philosophy, it makes it possible to change or adapt the structure of the application as it becomes larger, or as your needs or level of experience change.

In this chapter I'm going to discuss some patterns that apply to large applications, and to demonstrate them I'm going to make some changes to the way my Microblog project is structured, with the goal of making the code more maintainable and better organized. But of course, in true Flask spirit, I encourage you to take these changes just as a recommendation when trying to decide on a way to organize your own projects.

The GitHub links for this chapter are: Browse[1], Zip[2], Diff[3].

15.1 Current Limitations

There are two basic problems with the application in its current state. If you look at how the application is structured, you are going to notice that there are a few different subsystems that can be identified, but the code that supports them is all intermixed, without any clear boundaries. Let's review what those subsystems are:

- The user authentication subsystem, which includes some view functions in

---

[1] https://github.com/miguelgrinberg/microblog/tree/v0.15
[2] https://github.com/miguelgrinberg/microblog/archive/v0.15.zip
[3] https://github.com/miguelgrinberg/microblog/compare/v0.14...v0.15

app/routes.py, some forms in *app/forms.py*, some templates in *app/templates* and the email support in *app/email.py*.

- The error subsystem, which defines error handlers in *app/errors.py* and templates in *app/templates*.

- The core application functionality, which includes displaying and writing blog posts, user profiles and following, and live translations of blog posts, which is spread through most of the application modules and templates.

Thinking about these three subsystems that I have identified and how they are structured, you can probably notice a pattern. So far, the organization logic that I've been following is based on having modules dedicated to different application functions. There is a module for view functions, another one for web forms, one for errors, one for emails, a directory for HTML templates, and so on. While this is a structure that makes sense for small projects, once a project starts to grow, it tends to make some of these modules really large and messy.

One way to clearly see the problem is to consider how you would start a second project by reusing as much as you can from this one. For example, the user authentication portion should work well in other applications, but if you wanted to use that code as it is, you would have to go into several modules and copy/paste the pertinent sections into new files in the new project. See how inconvenient that is? Wouldn't it be better if this project had all the authentication related files separated from the rest of the application? The *blueprints* feature of Flask helps achieve a more practical organization that makes it easier to reuse code.

There is a second problem that is not that evident. The Flask application instance is created as a global variable in *app/__init__.py*, and then imported by a lot of application modules. While this in itself is not a problem, having the application as a global variable can complicate certain scenarios, in particular those related to testing. Imagine you want to test this application under different configurations. Because the application is defined as a global variable, there is really no way to instantiate two applications that use different configuration variables. Another situation that is not ideal is that all the tests use the same application, so a test could be making changes to the application that affect another test that runs later. Ideally you want all tests to run on a pristine application instance.

You can actually see in the *tests.py* module that I'm resorting to the trick of modifying the configuration after it was set in the application to direct the tests to use an in-memory database instead of the default SQLite database based on disk. I really have no other way to change the configured database, because by the time the tests start the application has been created and configured. For this particular situation, changing the configuration after it was applied to the application appears to work fine, but in other cases it may not, and in any case, it is a bad practice that can lead to obscure and difficult to find bugs.

15.2. BLUEPRINTS

A better solution would be to not use a global variable for the application, and instead use an *application factory* function to create the function at runtime. This would be a function that accepts a configuration object as an argument, and returns a Flask application instance, configured with those settings. If I could modify the application to work with an application factory function, then writing tests that require special configuration would become easy, because each test can create its own application.

In this chapter I'm going to refactor the application to introduce blueprints for the three subsystems I have identified above, and an application factory function. Showing you the detailed list of changes is going to be impractical, because there are little changes in pretty much every file that is part of the application, so I'm going to discuss the steps that I took to do the refactoring, and you can then download[4] the application with these changes made.

15.2 Blueprints

In Flask, a blueprint is a logical structure that represents a subset of the application. A blueprint can include elements such as routes, view functions, forms, templates and static files. If you write your blueprint in a separate Python package, then you have a component that encapsulates the elements related to specific feature of the application.

The contents of a blueprint are initially in a dormant state. To associate these elements, the blueprint needs to be registered with the application. During the registration, all the elements that were added to the blueprint are passed on to the application. So you can think of a blueprint as a temporary storage for application functionality that helps in organizing your code.

15.2.1 Error Handling Blueprint

The first blueprint that I created was one that encapsulates the support for error handlers. The structure of this blueprint is as follows:

```
app/
    errors/                       <-- blueprint package
        __init__.py               <-- blueprint creation
        handlers.py               <-- error handlers
    templates/
        errors/
            404.html
            500.html
    __init__.py                   <-- blueprint registration
```

[4] https://github.com/miguelgrinberg/microblog/archive/v0.15.zip

In essence, what I did is move the *app/errors.py* module into *app/errors/handlers.py* and the two error templates into *app/templates/errors*, so that they are separated from the other templates. I also had to change the `render_template()` calls in both error handlers to use the new *errors* template sub-directory. After that I added the blueprint creation to the *app/errors/__init__.py* module, and the blueprint registration to *app/__init__.py*, after the application instance is created.

I should note that Flask blueprints can be configured to have a separate directory for templates or static files. I have decided to move the templates into a sub-directory of the application's template directory so that all templates are in a single hierarchy, but if you prefer to have the templates that belong to a blueprint inside the blueprint package, that is supported. For example, if you add a `template_folder='templates'` argument to the `Blueprint()` constructor, you can then store the blueprint's templates in *app/errors/templates*.

The creation of a blueprint is fairly similar to the creation of an application. This is done in the ___init___.py module of the blueprint package:

Listing 15.1: *app/errors/__init__.py*: Errors blueprint.

```
from flask import Blueprint

bp = Blueprint('errors', __name__)

from app.errors import handlers
```

The `Blueprint` class takes the name of the blueprint, the name of the base module (typically set to `__name__` like in the Flask application instance), and a few optional arguments, which in this case I do not need. After the blueprint object is created, I import the *handlers.py* module, so that the error handlers in it are registered with the blueprint. This import is at the bottom to avoid circular dependencies.

In the *handlers.py* module, instead of attaching the error handlers to the application with the `@app.errorhandler` decorator, I use the blueprint's `@bp.app_errorhandler` decorator. While both decorators achieve the same end result, the idea is to try to make the blueprint independent of the application so that it is more portable. I also need to modify the path to the two error templates to account for the new *errors* sub-directory where they were moved.

The final step to complete the refactoring of the error handlers is to register the blueprint with the application:

Listing 15.2: *app/__init__.py*: Register the errors blueprint with the application.

```
app = Flask(__name__)
```

15.2. BLUEPRINTS

```
# ...
from app.errors import bp as errors_bp
app.register_blueprint(errors_bp)

# ...

from app import routes, models  # <-- remove errors from this import!
```

To register a blueprint, the `register_blueprint()` method of the Flask application instance is used. When a blueprint is registered, any view functions, templates, static files, error handlers, etc. are connected to the application. I put the import of the blueprint right above the `app.register_blueprint()` to avoid circular dependencies.

15.2.2 Authentication Blueprint

The process to refactor the authentication functions of the application into a blueprint is fairly similar to that of the error handlers. Here is a diagram of the refactored blueprint:

```
app/
    auth/                                   <-- blueprint package
        __init__.py                         <-- blueprint creation
        email.py                            <-- authentication emails
        forms.py                            <-- authentication forms
        routes.py                           <-- authentication routes
    templates/
        auth/                               <-- blueprint templates
            login.html
            register.html
            reset_password_request.html
            reset_password.html
    __init__.py                             <-- blueprint registration
```

To create this blueprint I had to move all the authentication related functionality to new modules I created in the blueprint. This includes a few view functions, web forms, and support functions such as the one that sends password reset tokens by email. I also moved the templates into a sub-directory to separate them from the rest of the application, like I did with the error pages.

When defining routes in a blueprint, the `@bp.route` decorate is used instead of `@app.route`. There is also a required change in the syntax used in the `url_for()` to build URLs. For regular view functions attached directly to the application, the first argument to `url_for()` is the view function name. When a route is defined in a blueprint, this argument must include the blueprint name and the view function name, separated by a period. So for example, I had to replace all occurrences of `url_for('login')` with `url_for('auth.login')`, and same for the remaining view functions.

To register the `auth` blueprint with the application, I used a slightly different format:

Listing 15.3: *app/__init__.py*: Register the authentication blueprint with the application.

```
# ...
from app.auth import bp as auth_bp
app.register_blueprint(auth_bp, url_prefix='/auth')
# ...
```

The `register_blueprint()` call in this case has an extra argument, `url_prefix`. This is entirely optional, but Flask gives you the option to attach a blueprint under a URL prefix, so any routes defined in the blueprint get this prefix in their URLs. In many cases this is useful as a sort of "namespacing" that keeps all the routes in the blueprint separated from other routes in the application or other blueprints. For authentication, I thought it was nice to have all the routes starting with */auth*, so I added the prefix. So now the login URL is going to be *http://localhost:5000/auth/login*. Because I'm using `url_for()` to generate the URLs, all URLs will automatically incorporate the prefix.

15.2.3 Main Application Blueprint

The third blueprint contains the core application logic. Refactoring this blueprint requires the same process that I used with the previous two blueprints. I gave this blueprint the name `main`, so all `url_for()` calls that referenced view functions had to get a `main.` prefix. Given that this is the core functionality of the application, I decided to leave the templates in the same locations. This is not a problem because I have moved the templates from the other two blueprints into sub-directories.

15.3 The Application Factory Pattern

As I mentioned in the introduction to this chapter, having the application as a global variable introduces some complications, mainly in the form of limitations for some testing scenarios. Before I introduced blueprints, the application had to be a global variable, because all the view functions and error handlers needed to be decorated with decorators that come from `app`, such as `@app.route`. But now that all routes and error handlers were moved to blueprints, there are a lot less reasons to keep the application global.

So what I'm going to do, is add a function called `create_app()` that constructs a Flask application instance, and eliminate the global variable. The transformation was not trivial, I had to sort out a few complications, but let's first look at the application factory function:

15.3. THE APPLICATION FACTORY PATTERN

Listing 15.4: *app/__init__.py*: Application factory function.

```
# ...
db = SQLAlchemy()
migrate = Migrate()
login = LoginManager()
login.login_view = 'auth.login'
login.login_message = _l('Please log in to access this page.')
mail = Mail()
bootstrap = Bootstrap()
moment = Moment()
babel = Babel()

def create_app(config_class=Config):
    app = Flask(__name__)
    app.config.from_object(config_class)

    db.init_app(app)
    migrate.init_app(app, db)
    login.init_app(app)
    mail.init_app(app)
    bootstrap.init_app(app)
    moment.init_app(app)
    babel.init_app(app)

    # ... no changes to blueprint registration

    if not app.debug and not app.testing:
        # ... no changes to logging setup

    return app
```

You have seen that most Flask extensions are initialized by creating an instance of the extension and passing the application as an argument. When the application does not exist as a global variable, there is an alternative mode in which extensions are initialized in two phases. The extension instance is first created in the global scope as before, but no arguments are passed to it. This creates an instance of the extension that is not attached to the application. At the time the application instance is created in the factory function, the `init_app()` method must be invoked on the extension instances to bind it to the now known application.

Other tasks performed during initialization remain the same, but are moved to the factory function instead of being in the global scope. This includes the registration of blueprints and logging configuration. Note that I have added a `not app.testing` clause to the conditional that decides if email and file logging should be enabled or not, so that all this logging is skipped during unit tests. The `app.testing` flag is going to be `True` when running unit tests, due to the `TESTING` variable being set to `True` in the configuration.

So who calls the application factory function? The obvious place to use this function is the top-level *microblog.py* script, which is the only module in which the application now exists in the global scope. The other place is in *tests.py*, and I will discuss unit testing in more detail in the next section.

As I mentioned above, most references to `app` went away with the introduction of blueprints, but there were some still in the code that I had to address. For example, the *app/models.py*, *app/translate.py*, and *app/main/routes.py* modules all had references to `app.config`. Fortunately, the Flask developers tried to make it easy for view functions to access the application instance without having to import it like I have been doing until now. The `current_app` variable that Flask provides is a special "context" variable that Flask initializes with the application before it dispatches a request. You have already seen another context variable before, the `g` variable in which I'm storing the current locale. These two, along with Flask-Login's `current_user` and a few others you haven't seen yet, are somewhat "magical" variables, in that they work like global variables, but are only accessible during the handling of a request, and only in the thread that is handling it.

Replacing `app` with Flask's `current_app` variable eliminates the need of importing the application instance as a global variable. I was able to change all references to `app.config` with `current_app.config` without any difficulty through simple search and replace.

The *app/email.py* module presented a slightly bigger challenge, so I had to use a small trick:

Listing 15.5: *app/email.py*: Pass application instance to another thread.

```
from app import current_app

def send_async_email(app, msg):
    with app.app_context():
        mail.send(msg)

def send_email(subject, sender, recipients, text_body, html_body):
    msg = Message(subject, sender=sender, recipients=recipients)
    msg.body = text_body
    msg.html = html_body
    Thread(target=send_async_email,
        args=(current_app._get_current_object(), msg)).start()
```

In the `send_email()` function, the application instance is passed as an argument to a background thread that will then deliver the email without blocking the main application. Using `current_app` directly in the `send_async_email()` function that runs as a background thread would not have worked, because `current_app` is a context-aware variable that is tied to the thread that is handling the client request. In a different thread, `current_app` would not have a value assigned. Passing `current_app` directly as an argument to the thread object would not have worked either, because `current_app` is really a *proxy object* that is dynamically mapped to the application instance. So passing the proxy object would be the same as using `current_app` directly in the thread. What I needed to do is access the real application instance that is stored inside the proxy object, and pass that as the `app` argument.

15.3. THE APPLICATION FACTORY PATTERN

The `current_app._get_current_object()` expression extracts the actual application instance from inside the proxy object, so that is what I passed to the thread as an argument.

Another module that was tricky was *app/cli.py*, which implements a few shortcut commands for managing language translations. The `current_app` variable does not work in this case because these commands are registered at start up, not during the handling of a request, which is the only time when `current_app` can be used. To remove the reference to `app` in this module, I resorted to another trick, which is to move these custom commands inside a `register()` function that takes the `app` instance as an argument:

Listing 15.6: *app/cli.py*: Register custom application commands.

```python
import os
import click

def register(app):
    @app.cli.group()
    def translate():
        """Translation and localization commands."""
        pass

    @translate.command()
    @click.argument('lang')
    def init(lang):
        """Initialize a new language."""
        # ...

    @translate.command()
    def update():
        """Update all languages."""
        # ...

    @translate.command()
    def compile():
        """Compile all languages."""
        # ...
```

Then I called this `register()` function from *microblog.py*. Here is the complete *microblog.py* after all the refactoring:

Listing 15.7: *microblog.py*: Main application module refactored.

```python
from app import create_app, db, cli
from app.models import User, Post

app = create_app()
cli.register(app)

@app.shell_context_processor
def make_shell_context():
    return {'db': db, 'User': User, 'Post' :Post}
```

15.4 Unit Testing Improvements

As I hinted in the beginning of this chapter, a lot of the work that I did so far had the goal of improving the unit testing workflow. When you are running unit tests you want to make sure the application is configured in a way that it does not interfere with your development resources, such as your database.

The current version of *tests.py* resorts to the trick of modifying the configuration after it was applied to the application instance, which is a dangerous practice as not all types of changes will work when done that late. What I want is to have a chance to specify my testing configuration before it gets added to the application.

The `create_app()` function now accepts a configuration class as an argument. By default, the `Config` class defined in *config.py* is used, but I can now create an application instance that uses different configuration simply by passing a new class to the factory function. Here is an example configuration class that would be suitable to use for my unit tests:

Listing 15.8: *tests.py*: Testing configuration.

```
from config import Config

class TestConfig(Config):
    TESTING = True
    SQLALCHEMY_DATABASE_URI = 'sqlite://'
```

What I'm doing here is creating a subclass of the application's `Config` class, and overriding the SQLAlchemy configuration to use an in-memory SQLite database. I also added a `TESTING` attribute set to `True`, which I currently do not need, but could be useful if the application needs to determine if it is running under unit tests or not.

If you recall, my unit tests relied on the `setUp()` and `tearDown()` methods, invoked automatically by the unit testing framework to create and destroy an environment that is appropriate for each test to run. I can now use these two methods to create and destroy a brand new application for each test:

Listing 15.9: *tests.py*: Create an application for each test.

```
class UserModelCase(unittest.TestCase):
    def setUp(self):
        self.app = create_app(TestConfig)
        self.app_context = self.app.app_context()
        self.app_context.push()
        db.create_all()
```

15.4. UNIT TESTING IMPROVEMENTS

```
    def tearDown(self):
        db.session.remove()
        db.drop_all()
        self.app_context.pop()
```

The new application will be stored in `self.app`, but creating an application isn't enough to make everything work. Consider the `db.create_all()` statement that creates the database tables. The `db` instance needs to know what the application instance is, because it needs to get the database URI from `app.config`, but when you are working with an application factory you are not really limited to a single application, there could be more than one created. So how does `db` know to use the `self.app` instance that I just created?

The answer is in the *application context*. Remember the `current_app` variable, which somehow acts as a proxy for the application when there is no global application to import? This variable looks for an active application context in the current thread, and if it finds one, it gets the application from it. If there is no context, then there is no way to know what application is active, so `current_app` raises an exception. Below you can see how this works in a Python console. This needs to be a console started by running `python`, because the `flask shell` command automatically activates an application context for convenience.

```
>>> from flask import current_app
>>> current_app.config['SQLALCHEMY_DATABASE_URI']
Traceback (most recent call last):
...
RuntimeError: Working outside of application context.

>>> from app import create_app
>>> app = create_app()
>>> app.app_context().push()
>>> current_app.config['SQLALCHEMY_DATABASE_URI']
'sqlite:////home/miguel/microblog/app.db'
```

So that's the secret! Before invoking your view functions, Flask pushes an application context, which brings `current_app` and `g` to life. When the request is complete, the context is removed, along with these variables. For the `db.create_all()` call to work in the unit testing `setUp()` method, I pushed an application context for the application instance I just created, and in that way, `db.create_all()` can use `current_app.config` to know where is the database. Then in the `tearDown()` method I pop the context to reset everything to a clean state.

You should also know that the application context is one of two contexts that Flask uses. There is also a *request context*, which is more specific, as it applies to a request. When a request context is activated right before a request is handled, Flask's `request` and `session` variables become available, as well as Flask-Login's `current_user`.

15.5 Environment Variables

As you have seen as I built this application, there are a number of configuration options that depend on having variables set up in your environment before you start the server. This includes your secret key, email server information, database URL, and Microsoft Translator API key. You'll probably agree with me that this is inconvenient, because each time you open a new terminal session those variables need to be set again.

A common pattern for applications that depend on lots of environment variables is to store these in a *.env* file in the root application directory. The application imports the variables in this file when it starts, and that way, there is no need to have all these variables manually set by you.

There is a Python package that supports *.env* files, called `python-dotenv`. So let's install that package:

```
(venv) $ pip install python-dotenv
```

Since the *config.py* module is where I read all the environment variables, I'm going to import a *.env* file before the `Config` class is created, so that the variables are set when the class is constructed:

Listing 15.10: *config.py*: Import a .env file with environment variables.

```python
import os
from dotenv import load_dotenv

basedir = os.path.abspath(os.path.dirname(__file__))
load_dotenv(os.path.join(basedir, '.env'))

class Config(object):
    # ...
```

So now you can create a *.env* file with all the environment variables that your application needs. It is important that you do not add your *.env* file to source control. You do not want to have a file that contains passwords and other sensitive information included in your source code repository.

The *.env* file can be used for all the configuration-time variables, but it cannot be used for Flask's `FLASK_APP` and `FLASK_DEBUG` environment variables, because these are needed very early in the application bootstrap process, before the application instance and its configuration object exist.

The following example shows a *.env* file that defines a secret ket, configures email to go out on a locally running mail server on port 25 and no authentication, sets up the Microsoft Translator API key, and leaves the database configuration to use the defaults:

```
SECRET_KEY=a-really-long-and-unique-key-that-nobody-knows
MAIL_SERVER=localhost
MAIL_PORT=25
MS_TRANSLATOR_KEY=<your-translator-key-here>
```

15.6 Requirements File

At this point I have installed a fair number of packages in the Python virtual environment. If you ever need to regenerate your environment on another machine, you are going to have trouble remembering what packages you had to install, so the generally accepted practice is to write a *requirements.txt* file in the root folder of your project listing all the dependencies, along with their versions. Producing this list is actually easy:

```
(venv) $ pip freeze > requirements.txt
```

The `pip freeze` command will dump all the packages that are installed on your virtual environment in the correct format for the *requirements.txt* file. Now, if you need to create the same virtual environment on another machine, instead of installing packages one by one, you can run:

```
(venv) $ pip install -r requirements.txt
```

Chapter 16

Full-Text Search

The goal of this chapter is to implement a search feature for Microblog, so that users can find interesting posts using natural language. For many types of web sites, it is possible to just let Google, Bing, etc. index all the content and provide search results through their search APIs. This works well for sites that have mostly static pages, like a forum. But in my application the basic unit of content is a user post, which is a small portion of the entire web page. The type of search results that I want are for these individual blog posts and not entire pages. For example, if I search for the word "dog" I want to see blog posts from any users that include that word. Obviously a page that shows all blog posts that have the word "dog" (or any other possible search term) does not really exist as a page that the big search engines can find and index, so clearly I have no choice other than to roll my own search feature.

The GitHub links for this chapter are: Browse[1], Zip[2], Diff[3].

16.1 Introduction to Full-Text Search Engines

Support for full-text search is not standardized like relational databases are. There are several open-source full-text engines: Elasticsearch[4], Apache Solr[5], Whoosh[6], Xapian[7], Sphinx[8], etc.

---

[1] https://github.com/miguelgrinberg/microblog/tree/v0.16
[2] https://github.com/miguelgrinberg/microblog/archive/v0.16.zip
[3] https://github.com/miguelgrinberg/microblog/compare/v0.15...v0.16
[4] https://www.elastic.co/products/elasticsearch
[5] http://lucene.apache.org/solr/
[6] http://whoosh.readthedocs.io/
[7] https://xapian.org/
[8] http://sphinxsearch.com/

As if this isn't enough choice, there are several databases that also provide searching capabilities that are comparable to dedicated search engines like the ones I enumerated above. SQLite[9], MySQL[10] and PostgreSQL[11] all offer some support for searching text, and NoSQL databases such as MongoDB[12] and CouchDB[13] do too.

If you are wondering which of these can work within a Flask application, the answer is all of them! That is one of the strengths of Flask, it does its job while not being opinionated. So what's the best choice?

From the list of dedicated search engines, Elasticsearch is one that stands out to me as being fairly popular, in part due to its popularity as the "E" in the ELK stack for indexing logs, along with Logstash and Kibana. Using the searching capabilities of one of the relational databases could also be a good choice, but given the fact that SQLAlchemy does not support this functionality, I would have to handle the searching with raw SQL statements, or else find a package that provides high-level access to text searches while being able to coexist with SQLAlchemy.

Based on the above analysis, I'm going to use Elasticsearch, but I'm going to implement all the text indexing and searching functions in a way that is very easy to switch to another engine. That will allow you to replace my implementation with an alternative one based on a different engine just by rewriting a few functions in a single module.

16.2 Installing Elasticsearch

There are several ways to install Elasticsearch, including one-click installers, zip file with the binaries that you need to install yourself, and even a Docker image. The documentation has an Installation[14] page with detailed information on all these options. If you are using Linux, you will likely have a package available for your distribution. If you are using a Mac and have Homebrew installed, then you can simply run `brew install elasticsearch`.

Once you install Elasticsearch on your computer, you can verify that it is running by typing `http://localhost:9200` in your browser's address bar, which should return some basic information about the service in JSON format.

---

[9] https://www.sqlite.org
[10] https://www.mysql.com/
[11] https://www.postgresql.org/
[12] https://www.mongodb.com/
[13] http://couchdb.apache.org/
[14] https://www.elastic.co/guide/en/elasticsearch/reference/current/install-elasticsearch.html

16.3. ELASTICSEARCH TUTORIAL

Since I will be managing Elasticsearch from Python, I will also be using the Python client library:

```
(venv) $ pip install elasticsearch
```

You may also want to update your *requirements.txt* file:

```
(venv) $ pip freeze > requirements.txt
```

16.3 Elasticsearch Tutorial

I'm going to start by showing you the basics of working with Elasticsearch from a Python shell. This will help you familiarize with this service, so that you can understand the implementation that I will discuss later.

To create a connection to Elasticsearch, create an instance of class `Elasticsearch`, passing a connection URL as an argument:

```
>>> from elasticsearch import Elasticsearch
>>> es = Elasticsearch('http://localhost:9200')
```

Data in Elasticsearch is written to *indexes*. Unlike a relational database, the data is just a JSON[15] object. The following example writes an object with a field called `text` to an index called `my_index`:

```
>>> es.index(index='my_index', doc_type='my_index', id=1, body={'text': 'this is a test'})
```

An index can store documents of different types if desired, and in that case the `doc_type` argument can be set to different values according to those different formats. I'm going to be storing all documents with the same format, so I'm setting the document type to the index name.

For each document stored, Elasticsearch takes a unique id and the JSON object with the data.

Let's store a second document on this index:

---

[15] http://www.json.org/

```
>>> es.index(index='my_index', doc_type='my_index', id=2, body={'text': 'a second test'})
```

And now that there are two documents in this index, I can issue a free-form search. In this example, I'm going to search for `this test`:

```
>>> es.search(index='my_index', doc_type='my_index',
... body={'query': {'match': {'text': 'this test'}}})
```

The response from the `es.search()` call is a Python dictionary with the search results:

```
{
    'took': 1,
    'timed_out': False,
    '_shards': {'total': 5, 'successful': 5, 'skipped': 0, 'failed': 0},
    'hits': {
        'total': 2,
        'max_score': 0.5753642,
        'hits': [
            {
                '_index': 'my_index',
                '_type': 'my_index',
                '_id': '1',
                '_score': 0.5753642,
                '_source': {'text': 'this is a test'}
            },
            {
                '_index': 'my_index',
                '_type': 'my_index',
                '_id': '2',
                '_score': 0.25316024,
                '_source': {'text': 'a second test'}
            }
        ]
    }
}
```

Here you can see that the search returned the two documents, each with an assigned score. The document with the highest score contains the two words I searched for, and the other document contains only one. You can see that even the best result does not have a great score, because the words do not exactly match the text.

Now this is the result if I search for the word `second`:

```
>>> es.search(index='my_index', doc_type='my_index',
... body={'query': {'match': {'text': 'second'}}})
{
```

```
    'took': 1,
    'timed_out': False,
    '_shards': {'total': 5, 'successful': 5, 'skipped': 0, 'failed': 0},
    'hits': {
        'total': 1,
        'max_score': 0.25316024,
        'hits': [
            {
                '_index': 'my_index',
                '_type': 'my_index',
                '_id': '2',
                '_score': 0.25316024,
                '_source': {'text': 'a second test'}
            }
        ]
    }
}
```

I still get a fairly low score because my search does not match the text in this document, but since only one of the two documents contains the word "second", the other document does not show up at all.

The Elasticsearch query object has more options, all well documented[16], and includes options such as pagination and sorting, just like relational databases.

Feel free to add more entries to this index and try different searches. When you are done experimenting, you can delete the index with the following command:

```
>>> es.indices.delete('my_index')
```

16.4 Elasticsearch Configuration

Integrating Elasticsearch into the application is a great example of the power of Flask. This is a service and Python package that does not have anything to do with Flask, yet, I'm going to get a pretty good level of integration, starting from the configuration, which I'm going to write in the `app.config` dictionary from Flask:

Listing 16.1: *config.py*: Elasticsearch configuration.

```
class Config(object):
    # ...
    ELASTICSEARCH_URL = os.environ.get('ELASTICSEARCH_URL')
```

---

[16]https://www.elastic.co/guide/en/elasticsearch/reference/current/search-request-body.html

Like with many other configuration entries, the connection URL for Elasticsearch is going to be sourced from an environment variable. If the variable is not defined, I'm going to let the setting be set to `None`, and I'll use that as a signal to disable Elasticsearch. This is mainly for convenience, so that you are not forced to always have the Elasticsearch service up and running when you work on the application, and in particular when you run unit tests. So to make sure the service is used, I need to define the `ELASTICSEARCH_URL` environment variable, either directly in the terminal or by adding it to the *.env* file as follows:

```
ELASTICSEARCH_URL=http://localhost:9200
```

Elasticsearch presents the challenge that it isn't wrapped by a Flask extension. I cannot create the Elasticsearch instance in the global scope like I did in the examples above because to initialize it I need access to `app.config`, which only becomes available after the `create_app()` function is invoked. So I decided to add a `elasticsearch` attribute to the `app` instance in the application factory function:

Listing 16.2: *app/__init__.py*: Elasticsearch instance.

```python
# ...
from elasticsearch import Elasticsearch

# ...

def create_app(config_class=Config):
    app = Flask(__name__)
    app.config.from_object(config_class)

    # ...
    app.elasticsearch = Elasticsearch([app.config['ELASTICSEARCH_URL']]) \
        if app.config['ELASTICSEARCH_URL'] else None

    # ...
```

Adding a new attribute to the `app` instance may seem a little strange, but Python objects are not strict in their structure, new attributes can be added to them at any time. An alternative that you may also consider is to create a subclass of `Flask` (maybe call it `Microblog`), with the `elasticsearch` attribute defined in its `__init__()` function.

Note how I use a conditional expression[17] to make the Elasticsearch instance `None` when a URL for the Elasticsearch service wasn't defined in the environment.

---

[17]https://docs.python.org/3/reference/expressions.html#conditional-expressions

16.5 A Full-Text Search Abstraction

As I said in the chapter's introduction, I want to make it easy to switch from Elasticsearch to other search engines, and I also don't want to code this feature specifically for searching blog posts, I prefer to design a solution that in the future I can easily extend to other models if I need to. For all these reasons, I decided to create an *abstraction* for the search functionality. The idea is to design the feature in generic terms, so I will not be assuming that the `Post` model is the only one that needs to be indexed, and I will also not be assuming that Elasticsearch is the index engine of choice. But if I can't make any assumptions about anything, how can I get this work done?

The first thing that I need, is to somehow find a generic way to indicate which model and which field or fields in it are to be indexed. I'm going to say that any model that needs indexing needs to define a `__searchable__` class attribute that lists the fields that need to be included in the index. For the `Post` model, these are the changes:

Listing 16.3: *app/models.py*: Add a __searchable__ attribute to the Post model.

```
class Post(db.Model):
    __searchable__ = ['body']
    # ...
```

So here I'm saying that this model needs to have its `body` field indexed. But just to make sure this is perfectly clear, this `__searchable__` attribute that I added is just a variable, it does not have any behavior associated with it. It will just help me write my indexing functions in a generic way.

I'm going to write all the code that interacts with the Elasticsearch index in a *app/search.py* module. The idea is to keep all the Elasticsearch code in this module. The rest of the application will use the functions in this new module to access the index and will not have direct access to Elasticsearch. This is important, because if one day I decided I don't like Elasticsearch anymore and want to switch to a different engine, all I need to do is rewrite the functions in this module, and the application will continue to work as before.

For this application, I decided that I need three supporting functions related to text indexing: I need to add entries to a full-text index, I need to remove entries from the index (assuming one day I will support deleting blog posts), and I need to execute a search query. Here is the *app/search.py* module that implements these three functions for Elasticsearch, using the functionality I showed you above from the Python console:

Listing 16.4: *app/search.py*: Search functions.

```python
from flask import current_app

def add_to_index(index, model):
    if not current_app.elasticsearch:
        return
    payload = {}
    for field in model.__searchable__:
        payload[field] = getattr(model, field)
    current_app.elasticsearch.index(index=index, doc_type=index, id=model.id,
                                    body=payload)

def remove_from_index(index, model):
    if not current_app.elasticsearch:
        return
    current_app.elasticsearch.delete(index=index, doc_type=index, id=model.id)

def query_index(index, query, page, per_page):
    if not current_app.elasticsearch:
        return [], 0
    search = current_app.elasticsearch.search(
        index=index, doc_type=index,
        body={'query': {'multi_match': {'query': query, 'fields': ['*']}},
              'from': (page - 1) * per_page, 'size': per_page})
    ids = [int(hit['_id']) for hit in search['hits']['hits']]
    return ids, search['hits']['total']
```

These functions all start by checking if `app.elasticsearch` is `None`, and in that case return without doing anything. This is so that when the Elasticsearch server isn't configured, the application continues to run without the search capability and without giving any errors. This is just as a matter of convenience during development or when running unit tests.

The functions accept the index name as an argument. In all the calls I'm passing down to Elasticsearch, I'm using this name as the index name and also as the document type, as I did in the Python console examples.

The functions that add and remove entries from the index take the SQLAlchemy model as a second argument. The `add_to_index()` function uses the `__searchable__` class variable I added to the model to build the document that is inserted into the index. If you recall, Elasticsearch documents also needed a unique identifier. For that I'm using the `id` field of the SQLAlchemy model, which is also conveniently unique. Using the same `id` value for SQLAlchemy and Elasticsearch is very useful when running the searches, as it allows me to link entries in the two databases. Something I did not mention above is that if you attempt to add an entry with an existing `id`, then Elasticsearch replaces the old entry with the new one, so `add_to_index()` can be used for new objects as well as for modified ones.

I did not show you the `es.delete()` function that I'm using in `remove_from_index()` before. This function deletes the document stored under the given `id`. Here is a good example

16.5. A FULL-TEXT SEARCH ABSTRACTION

of the convenience of using the same `id` to link entries in both databases.

The `query_index()` function takes the index name and a text to search for, along with pagination controls, so that search results can be paginated like Flask-SQLAlchemy results are. You have already seen an example usage of the `es.search()` function from the Python console. The call I'm issuing here is fairly similar, but instead of using a `match` query type, I decided to use `multi_match`, which can search across multiple fields. By passing a field name of `*`, I'm telling Elasticsearch to look in all the fields, so basically I'm searching the entire index. This is useful to make this function generic, since different models can have different field names in the index.

The `body` argument to `es.search()` includes pagination arguments in addition to the query itself. The `from` and `size` arguments control what subset of the entire result set needs to be returned. Elasticsearch does not provide a nice `Pagination` object like the one from Flask-SQLAlchemy, so I have to do the pagination math to calculate the `from` value.

The `return` statement in the `query_index()` function is somewhat complex. It returns two values: the first is a list of `id` elements for the search results, and the second is the total number of results. Both are obtained from the Python dictionary returned by the `es.search()` function. If you are not familiar with the expression that I'm using to obtain the list of IDs, this is called a *list comprehension*, and is a fantastic feature of the Python language that allows you to transform lists from one format to another. In this case I'm using the list comprehension to extract the `id` values from the much larger list of results provided by Elasticsearch.

Is this too confusing? Maybe a demonstration of these functions from the Python console can help you understand them a bit more. In the following session, I manually add all the posts from the database to the Elasticsearch index. In my test database, I had a few posts that had the numbers "one", "two", "three", "four" and "five" in them, so I used that as a search query. You may need to adapt your query to match the contents of your database:

```
>>> from app.search import add_to_index, remove_from_index, query_index
>>> for post in Post.query.all():
...     add_to_index('posts', post)
>>> query_index('posts', 'one two three four five', 1, 100)
([15, 13, 12, 4, 11, 8, 14], 7)
>>> query_index('posts', 'one two three four five', 1, 3)
([15, 13, 12], 7)
>>> query_index('posts', 'one two three four five', 2, 3)
([4, 11, 8], 7)
>>> query_index('posts', 'one two three four five', 3, 3)
([14], 7)
```

The query that I issued returned seven results. When I asked for page 1 with 100 items per page I get all seven, but then the next three examples shows how I can paginate the results in a way that is very similar to what I did for Flask-SQLAlchemy, with the exception that the results come as a list of IDs instead of SQLAlchemy objects.

If you want to keep things clean, delete the `posts` index after you are doing experimenting with it:

```
>>> app.elasticsearch.indices.delete('posts')
```

16.6 Integrating Searches with SQLAlchemy

The solution that I showed you in the previous section is decent, but it still has a couple of problems. The most obvious problem is that results come as a list of numeric IDs. This is highly inconvenient, I need SQLAlchemy models so that I can pass them down to templates for rendering, and I need a way to replace that list of numbers with the corresponding models from the database. The second problem is that this solution requires the application to explicitly issue indexing calls as posts are added or removed, which is not terrible, but less than ideal, since a bug that causes a missed indexing call when making a change on the SQLAlchemy side is not going to be easily detected, the two databases will get out of sync more and more each time the bug occurs and you will probably not notice for a while. A better solution would be for these calls to be triggered automatically as changes are made on the SQLAlchemy database.

The problem of replacing the IDs with objects can be addressed by creating a SQLAlchemy query that reads those objects from the database. This sounds easy in practice, but doing it efficiently with a single query is actually a bit tricky to implement.

For the problem of triggering the indexing changes automatically, I decided to drive updates to the Elasticsearch index from SQLAlchemy *events*. SQLAlchemy provides a large list of events[18] that applications can be notified about. For example, each time a session is committed, I can have a function in the application invoked by SQLAlchemy, and in that function I can apply the same updates that were made on the SQLAlchemy session to the Elasticsearch index.

To implement the solutions to these two problems I'm going to write a *mixin* class. Remember mixin classes? In Chapter 5, I added the `UserMixin` class from Flask-Login to the `User` model, to give it some features that were required by Flask-Login. For the search support I'm going to define my own `SearchableMixin` class, that when attached to a model, will give it the ability to automatically manage a full-text index associated with a SQLAlchemy model. The mixin class will act as a "glue" layer between the SQLAlchemy and Elasticsearch worlds, providing solutions to the two problems I stated above.

---

[18] http://docs.sqlalchemy.org/en/latest/core/event.html

16.6. INTEGRATING SEARCHES WITH SQLALCHEMY

Let me show you the implementation, then I'll go over some interesting details. Note that this makes use of several advanced techniques, so you will need to study this code carefully to fully understand it.

Listing 16.5: *app/models.py*: SearchableMixin class.

```python
from app.search import add_to_index, remove_from_index, query_index

class SearchableMixin(object):
    @classmethod
    def search(cls, expression, page, per_page):
        ids, total = query_index(cls.__tablename__, expression, page, per_page)
        if total == 0:
            return cls.query.filter_by(id=0), 0
        when = []
        for i in range(len(ids)):
            when.append((ids[i], i))
        return cls.query.filter(cls.id.in_(ids)).order_by(
            db.case(when, value=cls.id)), total

    @classmethod
    def before_commit(cls, session):
        session._changes = {
            'add': [obj for obj in session.new if isinstance(obj, cls)],
            'update': [obj for obj in session.dirty if isinstance(obj, cls)],
            'delete': [obj for obj in session.deleted if isinstance(obj, cls)]
        }

    @classmethod
    def after_commit(cls, session):
        for obj in session._changes['add']:
            add_to_index(cls.__tablename__, obj)
        for obj in session._changes['update']:
            add_to_index(cls.__tablename__, obj)
        for obj in session._changes['delete']:
            remove_from_index(cls.__tablename__, obj)
        session._changes = None

    @classmethod
    def reindex(cls):
        for obj in cls.query:
            add_to_index(cls.__tablename__, obj)
```

There are four functions in this mixin class, all class methods. Just as a refresher, a class method is a special method that is associated with the class and not a particular instance. Note how I renamed the `self` argument used in regular instance methods to `cls`, to make it clear that this method receives a class and not an instance as its first argument. Once attached to the `Post` model for example, the `search()` method above would be invoked as `Post.search()`, without having to have an actual instance of class `Post`.

The `search()` class method wraps the `query_index()` function from *app/search.py* to replace the list of object IDs with actual objects. You can see that the first thing this function does is call `query_index()`, passing `cls.__tablename__` as the index name. This is going to be a convention, all indexes will be named with the name Flask-SQLAlchemy assigned to the relational table. The function returns the list of result IDs, and the total number of results. The SQLAlchemy query that retrieves the list of objects by their IDs is based on a `CASE` statement from the SQL language, which needs to be used to ensure that the results from the database come in the same order as the IDs are given. This is important because the Elasticsearch query returns results sorted from more to less relevant. If you want to learn more about the way this query works, you can consult the accepted answer to this StackOverflow question[19]. The `search()` function returns the query that replaces the list of IDs, and also passes through the total number of search results as a second return value.

The `before_commit()` and `after_commit()` methods are going to respond to two events from SQLAlchemy, which are triggered before and after a commit takes place respectively. The before handler is useful because the session hasn't been committed yet, so I can look at it and figure out what objects are going to be added, modified and deleted, available as `session.new`, `session.dirty` and `session.deleted` respectively. These objects are not going to be available anymore after the session is committed, so I need to save them before the commit takes place. I'm using a `session._changes` dictionary to write these objects in a place that is going to survive the session commit, because as soon as the session is committed I will be using them to update the Elasticsearch index.

When the `after_commit()` handler is invoked, the session has been successfully committed, so this is the proper time to make changes on the Elasticsearch side. The session object has the `_changes` variable that I added in `before_commit()`, so now I can iterate over the added, modified and deleted objects and make the corresponding calls to the indexing functions in *app/search.py*.

The `reindex()` class method is a simple helper method that you can use to refresh an index with all the data from the relational side. You saw me do something similar from the Python shell session above to do an initial load of all the posts into a test index. With this method in place, I can issue `Post.reindex()` to add all the posts in the database to the search index.

To incorporate the `SearchableMixin` class into the `Post` model I have to add it as a subclass, and I also need to hook up the before and after commit events:

Listing 16.6: *app/models.py*: Adding the SearchableMixin class to the Post model.

```
class Post(SearchableMixin, db.Model):
    # ...

db.event.listen(db.session, 'before_commit', Post.before_commit)
db.event.listen(db.session, 'after_commit', Post.after_commit)
```

---

[19]https://stackoverflow.com/a/6332081/904393

Note that the `db.event.listen()` calls are not inside the class, but after it. These set up the event handlers that are invoked before and after each commit. Now the `Post` model is automatically maintaining a full-text search index for posts. I can use the `reindex()` method to initialize the index from all the posts currently in the database:

```
>>> Post.reindex()
```

And I can search posts working with SQLAlchemy models by running `Post.search()`. In the following example, I ask for the first page of five elements for my query:

```
>>> query, total = Post.search('one two three four five', 1, 5)
>>> total
7
>>> query.all()
[<Post five>, <Post two>, <Post one>, <Post one more>, <Post one>]
```

16.7 Search Form

This was very intense. The work that I've done above to keep things generic touches on several advanced topics, so it may take you time to fully understand it. But now I have a complete system to work with natural language searches for blog posts. What I need to do now is integrate all this functionality with the application.

A fairly standard approach for web-based searches is to have the search term as a `q` argument in the query string of the URL. For example, if you wanted to search for `Python` on Google, and you want to save a couple of seconds, you can just type the following URL in your browser's address bar to go directly to the results:

```
https://www.google.com/search?q=python
```

Allowing searches to be completely encapsulated in a URL is nice, because these can be shared with other people, who just by clicking on the link have access to the search results.

This introduces a change in the way I showed you to handle web forms in the past. I have used `POST` requests to submit form data for all the forms the application has so far, but to implement searches as above, the form submission will have to go as a `GET` request, which is the request method that is used when you type a URL in your browser or click a link. Another interesting difference is that the search form is going to be in the navigation bar, so it needs to be present in all pages of the application.

Here is the search form class, with just the `q` text field:

Listing 16.7: *app/main/forms.py*: Search form.

```python
from flask import request

class SearchForm(FlaskForm):
    q = StringField(_l('Search'), validators=[DataRequired()])

    def __init__(self, *args, **kwargs):
        if 'formdata' not in kwargs:
            kwargs['formdata'] = request.args
        if 'csrf_enabled' not in kwargs:
            kwargs['csrf_enabled'] = False
        super(SearchForm, self).__init__(*args, **kwargs)
```

The `q` field does not require any explanation, as it is similar to other text fields I've used in the past. For this form, I decided not to have a submit button. For a form that has a text field, the browser will submit the form when you press Enter with the focus on the field, so a button is not needed. I have also added a `__init__` constructor function, which provides values for the `formdata` and `csrf_enabled` arguments if they are not provided by the caller. The `formdata` argument determines from where Flask-WTF gets form submissions. The default is to use `request.form`, which is where Flask puts form values that are submitted via `POST` request. Forms that are submitted via `GET` request get have the field values in the query string, so I need to point Flask-WTF at `request.args`, which is where Flask writes the query string arguments. And as you remember, forms have CSRF protection added by default, with the inclusion of a CSRF token that is added to the form via the `form.hidden_tag()` construct in templates. For clickable search links to work, CSRF needs to be disabled, so I'm setting `csrf_enabled` to `False` so that Flask-WTF knows that it needs to bypass CSRF validation for this form.

Since I'm going to need to have this form visible in all pages, I need to create an instance of the `SearchForm` class regardless of the page the user is viewing. The only requirement is that the user is logged in, because for anonymous users I am not currently showing any content. Instead of creating a form object in every route, and then passing the form to all the templates, I'm going to show you a very useful trick that eliminates duplication of code when you need to implement a feature across the entire application. I already used a `before_request` handler before, back in Chapter 6, to record the time of last visit for each user. What I'm going to do is create my search form in that same function, but with a twist:

Listing 16.8: *app/main/routes.py*: Instantiate the search form in the before_request handler.

```python
from flask import g
from app.main.forms import SearchForm
```

16.7. SEARCH FORM

```
@bp.before_app_request
def before_request():
    if current_user.is_authenticated:
        current_user.last_seen = datetime.utcnow()
        db.session.commit()
        g.search_form = SearchForm()
    g.locale = str(get_locale())
```

Here I create an instance of the search form class when I have an authenticated user. But of course, I need this form object to persist until it can be rendered at the end of the request, so I need to store it somewhere. That somewhere is going to be the `g` container, provided by Flask. This `g` variable provided by Flask is a place where the application can store data that needs to persist through the life of a request. Here I'm storing the form in `g.search_form`, so then when the before request handler ends and Flask invokes the view function that handles the requested URL, the `g` object is going to be the same, and will still have the form attached to it. It's important to note that this `g` variable is specific to each request and each client, so even if your web server is handling multiple requests at a time for different clients, you can still rely on `g` to work as private storage for each request, independently of what goes on in other requests that are handled concurrently.

The next step is to render the form to the page. I said above that I wanted this form in all pages, so what makes more sense is to render it as part of the navigation bar. This is, in fact, simple, because templates can also see the data stored in the `g` variable, so I don't need to worry about adding the form as an explicit template argument in all the `render_template()` calls in the application. Here is how I can render the form in the base template:

Listing 16.9: *app/templates/base.html*: Render the search form in the navigation bar.

```
...
<div class="collapse navbar-collapse" id="bs-example-navbar-collapse-1">
    <ul class="nav navbar-nav">
        ... home and explore links ...
    </ul>
    {% if g.search_form %}
    <form class="navbar-form navbar-left" method="get"
            action="{{ url_for('main.search') }}">
        <div class="form-group">
            {{ g.search_form.q(size=20, class='form-control',
                placeholder=g.search_form.q.label.text) }}
        </div>
    </form>
    {% endif %}
    ...
```

The form is rendered only if `g.search_form` is defined. This check is necessary because some pages, such as error pages, may not have it defined. This form is slightly different than the ones I did previously. I'm setting its `method` attribute to `get`, because I want the form data to be submitted on the query string with a `GET` request. Also, the other forms I created had the `action` attribute empty, because they were submitted to the same page that rendered the form. This form is special because it appears in all pages, so I need to tell it explicitly where it needs to be submitted, which is a new route that is specifically dedicated to handling searches.

16.8 Search View Function

The last bit of functionality to complete the search feature is the view function that receives the search form submission. This view function is going to be attached to the */search* route, so that you can send a search request with a *http://localhost:5000/search?q=search-words*, just like Google.

Listing 16.10: *app/main/routes.py*: Search view function.

```python
@bp.route('/search')
@login_required
def search():
    if not g.search_form.validate():
        return redirect(url_for('main.explore'))
    page = request.args.get('page', 1, type=int)
    posts, total = Post.search(g.search_form.q.data, page,
                               current_app.config['POSTS_PER_PAGE'])
    next_url = url_for('main.search', q=g.search_form.q.data, page=page + 1) \
        if total > page * current_app.config['POSTS_PER_PAGE'] else None
    prev_url = url_for('main.search', q=g.search_form.q.data, page=page - 1) \
        if page > 1 else None
    return render_template('search.html', title=_('Search'), posts=posts,
                           next_url=next_url, prev_url=prev_url)
```

You have seen that in the other forms I used the `form.validate_on_submit()` method to check if the form submission was valid. Unfortunately that method only works for forms submitted via `POST` request, so for this form I need to use `form.validate()` which just validates field values, without checking how the data was submitted. If the validation fails, it is because the user submitted an empty search form, so in that case I just redirect to the explore page, which shows all blog posts.

The `Post.search()` method from my `SearchableMixin` class is used to obtain the list of search results. The pagination is handled in a very similar way to that of the index and explore pages, but generating the next and previous links is a little bit trickier without the help of the `Pagination` object from Flask-SQLAlchemy. This is where the total number of results passed as a second return value from `Post.search()` is useful.

16.8. SEARCH VIEW FUNCTION

Once the page of search results and pagination links are calculated, all that is left is to render a template with all this data. I could have figured out a way to reuse the *index.html* template to display search results, but given that there are a few differences I decided to create a dedicated *search.html* template that is dedicated to show search results, taking advantage of the *_post.html* sub-template to render the search results:

Listing 16.11: *app/templates/search.html*: Search results template.

```
{% extends "base.html" %}

{% block app_content %}
    <h1>{{ _('Search Results') }}</h1>
    {% for post in posts %}
        {% include '_post.html' %}
    {% endfor %}
    <nav aria-label="...">
        <ul class="pager">
            <li class="previous{% if not prev_url %} disabled{% endif %}">
                <a href="{{ prev_url or '#' }}">
                    <span aria-hidden="true">&larr;</span>
                    {{ _('Previous results') }}
                </a>
            </li>
            <li class="next{% if not next_url %} disabled{% endif %}">
                <a href="{{ next_url or '#' }}">
                    {{ _('Next results') }}
                    <span aria-hidden="true">&rarr;</span>
                </a>
            </li>
        </ul>
    </nav>
{% endblock %}
```

If the rendering logic for the previous and next links gets a bit confusing it might help to review the Bootstrap documentation for the pagination component[20].

---

[20]https://getbootstrap.com/docs/3.3/components/#pagination

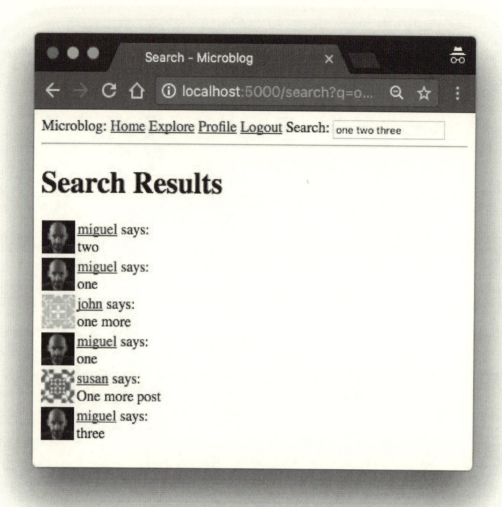

What do you think? This was an intense chapter, where I presented some fairly advanced techniques. Some of the concepts in this chapter may take some time to sink in. The most important take away from this chapter is that if you want to use a different search engine than Elasticsearch, all you need to do is re-implement the three functions in *app/search.py*. The other important benefit of going through this effort is that in the future, if I need to add search support for a different database model, I can simply do so by adding the `SearchableMixin` class to it, the `__searchable__` attribute with the list of fields to index and the SQLAlchemy event handler connections. I think it was well worth the effort, because from now on, it is going to be easy to deal with full-text indexes.

Chapter 17

Deployment on Linux

In this chapter I'm reaching a milestone in the life of my Microblog application, as I'm going to discuss ways in which the application can be deployed on a production server so that it is accessible to real users.

The topic of deployment is extensive, and for that reason it is impossible to cover all the possible options here. This chapter is dedicated to explore traditional hosting options, and as subjects I'm going to use a dedicated Linux server running Ubuntu, and also the widely popular Raspberry Pi mini-computer. I will cover other options such as cloud and container deployments in later chapters.

The GitHub links for this chapter are: Browse[1], Zip[2], Diff[3].

17.1 Traditional Hosting

When I refer to "traditional hosting", what I mean is that the application is installed manually or through a scripted installer on a stock server machine. The process involves installing the application, its dependencies and a production scale web server and configure the system so that it is secure.

The first question you need to ask when you are about to deploy your own project is where to find a server. These days there are many economic hosting services. For example, for $5 per

---

[1] https://github.com/miguelgrinberg/microblog/tree/v0.17
[2] https://github.com/miguelgrinberg/microblog/archive/v0.17.zip
[3] https://github.com/miguelgrinberg/microblog/compare/v0.16...v0.17

month, Digital Ocean[4], Linode[5], or Amazon Lightsail[6] will rent you a virtualized Linux server in which to run your deployment experiments (Linode provisions their entry level servers with 1GB of RAM, while Digital Ocean and Amazon provide only 512MB). If you prefer to practice deployments without spending any money, then Vagrant[7] and VirtualBox[8] are two tools that combined allow you to create a virtual server similar to the paid ones on your own computer.

As far as operating system choices, from a technical point of view, this application can be deployed on any of the major operating systems, a list which includes a large variety of open-source Linux and BSD distributions, and the commercial OS X and Microsoft Windows (though OS X is a hybrid open-source/commercial option as it is based on Darwin, an open-source BSD derivative).

Since OS X and Windows are desktop operating systems that are not optimized to work as servers, I'm going to discard those as candidates. The choice between a Linux or a BSD operating system is largely based on preference, so I'm going to pick the most popular of the two, which is Linux. As far as Linux distributions, once again I'm going to choose by popularity and go with Ubuntu.

17.2 Creating an Ubuntu Server

If you are interested in doing this deployment along with me, you obviously need a server to work on. I'm going to recommend two options for you to acquire a server, one paid and one free. If you are willing to spend a little bit of money, you can get an account at Digital Ocean, Linode or Amazon Lightsail and create a Ubuntu 16.04 virtual server. You should use the smallest server option, which at the time I'm writing this, costs $5 per month for all three providers. The cost is prorated to the number of hours that you have the server up, so if you create the server, play with it for a few hours and then delete it, you would be paying just cents.

The free alternative is based on a virtual machine that you can run on your own computer. To use this option, install Vagrant[9] and VirtualBox[10] on your machine, and then create file named *Vagrantfile* to describe the specs of your VM with the following contents:

---

[4]https://www.digitalocean.com/
[5]https://www.linode.com/
[6]https://amazonlightsail.com/
[7]https://www.vagrantup.com/
[8]https://www.virtualbox.org/
[9]https://www.vagrantup.com/
[10]https://www.virtualbox.org/

17.3 Using a SSH Client

Listing 17.1: *Vagrantfile*: Vagrant configuration.

```
Vagrant.configure("2") do |config|
  config.vm.box = "ubuntu/xenial64"
  config.vm.network "private_network", ip: "192.168.33.10"
  config.vm.provider "virtualbox" do |vb|
    vb.memory = "1024"
  end
end
```

This file configures a Ubuntu 16.04 server with 1GB of RAM, which you will be able to access from the host computer at IP address 192.168.33.10. To create the server, run the following command:

```
$ vagrant up
```

Consult the Vagrant command-line documentation[11] to learn about other options to manage your virtual server.

17.3 Using a SSH Client

Your server is headless, so you are not going to have a desktop on it like you have on your own computer. You are going to connect to your server through a SSH client and work on it through the command-line. If you are using Linux or Mac OS X, you likely have OpenSSH[12] already installed. If you are using Microsoft Windows, Cygwin[13], Git[14], and the Windows Subsystem for Linux[15] provide OpenSSH, so you can install any of these options.

If you are using a virtual server from a third-party provider, when you created the server you were given an IP address for it. You can open a terminal session with your brand new server with the following command:

```
$ ssh root@<server-ip-address>
```

---

[11] https://www.vagrantup.com/docs/cli/
[12] http://www.openssh.org/
[13] https://www.cygwin.com/
[14] https://git-scm.com/
[15] https://msdn.microsoft.com/en-us/commandline/wsl/about

You will be prompted to enter a password. Depending on the service, the password may have been automatically generated and shown to you after you created the server, or you may have given the option to choose your own password.

If you are using a Vagrant VM, you can open a terminal session using the command:

```
$ vagrant ssh
```

If you are using Windows and have a Vagrant VM, note that you will need to run the above command from a shell that can invoke the `ssh` command from OpenSSH.

17.4 Password-less Logins

If you are using a Vagrant VM, you can skip this section, since your VM is properly configured to use a non-root account named `ubuntu`, without password automatically by Vagrant.

If you are using a virtual server, it is recommended that you create a regular user account to do your deployment work, and configure this account to log you in without using a password, which at first may seem like a bad idea, but you'll see that it is not only more convenient but also more secure.

I'm going to create a user account named `ubuntu` (you can use a different name if you prefer). To create this user account, log in to your server's root account using the `ssh` instructions from the previous section, and then type the following commands to create the user, give it `sudo` powers, and finally switch to it:

```
$ adduser --gecos "" ubuntu
$ usermod -aG sudo ubuntu
$ su ubuntu
```

Now I'm going to configure this new `ubuntu` account to use public key[16] authentication so that you can log in without having to type a password.

Leave the terminal session you have open on your server for a moment, and start a second terminal on your local machine. If you are using Windows, this needs to be the terminal from where you have access to the `ssh` command, so it will probably be a `bash` or similar prompt and not a native Windows terminal. In that terminal session, check the contents of the ~/.ssh directory:

---

[16]http://en.wikipedia.org/wiki/Public-key_cryptography

17.4. PASSWORD-LESS LOGINS

```
$ ls ~/.ssh
id_rsa   id_rsa.pub
```

If the directory listing shows files named *id_rsa* and *id_rsa.pub* like above, then you already have a key. If you don't have these two files, or if you don't have the *~/.ssh* directory at all, then you need to create your SSH keypair by running the following command, also part of the OpenSSH toolset:

```
$ ssh-keygen
```

This application will prompt you to enter a few things, for which I recommend you accept the defaults by pressing Enter on all the prompts. If you know what you are doing and want to do otherwise, you certainly can.

After this command runs, you should have the two files listed above. The file *id_rsa.pub* is your *public key*, which is a file that you will provide to third parties as a way to identify you. The *id_rsa* file is your *private key*, which should not be shared with anyone.

You now need to configure your public key as an *authorized host* in your server. On the terminal that you opened on your own computer, print your public key to the screen:

```
$ cat ~/.ssh/id_rsa.pub
ssh-rsa AAAAB3NzaC1yc2EAAAADAQABAAABAQCjw....F8Xv4f/0+7WT miguel@miguelspc
```

This is going to be a very long sequence of characters, possibly spanning multiple lines. You need to copy this data to the clipboard, and then switch back to the terminal on your remote server, where you will issue these commands to store the public key:

```
$ echo <paste-your-key-here> >> ~/.ssh/authorized_keys
$ chmod 600 ~/.ssh/authorized_keys
```

The password-less login should now be working. The idea is that `ssh` on your machine will identify itself to the server by performing a cryptographic operation that requires the private key. The server then verifies that the operation is valid using your public key.

You can now log out of your `ubuntu` session, and then from your `root` session, and then try to login directly to the `ubuntu` account with:

```
$ ssh ubuntu@<server-ip-address>
```

This time you should not have to enter a password!

17.5 Securing Your Server

To minimize the risk of your server being compromised, there are a few steps that you can take, directed at closing a number of potential doors through which an attacker may gain access.

The first change I'm going to make is to disable root logins via SSH. You now have password-less access into the `ubuntu` account, and you can run administrator commands from this account via `sudo`, so there is really no need to expose the root account. To disable root logins, you need to edit the */etc/ssh/sshd_config* file on your server. You probably have the `vi` and `nano` text editors installed in your server that you can use to edit files (if you are not familiar with either one, try `nano` first). You will need to prefix your editor with `sudo`, because the SSH configuration is not accessible to regular users (i.e. `sudo vi /etc/ssh/sshd_config`). You need to change a single line in this file:

Listing 17.2: */etc/ssh/sshd_config*: Disable root logins.
```
PermitRootLogin no
```

Note that to make this change you need to locate the line that starts with `PermitRootLogin` and change the value, whatever that might be in your server, to `no`.

The next change is in the same file. Now I'm going to disable password logins for all accounts. You have a password-less login set up, so there is no need to allow passwords at all. If you feel nervous about disabling passwords altogether you can skip this change, but for a production server it is a really good idea, since attackers are constantly trying random account names and passwords on all servers hoping to get lucky. To disable password logins, change the following line in */etc/ssh/sshd_config*:

Listing 17.3: */etc/ssh/sshd_config*: Disable password logins.
```
PasswordAuthentication no
```

After you are done editing the SSH configuration, the service needs to be restarted for the changes to take effect:

```
$ sudo service ssh restart
```

The third change I'm going to make is to install a *firewall*. This is a software that blocks accesses to the server on any ports that are not explicitly enabled:

```
$ sudo apt-get install -y ufw
$ sudo ufw allow ssh
$ sudo ufw allow http
$ sudo ufw allow 443/tcp
$ sudo ufw --force enable
$ sudo ufw status
```

These commands install ufw[17], the Uncomplicated Firewall, and configure it to only allow external traffic on port 22 (ssh), 80 (http) and 443 (https). Any other ports will not be allowed.

17.6 Installing Base Dependencies

If you followed my advice and provisioned your server with the Ubuntu 16.04 release, then you have a system that comes with full support for Python 3.5, so this is the release that I'm going to use for the deployment.

The base Python interpreter is probably pre-installed on your server, but there are some extra packages that are likely not, and there are also a few other packages outside of Python that are going to be useful in creating a robust, production-ready deployment. For a database server, I'm going to switch from SQLite to MySQL. The postfix package is a mail transfer agent, that I will use to send out emails. The supervisor tool will monitor the Flask server process and automatically restart it if it ever crashes, or also if the server is rebooted. The nginx server is going to accept all request that come from the outside world, and forward them to the application. Finally, I'm going to use git as my tool of choice to download the application directly from its git repository.

```
$ sudo apt-get -y update
$ sudo apt-get -y install python3 python3-venv python3-dev
$ sudo apt-get -y install mysql-server postfix supervisor nginx git
```

These installations run mostly unattended, but at some point while you run the third install statement you will be prompted to choose a root password for the MySQL service, and you'll

---

[17]https://wiki.ubuntu.com/UncomplicatedFirewall

also be asked a couple of questions regarding the installation of the postfix package which you can accept with their default answers.

Note that for this deployment I'm choosing not to install Elasticsearch. This service requires a large amount of RAM, so it is only viable if you have a large server with more than 2GB of RAM. To avoid problems with servers running out of memory I will leave the search functionality out. If you have a big enough server, you can download the official .deb package from the Elasticsearch site[18] and follow their installation instructions to add it to your server. Note that the Elasticsearch package available in the Ubuntu 16.04 package repository is too old and will not work, you need version 6.x or newer.

I should also note that the default installation of postfix is likely insufficient for sending email in a production environment. To avoid spam and malicious emails, many servers require the sender server to identify itself through security extensions, which means at the very least you have to have a domain name associated with your server. If you want to learn how to fully configure an email server so that it passes standard security tests, see the following Digital Ocean guides:

- Postfix Configuration[19]
- Adding an SPF Record[20]
- DKIM Installation and Configuration[21]

17.7 Installing the Application

Now I'm going to use `git` to download the Microblog source code from my GitHub repository. I recommend that you read git for beginners[22] if you are not familiar with git source control.

To download the application to the server, make sure you are in the `ubuntu` user's home directory and then run:

```
$ git clone https://github.com/miguelgrinberg/microblog
$ cd microblog
$ git checkout v0.17
```

[18] https://elastic.co
[19] http://do.co/2FhdIes
[20] http://do.co/2Ff8ksk
[21] http://do.co/2HW2oTD
[22] http://ryanflorence.com/git-for-beginners/

17.7. INSTALLING THE APPLICATION

This installs the code on your server, and syncs it to this chapter. If you are keeping your version of this tutorial's code on your own git repository, you can change the repository URL to yours, and in that case you can skip the `git checkout` command.

Now I need to create a virtual environment and populate it with all the package dependencies, which I conveniently saved to the *requirements.txt* file in Chapter 15:

```
$ python3 -m venv venv
$ source venv/bin/activate
(venv) $ pip install -r requirements.txt
```

In addition to the common requirements in *requirements.txt*, I'm going to use two packages that are specific to this production deployment, so they are not included in the requirements file. The `gunicorn` package is a production web server for Python applications. The `pymysql` package contains the MySQL driver that enables SQLAlchemy to work with MySQL databases:

```
(venv) $ pip install gunicorn pymysql
```

I need to create a *.env* file, with all the needed environment variables:

Listing 17.4: */home/ubuntu/microblog/.env*: Environment configuration.

```
SECRET_KEY=52cb883e323b48d78a0a36e8e951ba4a
MAIL_SERVER=localhost
MAIL_PORT=25
DATABASE_URL=mysql+pymysql://microblog:<db-password>@localhost:3306/microblog
MS_TRANSLATOR_KEY=<your-translator-key-here>
```

This *.env* file is mostly similar to the example I shown in Chapter 15, but I have used a random string for `SECRET_KEY`. To generate this random string I used the following command:

```
python3 -c "import uuid; print(uuid.uuid4().hex)"
```

For the `DATABASE_URL` variable I defined a MySQL URL. I will show you how to configure the database in the next section.

I need to set the `FLASK_APP` environment variable to the entry point of the application to enable the `flask` command to work, but this variable is needed before the *.env* file is parsed so it needs to be set manually. To avoid having to set it every time, I'm going to add it at the bottom of the *~/.profile* file for the `ubuntu` account, so that it is set automatically every time I log in:

```
$ echo "export FLASK_APP=microblog.py" >> ~/.profile
```

If you log out and back in, now `FLASK_APP` will be set for you. You can confirm that it is set by running `flask --help`. If the help message shows the `translate` command added by the application, then you know the application was found.

And now that the `flask` command is functional, I can compile the language translations:

```
(venv) $ flask translate compile
```

17.8 Setting Up MySQL

The sqlite database that I've used during development is great for simple applications, but when deploying a full blown web server that can potentially need to handle multiple requests at a time, it is better to use a more robust database. For that reason I'm going to set up a MySQL database that I will call `microblog`.

To manage the database server I'm going to use the `mysql` command, which should be already installed on your server:

```
$ mysql -u root -p
Enter password:
Welcome to the MySQL monitor.  Commands end with ; or \g.
Your MySQL connection id is 6
Server version: 5.7.19-0ubuntu0.16.04.1 (Ubuntu)

Copyright (c) 2000, 2017, Oracle and/or its affiliates. All rights reserved.

Oracle is a registered trademark of Oracle Corporation and/or its
affiliates. Other names may be trademarks of their respective
owners.

Type 'help;' or '\h' for help. Type '\c' to clear the current input statement.

mysql>
```

Note that you will need to type the MySQL root password that you selected when you installed MySQL to gain access to the MySQL command prompt.

These are the commands that create a new database called `microblog`, and a user with the same name that has full access to it:

```
mysql> create database microblog character set utf8 collate utf8_bin;
mysql> create user 'microblog'@'localhost' identified by '<db-password>';
mysql> grant all privileges on microblog.* to 'microblog'@'localhost';
mysql> flush privileges;
mysql> quit;
```

You will need to replace `<db-password>` with a password of your choice. This is going to be the password for the `microblog` database user, so it is a good idea to not use the same password you selected for the root user. The password for the `microblog` user needs to match the password that you included in the `DATABASE_URL` variable in the *.env* file.

If your database configuration is correct, you should now be able to run the database migrations that create all the tables:

```
(venv) $ flask db upgrade
```

Make sure the above command completes without producing any errors before you continue.

17.9 Setting Up Gunicorn and Supervisor

When you run the server with `flask run`, you are using a web server that comes with Flask. This server is very useful during development, but it isn't a good choice to use for a production server because it wasn't built with performance and robustness in mind. Instead of the Flask development server, for this deployment I decided to use gunicorn[23], which is also a pure Python web server, but unlike Flask's, it is a robust production server that is used by a lot of people, while at the same time it is very easy to use.

To start Microblog under gunicorn you can use the following command:

```
(venv) $ gunicorn -b localhost:8000 -w 4 microblog:app
```

The `-b` option tells gunicorn where to listen for requests, which I set to the internal network interface at port 8000. It is usually a good idea to run Python web applications without external access, and then have a very fast web server that is optimized to serve static files accepting all requests from clients. This fast web server will serve static files directly, and forward any

---

[23]http://gunicorn.org/

requests intended for the application to the internal server. I will show you how to set up nginx as the public facing server in the next section.

The `-w` option configures how many *workers* gunicorn will run. Having four workers allows the application to handle up to four clients concurrently, which for a web application is usually enough to handle a decent amount of clients, since not all of them are constantly requesting content. Depending on the amount of RAM your server has, you may need to adjust the number of workers so that you don't run out of memory.

The `microblog:app` argument tells gunicorn how to load the application instance. The name before the colon is the module that contains the application, and the name after the colon is the name of this application.

While gunicorn is very simple to set up, running the server from the command-line is actually not a good solution for a production server. What I want to do is have the server running in the background, and have it under constant monitoring, because if for any reason the server crashes and exits, I want to make sure a new server is automatically started to take its place. And I also want to make sure that if the machine is rebooted, the server runs automatically upon startup, without me having to log in and start things up myself. I'm going to use the supervisor[24] package that I installed above to do this.

The supervisor utility uses configuration files that tell it what programs to monitor and how to restart them when necessary. Configuration files must be stored in */etc/supervisor/conf.d*. Here is a configuration file for Microblog, which I'm going to call *microblog.conf*:

Listing 17.5: */etc/supervisor/conf.d/microblog.conf*: Supervisor configuration.

```
[program:microblog]
command=/home/ubuntu/microblog/venv/bin/gunicorn -b localhost:8000 -w 4 microblog:app
directory=/home/ubuntu/microblog
user=ubuntu
autostart=true
autorestart=true
stopasgroup=true
killasgroup=true
```

The `command`, `directory` and `user` settings tell supervisor how to run the application. The `autostart` and `autorestart` set up automatic restarts due to the computer starting up, or crashes. The `stopasgroup` and `killasgroup` options ensure that when supervisor needs to stop the application to restart it, it also reaches the child processes of the top-level gunicorn process.

---

[24]http://supervisord.org/

After you write this configuration file, you have to reload the supervisor service for it to be imported:

```
$ sudo supervisorctl reload
```

And just like that, the gunicorn web server should be up and running and monitored!

17.10 Setting Up Nginx

The microblog application server powered by gunicorn is now running privately port 8000. What I need to do now to expose the application to the outside world is to enable my public facing web server on ports 80 and 443, the two ports that I opened on the firewall to handle the web traffic of the application.

I want this to be a secure deployment, so I'm going to configure port 80 to forward all traffic to port 443, which is going to be encrypted. So I'm going to start by creating an SSL certificate. For now I'm going to create a *self-signed SSL certificate*, which is okay for testing everything but not good for a real deployment because web browsers will warn users that the certificate was not issued by a trusted certificate authority. The command to create the SSL certificate for microblog is:

```
$ mkdir certs
$ openssl req -new -newkey rsa:4096 -days 365 -nodes -x509 \
  -keyout certs/key.pem -out certs/cert.pem
```

The command is going to ask you for some information about your application and yourself. This is information that will be included in the SSL certificate, and that web browsers will show to users if they request to see it. The result of the command above is going to be two files called *key.pem* and *cert.pem*, which I placed in a *certs* sub-directory of the Microblog root directory.

To have a web site served by nginx, you need to write a configuration file for it. In most nginx installations this file needs to be in the */etc/nginx/sites-enabled* directory. Nginx installs a test site in this location that I don't really need, so I'm going to start by removing it:

```
$ sudo rm /etc/nginx/sites-enabled/default
```

Below you can see the nginx configuration file for Microblog, which goes in /etc/nginx/sites-enabled/microblog:

Listing 17.6: /etc/nginx/sites-enabled/microblog: Nginx configuration.

```
server {
    # listen on port 80 (http)
    listen 80;
    server_name _;
    location / {
        # redirect any requests to the same URL but on https
        return 301 https://$host$request_uri;
    }
}
server {
    # listen on port 443 (https)
    listen 443 ssl;
    server_name _;

    # location of the self-signed SSL certificate
    ssl_certificate /home/ubuntu/microblog/certs/cert.pem;
    ssl_certificate_key /home/ubuntu/microblog/certs/key.pem;

    # write access and error logs to /var/log
    access_log /var/log/microblog_access.log;
    error_log /var/log/microblog_error.log;

    location / {
        # forward application requests to the gunicorn server
        proxy_pass http://localhost:8000;
        proxy_redirect off;
        proxy_set_header Host $host;
        proxy_set_header X-Real-IP $remote_addr;
        proxy_set_header X-Forwarded-For $proxy_add_x_forwarded_for;
    }

    location /static {
        # handle static files directly, without forwarding to the application
        alias /home/ubuntu/microblog/static;
        expires 30d;
    }
}
```

The nginx configuration is far from trivial, but I've added some comments so that at least you know what each section does. If you want to have information about a specific directive, consult the nginx official documentation[25].

After you add this file, you need to tell nginx to reload the configuration to activate it:

---

[25]https://nginx.org/en/docs/

17.11. DEPLOYING APPLICATION UPDATES

```
$ sudo service nginx reload
```

And now the application should be deployed. In your web browser, you can type the the IP address of your server (or 192.168.33.10 if you are using a Vagrant VM) and that will connect to the application. Because you are using a self-signed certificate, you will get a warning from the web browser, which you will have to dismiss.

After you complete a deployment with the above instructions for your own projects, I strongly suggest that you replace the self-signed certificate with a real one, so that the browser does not warn your users about your site. For this you will first need to purchase a domain name and configure it to point to your server's IP address. Once you have a domain, you can request a free Let's Encrypt[26] SSL certificate. I have written a detailed article on my blog on how to Run your Flask application over HTTPS[27].

17.11 Deploying Application Updates

The last topic I want to discuss regarding the Linux based deployment is how to handle application upgrades. The application source code is installed in the server through `git`, so whenever you want to upgrade your application to the latest version, you can just run `git pull` to download the new commits that were made since the previous deployment.

But of course, downloading the new version of the code is not going to cause an upgrade. The server processes that are currently running will continue to run with the old code, which was already read and stored in memory. To trigger an upgrade you have to stop the current server and start a new one, to force all the code to be read again.

Doing an upgrade is in general more complicated than just restarting the server. You may need to apply database migrations, or compile new language translations, so in reality, the process to perform an upgrade involves a sequence of commands:

```
(venv) $ git pull                              # download the new version
(venv) $ sudo supervisorctl stop microblog     # stop the current server
(venv) $ flask db upgrade                      # upgrade the database
(venv) $ flask translate compile               # upgrade the translations
(venv) $ sudo supervisorctl start microblog    # start a new server
```

---

[26]https://letsencrypt.org/
[27]https://blog.miguelgrinberg.com/post/running-your-flask-application-over-https

17.12 Raspberry Pi Hosting

The Raspberry Pi[28] is a low-cost revolutionary little Linux computer that has very low power consumption, so it is the perfect device to host a home based web server that can be online 24/7 without tying up your desktop computer or laptop. There are several Linux distributions that run on the Raspberry Pi. My choice is Raspbian[29], which is the official distribution from the Raspberry Pi Foundation.

To prepare the Raspberry Pi, I'm going to install a fresh Raspbian release. I will be using the September 2017 version of Raspbian Stretch Lite, but by the time you read this there is likely going to be newer versions out, so check the official downloads page[30] to get the most current release.

The Raspbian image needs to be installed on an SD card, which you then plug into the Raspberry Pi so that it can boot with it. Instructions to copy the Raspbian image to an SD card from Windows, Mac OS X and Linux are available on the Raspberry Pi site[31].

When you boot your Raspberry Pi for the first time, do it while connected to a keyboard and a monitor, so that you can do the set up. At the very least you should enable SSH, so that you can log in from your computer to perform the deployment tasks more comfortably.

Like Ubuntu, Raspbian is a derivative of Debian, so the instructions above for Ubuntu Linux for the most part work just as well for the Raspberry Pi. However, you may decide to skip some of the steps if you are planning on running a small application on your home network, without external access. For example, you may not need the firewall, or the password-less logins. And You may want to use SQLite instead of MySQL in such a small computer. You may opt to not use nginx, and just have the gunicorn server listening directly to requests from clients. You will probably want just one gunicorn worker. The supervisor service is useful in ensuring the application is always up, so my recommendation is that you also use it on the Raspberry Pi.

---

[28] http://www.raspberrypi.org/
[29] http://www.raspbian.org/
[30] https://www.raspberrypi.org/downloads/raspbian/
[31] https://www.raspberrypi.org/documentation/installation/installing-images/

Chapter 18

Deployment on Heroku

In the previous article I showed you the "traditional" way to host a Python application, and I gave you two actual examples of deployment to Linux based servers. If you are not used to manage a Linux system, you probably thought that the amount of effort that needs to be put into the task was big, and that surely there must be an easier way.

In this chapter I'm going to show you a completely different approach, in which you rely on a third-party *cloud* hosting provider to perform most of the administration tasks, freeing you to spend more time working on your application.

Many cloud hosting providers offer a managed platform on which applications can run. All you need to provide to have your application deployed on these platforms is the actual application, because the hardware, operating system, scripting language interpreters, database, etc. are all managed by the service. This type of service is called Platform as a Service[1], or PaaS.

Sounds too good to be true, right?

I will look at deploying Microblog to Heroku[2], a popular cloud hosting service that is also very friendly for Python applications. I picked Heroku not only because it is popular, but also because it has a free service level that will allow you to follow me and do a complete deployment without spending any money.

The GitHub links for this chapter are: Browse[3], Zip[4], Diff[5].

---

[1] https://en.wikipedia.org/wiki/Platform_as_a_service
[2] http://heroku.com
[3] https://github.com/miguelgrinberg/microblog/tree/v0.18
[4] https://github.com/miguelgrinberg/microblog/archive/v0.18.zip
[5] https://github.com/miguelgrinberg/microblog/compare/v0.17...v0.18

18.1 Hosting on Heroku

Heroku was one of the first platform as a service providers. It started as a hosting option for Ruby based applications, but then grew to support many other languages like Java, Node.js and of course Python.

Deploying a web application to Heroku is done through the `git` version control tool, so you must have your application in a git repository. Heroku looks for a file called *Procfile* in the application's root directory for instructions on how to start the application. For Python projects, Heroku also expects a *requirements.txt* file that lists all the module dependencies that need to be installed. After the application is uploaded to Heroku's servers through git, you are essentially done and just need to wait a few seconds until the application is online. It's really that simple.

The different service tiers Heroku offers allow you to choose how much computing power and time you get for your application, so as your user base grows you will need to buy more units of computing, which Heroku calls "dynos".

Ready to try Heroku? Let's get started!

18.2 Creating Heroku account

Before you can deploy to Heroku you need to have an account with them. So visit heroku.com[6] and create a free account. Once you have an account and log in to Heroku, you will have access to a dashboard, where all your applications are listed.

18.3 Installing the Heroku CLI

Heroku provides a command-line tool for interacting with their service called Heroku CLI[7], available for Windows, Mac OS X and Linux. The documentation includes installation instructions for all the supported platforms. Go ahead and install it on your system if you plan on deploying the application to test the service.

The first thing you should do once the CLI is installed is login to your Heroku account:

---

[6]`https://id.heroku.com/signup`
[7]`https://devcenter.heroku.com/articles/heroku-cli`

18.4 Setting Up Git

```
$ heroku login
```

Heroku CLI will ask you to enter your email address and your account password. Your authenticated status will be remembered in subsequent commands.

18.4 Setting Up Git

The `git` tool is core to the deployment of applications to Heroku, so you must install it on your system if you don't have it yet. If you don't have a package available for your operating system, you can visit the git site[8] to download an installer.

There are a lot of reasons why using `git` for your projects makes sense. If you plan to deploy to Heroku, you have one more, because to deploy to Heroku, your application must be in a `git` repository. If you are going to do a test deployment for Microblog, you can clone the application from GitHub:

```
$ git clone https://github.com/miguelgrinberg/microblog
$ cd microblog
$ git checkout v0.18
```

The `git checkout` command selects the specific commit that has the application at the point in its history that corresponds to this chapter.

If you prefer to work with your own code instead of mine, you can transform your own project into a `git` repository by running `git init .` on the top-level directory (note the period after `init`, which tells git that you want to create the repository in the current directory).

18.5 Creating a Heroku Application

To register a new application with Heroku, you use the `apps:create` command from the root directory of the application, passing the application name as the only argument:

```
$ heroku apps:create flask-microblog
Creating flask-microblog... done
http://flask-microblog.herokuapp.com/ | https://git.heroku.com/flask-microblog.git
```

---

[8]https://git-scm.com/

Heroku requires that applications have a unique name. The name `flask-microblog` that I used above is not going to be available to you because I'm using it, so you will need to pick a different name for your deployment.

The output of this command will include the URL that Heroku assigned to the application, and also its git repository. Your local git repository will be configured with an extra *remote*, called `heroku`. You can verify that it exists with the `git remote` command:

```
$ git remote -v
heroku          https://git.heroku.com/flask-microblog.git (fetch)
heroku          https://git.heroku.com/flask-microblog.git (push)
```

Depending on how you created your git repository, the output of the above command could also include another remote called `origin`.

18.6 The Ephemeral File System

The Heroku platform is different to other deployment platforms in that it features an *ephemeral* file system that runs on a virtualized platform. What does that mean? It means that at any time, Heroku can reset the virtual server on which your server runs back to a clean state. You cannot assume that any data that you save to the file system will persist, and in fact, Heroku recycles servers very often.

Working under these conditions introduces some problems for my application, which uses a few files:

- The default SQLite database engine writes data in a disk file
- Logs for the application are also written to the file system
- The compiled language translation repositories are also written to local files

The following sections will address these three areas.

18.7 Working with a Heroku Postgres Database

To address the first problem, I'm going to switch to a different database engine. In Chapter 17 you saw me use a MySQL database to add robustness to the Ubuntu deployment. Heroku has

18.8. LOGGING TO STDOUT

a database offering of its own, based on the Postgres database, so I'm going to switch to that to avoid the file-based SQLite.

Databases for Heroku applications are provisioned with the same Heroku CLI. In this case I'm going to create a database on the free tier:

```
$ heroku addons:add heroku-postgresql:hobby-dev
Creating heroku-postgresql:hobby-dev on flask-microblog... free
Database has been created and is available
 ! This database is empty. If upgrading, you can transfer
 ! data from another database with pg:copy
Created postgresql-parallel-56076 as DATABASE_URL
Use heroku addons:docs heroku-postgresql to view documentation
```

The URL for the newly created database is stored in a `DATABASE_URL` environment variable that will be available when the application runs. This is very convenient, because the application already looks for the database URL in that variable.

18.8 Logging to stdout

Heroku expects applications to log directly to `stdout`. Anything the application prints to the standard output is saved and returned when you use the `heroku logs` command. So I'm going to add a configuration variable that indicates if I need to log to `stdout` or to a file like I've been doing. Here is the change in the configuration:

Listing 18.1: *config.py*: Option to log to stdout.

```python
class Config(object):
    # ...
    LOG_TO_STDOUT = os.environ.get('LOG_TO_STDOUT')
```

Then in the application factory function I can check this configuration to know how to configure the application's logger:

Listing 18.2: *app/__init__.py*: Log to stdout or file.

```python
def create_app(config_class=Config):
    # ...
    if not app.debug and not app.testing:
        # ...
```

```
    if app.config['LOG_TO_STDOUT']:
        stream_handler = logging.StreamHandler()
        stream_handler.setLevel(logging.INFO)
        app.logger.addHandler(stream_handler)
    else:
        if not os.path.exists('logs'):
            os.mkdir('logs')
        file_handler = RotatingFileHandler('logs/microblog.log',
                                           maxBytes=10240, backupCount=10)
        file_handler.setFormatter(logging.Formatter(
            '%(asctime)s %(levelname)s: %(message)s '
            '[in %(pathname)s:%(lineno)d]'))
        file_handler.setLevel(logging.INFO)
        app.logger.addHandler(file_handler)

    app.logger.setLevel(logging.INFO)
    app.logger.info('Microblog startup')

    return app
```

So now I need to set the `LOG_TO_STDOUT` environment variable when the application runs in Heroku, but not in other configurations. The Heroku CLI makes this easy, as it provides an option to set environment variables to be used at runtime:

```
$ heroku config:set LOG_TO_STDOUT=1
Setting LOG_TO_STDOUT and restarting flask-microblog... done, v4
LOG_TO_STDOUT: 1
```

18.9 Compiled Translations

The third aspect of Microblog that relies on local files is the compiled language translation files. The more direct option to ensure those files never disappear from the ephemeral file system is to add the compiled language files to the git repository, so that they become part of the initial state of the application once it is deployed to Heroku.

A more elegant option, in my opinion, is to include the `flask translate compile` command in the start up command given to Heroku, so that any time the server is restarted those files are compiled again. I'm going to go with this option, since I know that my start up procedure is going to require more than one command anyway, since I also need to run the database migrations. So for now, I will set this problem aside, and will revisit it later when I write the *Procfile*.

18.10 Elasticsearch Hosting

Elasticsearch is one of the many services that can be added to a Heroku project, but unlike Postgres, this is not a service provided by Heroku, but by third parties that partner with Heroku to provide add-ons. At the time I'm writing this, there are three different providers of an integrated Elasticsearch service.

Before you configure Elasticsearch, be aware that Heroku requires your account to have a credit card on file before any third party add-on is installed, even if you stay within their free tiers. If you prefer not to provide your credit card to Heroku, then skip this section. You will still be able to deploy the application, but the search functionality is not going to work.

Out of the Elasticsearch options that are available as add-ons, I decided to try SearchBox[9], which comes with a free starter plan. To add SearchBox to your account, you have to run the following command while being logged in to Heroku:

```
$ heroku addons:create searchbox:starter
```

This command will deploy an Elasticsearch service and leave the connection URL for the service in a `SEARCHBOX_URL` environment variable associated with your application. Once more keep in mind that this command will fail unless you add your credit card to your Heroku account.

If you recall from Chapter 16, my application looks for the Elasticsearch connection URL in the `ELASTICSEARCH_URL` variable, so I need to add this variable and set it to the connection URL assigned by SearchBox:

```
$ heroku config:get SEARCHBOX_URL
<your-elasticsearch-url>
$ heroku config:set ELASTICSEARCH_URL=<your-elasticsearch-url>
```

Here I first asked Heroku to print the value of `SEARCHBOX_URL`, and then I added a new environment variable with the name `ELASTICSEARCH_URL` set to that same value.

18.11 Updates to Requirements

Heroku expects the dependencies to be in the *requirements.txt* file, exactly like I defined it in Chapter 15. But for the application to run on Heroku I need to add two new dependencies to

---
[9]https://elements.heroku.com/addons/searchbox

this file.

Heroku does not provide a web server of its own. Instead, it expects the application to start its own web server on the port number given in the environment variable $PORT. Since the Flask development web server is not robust enough to use for production, I'm going to use gunicorn[10] again, the server recommended by Heroku for Python applications.

The application will also be connecting to a Postgres database, and for that SQLAlchemy requires the psycopg2 package to be installed.

Both gunicorn and psycopg2 need to be added to the *requirements.txt* file.

18.12 The Procfile

Heroku needs to know how to execute the application, and for that it uses a file named *Procfile* in the root directory of the application. The format of this file is simple, each line includes a process name, a colon, and then the command that starts the process. The most common type of application that runs on Heroku is a web application, and for this type of application the process name should be web. Below you can see a *Procfile* for Microblog:

Listing 18.3: *Procfile*: Heroku Procfile.

```
web: flask db upgrade; flask translate compile; gunicorn microblog:app
```

Here I defined the command to start the web application as three commands in sequence. First I run a database migration upgrade, then I compile the language translations, and finally I start the server.

Because the first two sub-commands are based on the `flask` command, I need to add the `FLASK_APP` environment variable:

```
$ heroku config:set FLASK_APP=microblog.py
Setting FLASK_APP and restarting flask-microblog... done, v4
FLASK_APP: microblog.py
```

The `gunicorn` command is simpler than what I used for the Ubuntu deployment, because this server has a very good integration with the Heroku environment. For example, the $PORT environment variable is honored by default, and instead of using the -w option to set the number of

---

[10]http://gunicorn.org/

workers, heroku recommends adding a variable called `WEB_CONCURRENCY`, which `gunicorn` uses when `-w` is not provided, giving you the flexibility to control the number of workers without having to modify the Procfile.

18.13 Deploying the Application

All the preparatory steps are complete, so now it is time to run the deployment. To upload the application to Heroku's servers for deployment, the `git push` command is used. This is similar to how you push changes in your local git repository to GitHub or other remote git server.

And now I have reached the most interesting part, where I push the application to our Heroku hosting account. This is actually pretty simple, I just have to use `git` to push the application to the master branch of the Heroku git repository. There are a couple of variations on how to do this, depending on how you created your git repository. If you are using my `v0.18` code, then you need to create a branch based on this tag, and push it as the remote master branch, as follows:

```
$ git checkout -b deploy
$ git push heroku deploy:master
```

If instead, you are working with your own repository, then your code is already in a `master` branch, so you first need to make sure that your changes are committed:

```
$ git commit -a -m "heroku deployment changes"
```

And then you can run the following to start the deployment:

```
$ git push heroku master
```

Regardless of how you push the branch, you should see the following output from Heroku:

```
$ git push heroku deploy:master
Counting objects: 247, done.
Delta compression using up to 8 threads.
Compressing objects: 100% (238/238), done.
Writing objects: 100% (247/247), 53.26 KiB | 3.80 MiB/s, done.
```

```
Total 247 (delta 136), reused 3 (delta 0)
remote: Compressing source files... done.
remote: Building source:
remote:
remote: -----> Python app detected
remote: -----> Installing python-3.6.2
remote: -----> Installing pip
remote: -----> Installing requirements with pip
...
remote:
remote: -----> Discovering process types
remote:        Procfile declares types -> web
remote:
remote: -----> Compressing...
remote:        Done: 57M
remote: -----> Launching...
remote:        Released v5
remote:        https://flask-microblog.herokuapp.com/ deployed to Heroku
remote:
remote: Verifying deploy... done.
To https://git.heroku.com/flask-microblog.git
 * [new branch]      deploy -> master
```

The label `heroku` that we used in the `git push` command is the remote that was automatically added by the Heroku CLI when the application was created. The `deploy:master` argument means that I'm pushing the code from the local repository referenced by the `deploy` branch to the `master` branch on the Heroku repository. When you work with your own projects, you will likely be pushing with the command `git push heroku master`, which pushes your local `master` branch. Because of the way this project is structured, I'm pushing a branch that is not `master`, but the destination branch on the Heroku side always needs to be `master` as that is the only branch that Heroku accepts for deployment.

And that is it, the application should now be deployed at the URL that you were given in the output of the command that created the application. In my case, the URL was *https://flask-microblog.herokuapp.com*, so that is what I need to type to access the application.

If you want to see the log entries for the running application, use the `heroku logs` command. This can be useful if for any reason the application fails to start. If there were any errors, those will be in the logs.

18.14 Deploying Application Updates

To deploy a new version of the application, you just need to run a new `git push` command with the new code. This will repeat the deployment process, take the old deployment offline, and then replace it with the new code. The commands in the Procfile will run again as part of

18.14. DEPLOYING APPLICATION UPDATES

the new deployment, so any new database migrations or translations will be updated during the process.

Chapter 19

Deployment on Docker Containers

In Chapter 17 you learned about traditional deployments, in which you have to take care of every little aspect of the server configuration. Then in Chapter 18 I took you to the other extreme when I introduced you to Heroku, a service that takes complete control of the configuration and deployment tasks, allowing you to fully concentrate on your application. In this chapter you are going to learn about a third application deployment strategy based on *containers*, more particularly on the Docker[1] container platform. This third option sits somewhere in between the other two in terms of the amount of deployment work needed on your part.

Containers are built on a lightweight virtualization technology that allows an application, along with its dependencies and configuration to run in complete isolation, but without the need to use a full blown virtualization solution such as virtual machines, which need a lot more resources and can sometimes have a significant performance degradation in comparison to the host. A system configured as a container host can execute many containers, all of them sharing the host's kernel and direct access to the host's hardware. This is in contrast to virtual machines, which have to emulate a complete system, including CPU, disk, other hardware, kernel, etc.

In spite of having to share the kernel, the level of isolation in a container is pretty high. A container has its own file system, and can be based on an operating system that is different than the one used by the container host. For example, you can run containers based on Ubuntu Linux on a Fedora host, or vice versa. While containers are a technology that is native to the Linux operating system, thanks to virtualization it is also possible to run Linux containers on Windows and Mac OS X hosts. This allows you to test your deployments on your development system, and also incorporate containers in your development workflow if you wish to do so.

---

[1] https://www.docker.com/

The GitHub links for this chapter are: Browse[2], Zip[3], Diff[4].

19.1 Installing Docker CE

While Docker isn't the only container platform, it is by far the most popular, so that's going to be my choice. There are two editions of Docker, a free community edition (CE) and a subscription based enterprise edition (EE). For the purposes of this tutorial Docker CE is perfectly adequate.

To work with Docker CE, you first have to install it on your system. There are installers for Windows, Mac OS X and several Linux distributions available at the Docker website[5]. If you are working on a Microsoft Windows system, it is important to note that Docker CE requires Hyper-V. The installer will enable this for you if necessary, but keep in mind that enabling Hyper-V prevents other virtualization technologies such as VirtualBox from working.

Once Docker CE is installed on your system, you can verify that the install was successful by typing the following command on a terminal window or command prompt:

```
$ docker version
Client:
 Version:      17.09.0-ce
 API version:  1.32
 Go version:   go1.8.3
 Git commit:   afdb6d4
 Built:        Tue Sep 26 22:40:09 2017
 OS/Arch:      darwin/amd64

Server:
 Version:      17.09.0-ce
 API version:  1.32 (minimum version 1.12)
 Go version:   go1.8.3
 Git commit:   afdb6d4
 Built:        Tue Sep 26 22:45:38 2017
 OS/Arch:      linux/amd64
 Experimental: true
```

---

[2]https://github.com/miguelgrinberg/microblog/tree/v0.19
[3]https://github.com/miguelgrinberg/microblog/archive/v0.19.zip
[4]https://github.com/miguelgrinberg/microblog/compare/v0.18...v0.19
[5]https://www.docker.com/community-edition

19.2 Building a Container Image

The first step in creating a container for Microblog is to build an *image* for it. A container image is a template that is used to create a container. It contains a complete representation of the container file system, along with various settings pertaining to networking, start up options, etc.

The most basic way to create a container image for your application is to start a container for the base operating system you want to use (Ubuntu, Fedora, etc.), connect to a bash shell process running in it, and then manually install your application, maybe following the guidelines I presented in Chapter 17 for a traditional deployment. After you install everything, you can take a snapshot of the container and that becomes the image. This type of workflow is supported with the `docker` command, but I'm not going to discuss it because it is not convenient to have to manually install the application every time you need to generate a new image.

A better approach is to generate the container image through a script. The command that creates scripted container images is `docker build`. This command reads and executes build instructions from a file called *Dockerfile*, which I will need to create. The Dockerfile is basically an installer script of sorts that executes the installation steps to get the application deployed, plus some container specific settings.

Here is a basic *Dockerfile* for Microblog:

Listing 19.1: *Dockerfile*: Dockerfile for Microblog.

```
FROM python:3.6-alpine

RUN adduser -D microblog

WORKDIR /home/microblog

COPY requirements.txt requirements.txt
RUN python -m venv venv
RUN venv/bin/pip install -r requirements.txt
RUN venv/bin/pip install gunicorn

COPY app app
COPY migrations migrations
COPY microblog.py config.py boot.sh ./
RUN chmod +x boot.sh

ENV FLASK_APP microblog.py

RUN chown -R microblog:microblog ./
USER microblog

EXPOSE 5000
ENTRYPOINT ["./boot.sh"]
```

Each line in the Dockerfile is a command. The `FROM` command specifies the base container image on which the new image will be built. The idea is that you start from an existing image, add or change some things, and you end up with a derived image. Images are referenced by a name and a tag, separated by a colon. The tag is used as a versioning mechanism, allowing a container image to provide more than one variant. The name of my chosen image is `python`, which is the official Docker image for Python. The tags for this image allow you to specify the interpreter version and base operating system. The `3.6-alpine` tag selects a Python 3.6 interpreter installed on Alpine Linux. The Alpine Linux distribution is often used instead of more popular ones such as Ubuntu because of its small size. You can see what tags are available for the Python image in the Python image repository[6].

The `RUN` command executes an arbitrary command in the context of the container. This would be similar to you typing the command in a shell prompt. The `adduser -D microblog` command creates a new user named `microblog`. Most container images have `root` as the default user, but it is not a good practice to run an application as root, so I create my own user.

The `WORKDIR` command sets a default directory where the application is going to be installed. When I created the `microblog` user above, a home directory was created, so now I'm making that directory the default. The new default directory is going to apply to any remaining commands in the Dockerfile, and also later when the container is executed.

The `COPY` command transfers files from your machine to the container file system. This command takes two or more arguments, the source and destination files or directories. The source file(s) must be relative to the directory where the Dockerfile is located. The destination can be an absolute path, or a path relative to the directory that was set in a previous `WORKDIR` command. In this first `COPY` command, I'm copying the *requirements.txt* file to the `microblog` user's home directory in the container file system.

Now that I have the *requirements.txt* file in the container, I can create a virtual environment, using the `RUN` command. First I create it, and then I install all the requirements in it. Because the requirements file contains only generic dependencies, I then explicitly install *gunicorn*, which I'm going to use as a web server. Alternatively, I could have added gunicorn to my *requirements.txt* file.

The three `COPY` commands that follow install the application in the container, by copying the *app* package, the *migrations* directory with the database migrations, and the *microblog.py* and *config.py* scripts from the top-level directory. I'm also copying a new file, *boot.sh* that I will discuss below.

The `RUN chmod` command ensures that this new *boot.sh* file is correctly set as an executable file. If you are in a Unix based file system and your source file is already marked as executable,

---

[6]https://hub.docker.com/r/library/python/tags/

19.2. BUILDING A CONTAINER IMAGE

then the copied file will also have the executable bit set. I added an explicit set because on Windows it is harder to set executable bits. If you are working on Mac OS X or Linux you probably don't need this statement, but it does not hurt to have it anyway.

The `ENV` command sets an environment variable inside the container. I need to set `FLASK_APP`, which is required to use the `flask` command.

The `RUN chown` command that follows sets the owner of all the directories and files that were stored in */home/microblog* as the new `microblog` user. Even though I created this user near the top of the Dockerfile, the default user for all the commands remained `root`, so all these files need to be switched to the `microblog` user so that this user can work with them when the container is started.

The `USER` command in the next line makes this new `microblog` user the default for any subsequent instructions, and also for when the container is started.

The `EXPOSE` command configures the port that this container will be using for its server. This is necessary so that Docker can configure the network in the container appropriately. I've chosen the standard Flask port 5000, but this can be any port.

Finally, the `ENTRYPOINT` command defines the default command that should be executed when the container is started. This is the command that will start the application web server. To keep things well organized, I decided to create a separate script for this, and this is the *boot.sh* file that I copied to the container earlier. Here are the contents of this script:

Listing 19.2: *boot.sh*: Docker container start-up script.

```sh
#!/bin/sh
source venv/bin/activate
flask db upgrade
flask translate compile
exec gunicorn -b :5000 --access-logfile - --error-logfile - microblog:app
```

This is a fairly standard start up script that is fairly similar to how the deployments in Chapter 17 and Chapter 18 were started. I activate the virtual environment, upgrade the database though the migration framework, compile the language translations, and finally run the server with gunicorn.

Note the `exec` that precedes the gunicorn command. In a shell script, `exec` triggers the process running the script to be replaced with the command given, instead of starting it as a new process. This is important, because Docker associates the life of the container to the first process that runs on it. In cases like this one, where the start up process is not the main process of the container, you need to make sure that the main process takes the place of that first process to ensure that the container is not terminated early by Docker.

An interesting aspect of Docker is that anything that the container writes to `stdout` or `stderr` will be captured and stored as logs for the container. For that reason, the `--access-logfile` and `--error-logfile` are both configured with a `-`, which sends the log to standard output so that they are stored as logs by Docker.

With the Dockerfile created, I can now build a container image:

```
$ docker build -t microblog:latest .
```

The `-t` argument that I'm giving to the `docker build` command sets the name and tag for the new container image. The `.` indicates the base directory where the container is to be built. This is the directory where the *Dockerfile* is located. The build process is going to evaluate all the commands in the *Dockerfile* and create the image, which will be stored on your own machine.

You can obtain a list of the images that you have locally with the `docker images` command:

```
$ docker images
REPOSITORY     TAG          IMAGE ID        CREATED            SIZE
microblog      latest       54a47d0c27cf    About a minute ago 216MB
python         3.6-alpine   a6beab4fa70b    3 months ago       88.7MB
```

This listing will include your new image, and also the base image on which it was built. Any time you make changes to the application, you can update the container image by running the build command again.

19.3   Starting a Container

With an image already created, you can now run the container version of the application. This is done with the `docker run` command, which usually takes a large number of arguments. I'm going to start by showing you a basic example:

```
$ docker run --name microblog -d -p 8000:5000 --rm microblog:latest
021da2e1e0d390320248abf97dfbbe7b27c70fefed113d5a41bb67a68522e91c
```

The `--name` option provides a name for the new container. The `-d` option tells Docker to run the container in the background. Without `-d` the container runs as a foreground application, blocking your command prompt. The `-p` option maps container ports to host ports. The first

19.3. STARTING A CONTAINER

port is the port on the host computer, and the one on the right is the port inside the container. The above example exposes port 5000 in the container on port 8000 in the host, so you will access the application on 8000, even though internally the container is using 5000. The `-rm` option will delete the container once it is terminated. While this isn't required, containers that finish or are interrupted are usually not needed anymore, so they can be automatically deleted. The last argument is the container image name and tag to use for the container. After you run the above command, you can access the application at *http://localhost:8000*.

The output of `docker run` is the ID assigned to the new container. This is a long hexadecimal string, that you can use whenever you need to refer to the container in subsequent commands. In fact, only the first few characters are necessary, enough to make the ID unique.

If you want to see what containers are running, you can use the `docker ps` command:

```
$ docker ps
CONTAINER ID   IMAGE              COMMAND       PORTS                    NAMES
021da2e1e0d3   microblog:latest   "./boot.sh"   0.0.0.0:8000->5000/tcp   microblog
```

You can see that even the `docker ps` command shortens container IDs. If you now want to stop the container, you can use `docker stop`:

```
$ docker stop 021da2e1e0d3
021da2e1e0d3
```

If you recall, there are a number of options in the application's configuration that are sourced from environment variables. For example, the Flask secret key, database URL and email server options are all imported from environment variables. In the `docker run` example above I have not worried about those, so all those configuration options are going to use defaults.

In a more realistic example, you will be setting those environment variables inside the container. You saw in the previous section that the `ENV` command in the *Dockerfile* sets environment variables, and it is a handy option for variables that are going to be static. For variables that depend on the installation, however, it isn't convenient to have them as part of the build process, because you want to have a container image that is fairly portable. If you want to give your application to another person as a container image, you would want that person to be able to use it as is, and not have to rebuild it with different variables.

So build-time environment variables can be useful, but there is also a need to have run-time environment variables that can be set via the `docker run` command, and for these variables, the `-e` option can be used. The following example sets a secret key and sends email through a gmail account:

```
$ docker run --name microblog -d -p 8000:5000 --rm -e SECRET_KEY=my-secret-key \
    -e MAIL_SERVER=smtp.googlemail.com -e MAIL_PORT=587 -e MAIL_USE_TLS=true \
    -e MAIL_USERNAME=<your-gmail-username> -e MAIL_PASSWORD=<your-gmail-password> \
    microblog:latest
```

It is not uncommon for `docker run` command lines to be extremely long due to having many environment variable definitions.

19.4 Using Third-Party "Containerized" Services

The container version of Microblog is looking good, but I haven't really thought much about storage yet. In fact, since I haven't set a `DATABASE_URL` environment variable, the application is using the default SQLite database, which is supported by a file on disk. What do you think is going to happen to that SQLite file when you stop and delete the container? The file is going to disappear!

The file system in a container is *ephemeral*, meaning that it goes away when the container goes away. You can write data to the file system, and the data is going to be there if the container needs to read it, but if for any reason you need to recycle your container and replace it with a new one, any data that the application saved to disk is going to be lost forever.

A good design strategy for a container application is to make the application containers *stateless*. If you have a container that has application code and no data, you can throw it away and replace it with a new one without any problems, the container becomes truly disposable, which is great in terms of simplifying the deployment of upgrades.

But of course, this means that the data must be put somewhere outside of the application container. This is where the fantastic Docker ecosystem comes into play. The Docker Container Registry contains a large variety of container images. I have already told you about the Python container image, which I'm using as a base image for my Microblog container. In addition to that, Docker maintains images for many other languages, databases and other services in the Docker registry and if that isn't enough, the registry also allows companies to publish container images for their products, and also regular users like you or me to publish your own images. That means that the effort to install third party services is reduced to finding an appropriate image in the registry, and starting it with a `docker run` command with proper arguments.

So what I'm going to do now is create two additional containers, one for a MySQL database, and another one for the Elasticsearch service, and then I'm going to make the command line that starts the Microblog container even longer with options that enable it to access these two new containers.

19.4. USING THIRD-PARTY "CONTAINERIZED" SERVICES

19.4.1 Adding a MySQL Container

Like many other products and services, MySQL has public container images available on the Docker registry. Like my own Microblog container, MySQL relies on environment variables that need to be passed to `docker run`. These configure passwords, database names etc. While there are many MySQL images in the registry, I decided to use one that is officially maintained by the MySQL team. You can find detailed information about the MySQL container image in its registry page: *https://hub.docker.com/r/mysql/mysql-server/*.

If you remember the laborious process to set up MySQL in Chapter 17, you are going to appreciate Docker when you see how easy it is to deploy MySQL. Here is the `docker run` command that starts a MySQL server:

```
$ docker run --name mysql -d -e MYSQL_RANDOM_ROOT_PASSWORD=yes \
    -e MYSQL_DATABASE=microblog -e MYSQL_USER=microblog \
    -e MYSQL_PASSWORD=<database-password> \
    mysql/mysql-server:5.7
```

That is it! On any machine that you have Docker installed, you can run the above command and you'll get a fully installed MySQL server with a randomly generated root password, a brand new database called `microblog`, and a user with the same name that is configured with full permissions to access the database. Note that you will need to enter a proper password as the value for the `MYSQL_PASSWORD` environment variable.

Now on the application side, I need to add a MySQL client package, like I did for the traditional deployment on Ubuntu. I'm going to use `pymysql` once again, which I can add to the *Dockerfile*:

Listing 19.3: *Dockerfile*: Add pymysql to Dockerfile.

```
# ...
RUN venv/bin/pip install gunicorn pymysql
# ...
```

Any time a change is made to the application or the *Dockerfile*, the container image needs to be rebuilt:

```
$ docker build -t microblog:latest .
```

Any now I can start Microblog again, but this time with a link to the database container so that both can communicate through the network:

```
$ docker run --name microblog -d -p 8000:5000 --rm -e SECRET_KEY=my-secret-key \
    -e MAIL_SERVER=smtp.googlemail.com -e MAIL_PORT=587 -e MAIL_USE_TLS=true \
    -e MAIL_USERNAME=<your-gmail-username> -e MAIL_PASSWORD=<your-gmail-password> \
    --link mysql:dbserver \
    -e DATABASE_URL=mysql+pymysql://microblog:<database-password>@dbserver/microblog \
    microblog:latest
```

The `-link` option tells Docker to make another container accessible to this one. The argument contains two names separated by a colon. The first part is the name or ID of the container to link, in this case the one named `mysql` that I created above. The second part defines a hostname that can be used in this container to refer to the linked one. Here I'm using `dbserver` as generic name that represents the database server.

With the link between the two containers established, I can set the `DATABASE_URL` environment variable so that SQLAlchemy is directed to use the MySQL database in the other container. The database URL is going to use `dbserver` as the database hostname, `microblog` as the database name and user, and the password that you selected when you started MySQL.

One thing I noticed when I was experimenting with the MySQL container is that it takes a few seconds for this container to be fully running and ready to accept database connections. If you start the MySQL container and then start the application container immediately after, when the *boot.sh* script tries to run `flask db migrate` it may fail due to the database not being ready to accept connections. To make my solution more robust, I decided to add a retry loop in *boot.sh*:

Listing 19.4: *boot.sh*: Retry database connection.

```
#!/bin/sh
source venv/bin/activate
while true; do
    flask db upgrade
    if [[ "$?" == "0" ]]; then
        break
    fi
    echo Upgrade command failed, retrying in 5 secs...
    sleep 5
done
flask translate compile
exec gunicorn -b :5000 --access-logfile - --error-logfile - microblog:app
```

This loop checks the exit code of the `flask db upgrade` command, and if it is non-zero it assumes that something went wrong, so it waits five seconds and then retries.

19.4.2 Adding a Elasticsearch Container

The Elasticsearch documentation for Docker[7] shows how to run the service as a single-node for development, and as a two-node production-ready deployment. For now I'm going to go with the single-node option and use the "oss" image, which only has the open source engine. The container is started with the following command:

```
$ docker run --name elasticsearch -d -p 9200:9200 -p 9300:9300 --rm \
    -e "discovery.type=single-node" \
    docker.elastic.co/elasticsearch/elasticsearch-oss:6.1.1
```

This `docker run` command has many similarities with the ones I've used for Microblog and MySQL, but there are a couple of interesting differences. First, there are two -p options, which means that this container is going to listen on two ports instead of just one. Both ports 9200 and 9300 are mapped to the same ports in the host machine.

The other difference is in the syntax used to refer to the container image. For the images that I've been building locally, the syntax was `<name>:<tag>`. The MySQL container uses a slightly more complete syntax with the format `<account>/<name>:<tag>`, which is appropriate to reference container images on the Docker registry. The Elasticsearch image that I'm using follows the pattern `<registry>/<account><name>:<tag>`, which includes the address of the registry as the first component. This syntax is used for images that are not hosted in the Docker registry. In this case Elasticsearch runs their own container registry service at *docker.elastic.co* instead of using the main registry maintained by Docker.

So now that I have the Elasticsearch service up and running, I can modify the start command for my Microblog container to create a link to it and set the Elasticsearch service URL:

```
$ docker run --name microblog -d -p 8000:5000 --rm -e SECRET_KEY=my-secret-key \
    -e MAIL_SERVER=smtp.googlemail.com -e MAIL_PORT=587 -e MAIL_USE_TLS=true \
    -e MAIL_USERNAME=<your-gmail-username> -e MAIL_PASSWORD=<your-gmail-password> \
    --link mysql:dbserver \
    -e DATABASE_URL=mysql+pymysql://microblog:<database-password>@dbserver/microblog \
    --link elasticsearch:elasticsearch \
    -e ELASTICSEARCH_URL=http://elasticsearch:9200 \
    microblog:latest
```

Before you run this command, remember to stop your previous Microblog container if you still have it running. Also be careful in setting the correct passwords for the database and the Elasticsearch service in the proper places in the command.

---

[7]https://www.elastic.co/guide/en/elasticsearch/reference/current/docker.html

Now you should be able to visit *http://localhost:8000* and use the search feature. If you experience any errors, you can troubleshoot them by looking at the container logs. You'll most likely want to see logs for the Microblog container, where any Python stack traces will appear:

```
$ docker logs microblog
```

19.5 The Docker Container Registry

So now I have the complete application up and running on Docker, using three containers, two of which come from publicly available third-party images. If you would like to make your own container images available to others, then you have to *push* them to the Docker registry from where anybody can obtain images.

To have access to the Docker registry you need to go to *https://hub.docker.com* and create an account for yourself. Make sure you pick a username that you like, because that is going to be used in all the images that you publish.

To be able to access your account from the command line, you need to log in with the `docker login` command:

```
$ docker login
```

If you've been following my instructions, you now have an image called `microblog:latest` stored locally on your computer. To be able to push this image to the Docker registry, it needs to be renamed to include the account, like the image from MySQL. This is done with the `docker tag` command:

```
$ docker tag microblog:latest <your-docker-registry-account>/microblog:latest
```

If you list your images again with `docker images` you are not going to see two entries for Microblog, the original one with the `microblog:latest` name, and a new one that also includes your account name. These are really two alias for the same image.

To publish your image to the Docker registry, use the `docker push` command:

```
$ docker push <your-docker-registry-account>/microblog:latest
```

Now your image is publicly available and you can document how to install it and run from the Docker registry in the same way MySQL and others do.

19.6 Deployment of Containerized Applications

One of the best things about having your application running in Docker containers is that once you have the containers tested locally, you can take them to any platform that offers Docker support. For example, you could use the same servers I recommended in Chapter 17 from Digital Ocean, Linode or Amazon Lightsail. Even the cheapest offering from these providers is sufficient to run Docker with a handful of containers.

The Amazon Container Service (ECS)[8] gives you the ability to create a cluster of container hosts on which to run your containers, in a fully integrated AWS environment, with support for scaling and load balancing, plus the option to use a private container registry for your container images.

Finally, a container orchestration platform such as Kubernetes[9] provides an even greater level of automation and convenience, by allowing you to describe your multi-container deployments in simple text files in YAML format, with load balancing, scaling, secure management of secrets and rolling upgrades and rollbacks.

---

[8]https://aws.amazon.com/ecs/
[9]https://kubernetes.io/

Chapter 20

Some JavaScript Magic

Nowadays it is impossible to build a web application that doesn't use at least a little bit of JavaScript. As I'm sure you know, the reason is that JavaScript is the only language that runs natively in web browsers. In Chapter 14 you saw me add a simple JavaScript enabled link in a Flask template to provide real-time language translations of blog posts. In this chapter I'm going to dig deeper into the topic and show you another useful JavaScript trick to make the application more interesting and engaging to users.

A common user interface pattern for social sites in which users can interact with each other is to show a quick summary of a user in a popup panel when you hover over the user's name, anywhere it appears on the page. If you have never paid attention to this, go to Twitter, Facebook, LinkedIn, or any other major social network, and when you see a username, just leave your mouse pointer on top of it for a couple of seconds to see the popup appear. This chapter is going to be dedicated to building that feature for Microblog, of which you can see a preview below:

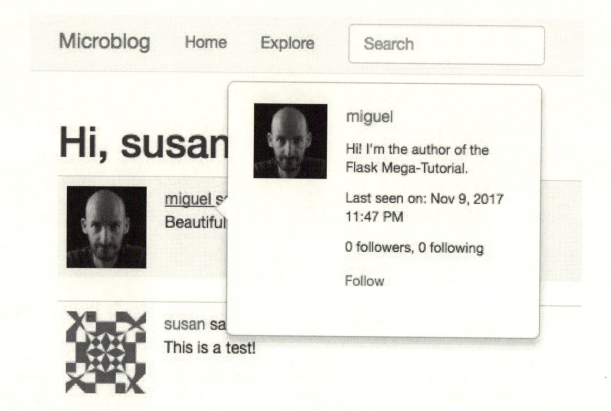

The GitHub links for this chapter are: Browse[1], Zip[2], Diff[3].

20.1 Server-side Support

Before we delve into the client-side, let's get the little bit of server work that is necessary to support these user popups out of the way. The contents of the user popup are going to be returned by a new route, which is going to be a simplified version of the existing user profile route. Here is the view function:

Listing 20.1: *app/main/routes.py*: User popup view function.

```
@bp.route('/user/<username>/popup')
@login_required
```

[1] https://github.com/miguelgrinberg/microblog/tree/v0.20
[2] https://github.com/miguelgrinberg/microblog/archive/v0.20.zip
[3] https://github.com/miguelgrinberg/microblog/compare/v0.19...v0.20

20.1. SERVER-SIDE SUPPORT

```python
def user_popup(username):
    user = User.query.filter_by(username=username).first_or_404()
    return render_template('user_popup.html', user=user)
```

This route is going to be attached to the */user/<username>/popup* URL, and will simply load the requested user and then render a template with it. The template is a shorter version of the one used for the user profile page:

Listing 20.2: *app/templates/user_popup.html*: User popup template.

```html
<table class="table">
    <tr>
        <td width="64" style="border: 0px;"><img src="{{ user.avatar(64) }}"></td>
        <td style="border: 0px;">
            <p>
                <a href="{{ url_for('main.user', username=user.username) }}">
                    {{ user.username }}
                </a>
            </p>
            <small>
                {% if user.about_me %}<p>{{ user.about_me }}</p>{% endif %}
                {% if user.last_seen %}
                <p>{{ _('Last seen on') }}:
                    {{ moment(user.last_seen).format('lll') }}</p>
                {% endif %}
                <p>{{ _('%(count)d followers', count=user.followers.count()) }},
                   {{ _('%(count)d following', count=user.followed.count()) }}</p>
                {% if user != current_user %}
                    {% if not current_user.is_following(user) %}
                    <a href="{{ url_for('main.follow', username=user.username) }}">
                        {{ _('Follow') }}
                    </a>
                    {% else %}
                    <a href="{{ url_for('main.unfollow', username=user.username) }}">
                        {{ _('Unfollow') }}
                    </a>
                    {% endif %}
                {% endif %}
            </small>
        </td>
    </tr>
</table>
```

The JavaScript code that I will write in the following sections will invoke this route when the user hovers the mouse pointer over a username. In response the server will return the HTML content for the popup, which the client then display. When the user moves the mouse away the popup will be removed. Sounds simple, right?

If you want to have an idea of how the popup will look, you can now run the application, go to any user's profile page and then append */popup* to the URL in the address bar to see a full-screen version of the popup content.

20.2 Introduction to the Bootstrap Popover Component

In Chapter 11 I introduced you to the Bootstrap framework as a convenient way to create great looking web pages. So far, I have used only a minimal portion of this framework. Bootstrap comes bundled with many common UI elements, all of which have demos and examples in the Bootstrap documentation at *https://getbootstrap.com*. One of these components is the Popover[4], which is described in the documentation as a "small overlay of content, for housing secondary information". Exactly what I need!

Most bootstrap components are defined through HTML markup that references the Bootstrap CSS definitions that add the nice styling. Some of the most advanced ones also require JavaScript. The standard way in which an application includes these components in a web page is by adding the HTML in the proper place, and then for the components that need scripting support, calling a JavaScript function that initializes it or activates it. The popover component does require JavaScript support.

The HTML portion to do a popover is really simple, you just need to define the element that is going to trigger the popover to appear. In my case, this is going to the clickable username that appears in each blog post. The *app/templates/_post.html* sub-template has the username already defined:

```
<a href="{{ url_for('main.user', username=post.author.username) }}">
    {{ post.author.username }}
</a>
```

Now according to the popover documentation, I need to invoke the `popover()` JavaScript function on each of the links like the one above that appear on the page, and this will initialize the popup. The initialization call accepts a number of options that configure the popup, including options that pass the content that you want displayed in the popup, what method to use to trigger the popup to appear or disappear (a click, hovering over the element, etc.), if the content is plain text or HTML, and a few more options that you can see in the documentation page. Unfortunately, after reading this information I ended up with more questions than answers, because this component does not appear to be designed to work in the way I need it to. The following is a list of problems I need to solve to implement this feature:

- There will be many username links in the page, one for each blog post displayed. I need to have a way to find all these links from JavaScript after the page is rendered, so that I can then initialize them as popovers.

---

[4]https://getbootstrap.com/docs/3.3/javascript/#popovers

- The popover examples in the Bootstrap documentation all provide the content of the popover as a `data-content` attribute added to the target HTML element, so when the hover event is triggered, all Bootstrap needs to do is display the popup. That is really inconvenient for me, because I want to make an Ajax call to the server to get the content, and only when the server's response is received I want the popup to appear.

- When using the "hover" mode, the popup will stay visible for as long as you keep the mouse pointer within the target element. When you move the mouse away, the popup will go away. This has the ugly side effect that if the user wants to move the mouse pointer into the popup itself, the popup will disappear. I will need to figure out a way to extend the hover behavior to also include the popup, so that the user can move into the popup and, for example, click on a link there.

It is actually not that uncommon when working with browser based applications that things get complicated really fast. You have to think very specifically in terms of how the DOM elements interact with each other and make them behave in a way that gives the user a good experience.

20.3 Executing a Function On Page Load

It is clear that I'm going to need to run some JavaScript code as soon as each page loads. The function that I'm going to run will search for all the links to usernames in the page, and configure those with a popover component from Bootstrap.

The jQuery JavaScript library is loaded as a dependency of Bootstrap, so I'm going to take advantage of it. When using jQuery, you can register a function to run when the page is loaded by wrapping it inside a `$( ... )`. I can add this in the *app/templates/base.html* template, so that this runs on every page of the application:

Listing 20.3: *app/templates/base.html*: Run function after page load.

```
...
<script>
    // ...

    $(function() {
        // write start up code here
    });
</script>
```

As you see, I have added my start up function inside the `<script>` element in which I defined the `translate()` function in Chapter 14.

20.4 Finding DOM Elements with Selectors

My first problem is to create a JavaScript function that finds all the user links in the page. This function is going to run when the page finishes loading, and when complete, will configure the hovering and popup behavior for all of them. For now I'm going to concentrate finding the links.

If you recall from Chapter 14, the HTML elements that were involved in the live translations had unique IDs. For example, a post with ID=123 had a `id="post123"` attribute added. Then using the jQuery, the expression `$('#post123')` was used in JavaScript to locate this element in the DOM. The `$()` function is extremely powerful and has a fairly sophisticated query language to search for DOM elements that is based on CSS Selectors[5].

The selector that I used for the translation feature was designed to find one specific element that had a unique identifier set as an `id` attribute. Another option to identify elements is by using the `class` attribute, which can be assigned to multiple elements in the page. For example, I could mark all the user links with a `class="user_popup"`, and then I could get the list of links from JavaScript with `$('.user_popup')` (in CSS selectors, the `#` prefix searches by ID, while the `.` prefix searches by class). The return value in this case would be a collection of all the elements that have the class.

20.5 Popovers and the DOM

By playing with the popover examples on the Bootstrap documentation and inspecting the DOM in the browser's debugger, I determined that Bootstrap creates the popover component as a sibling of the target element in the DOM. As I mentioned above, that affects the behavior of the hover event, which will trigger a "mouse out" as soon as the user moves the mouse away from the `<a>` link and into the popup itself.

A trick that I can use to extend the hover event to include the popover, is to make the popover a child of the target element, that way the hover event is inherited. Looking through the popover options in the documentation, this can be done by passing a parent element in the `container` option.

Making the popover a child of the hovered element would work well for buttons, or general `<div>` or `<span>` based elements, but in my case, the target for the popover is going to be an `<a>` element that displays the clickable link of a username. The problem with making the popover a child of a `<a>` element is that the popover will then acquire the link behavior of the

---

[5]https://api.jquery.com/category/selectors/

20.5. POPOVERS AND THE DOM

`<a>` parent. The end result would be something like this:

```
<a href="..." class="user_popup">
    username
    <div> ... popover elements here ... </div>
</a>
```

To avoid the popover being inside the `<a>` element, I'm going to use is another trick. I'm going to wrap the `<a>` element inside a `<span>` element, and then associate the hover event and the popover with the `<span>`. The resulting structure would be:

```
<span class="user_popup">
    <a href="...">
        username
    </a>
    <div> ... popover elements here ... </div>
</span>
```

The `<div>` and `<span>` elements are invisible, so they are great elements to use to help organize and structure your DOM. The `<div>` element is a *block element*, sort of like a paragraph in the HTML document, while the `<span>` element is an *inline element*, which would compare to a word. For this case I decided to go with the `<span>` element, since the `<a>` element that I'm wrapping is also an inline element.

So I'm going to go ahead and refactor my *app/templates/_post.html* sub-template to include the `<span>` element:

```
...
    {% set user_link %}
        <span class="user_popup">
            <a href="url_for('main.user', username=post.author.username)">
                {{ post.author.username }}
            </a>
        </span>
    {% endset %}
...
```

If you are wondering where the popover HTML elements are, the good news is that I don't have to worry about that. When I get to call the `popover()` initialization function on the `<span>` elements I just created, the Bootstrap framework will dynamically insert the popup component for me.

20.6 Hover Events

As I mentioned above, the hover behavior used by the popover component from Bootstrap is not flexible enough to accommodate my needs, but if you look at the documentation for the `trigger` option, "hover' is just one of the possible values. The one that caught my eye was the "manual" mode, in which the popover can be displayed or removed manually by making JavaScript calls. This mode will give me the freedom to implement the hover logic myself, so I'm going to use that option and implement my own hover event handlers that work the way I need them to.

So my next step is to attach a "hover" event to all the links in the page. Using jQuery, a hover event can be attached to any HTML element by calling `element.hover(handlerIn, handlerOut)`. If this function is called on a collection of elements, jQuery conveniently attaches the event to all of them. The two arguments are two functions, which are invoked when the user moves the mouse pointer into and out of the target element respectively.

Listing 20.4: *app/templates/base.html*: Hover event.

```
$(function() {
    $('.user_popup').hover(
        function(event) {
            // mouse in event handler
            var elem = event.currentTarget;
        },
        function(event) {
            // mouse out event handler
            var elem = event.currentTarget;
        }
    )
});
```

The `event` argument is the event object, which contains useful information. In this case, I'm extracting the element that was the target of the event using the `event.currentTarget`.

The browser dispatches the hover event immediately after the mouse enters the affected element. In the case of a popup, you want to activate only after waiting a short period of time where the mouse stays on the element, so that when the mouse pointer briefly passes over the element but doesn't stay on it there is no popups flashing. Since the event does not come with support for a delay, this is another thing that I'm going to need to implement myself. So I'm going to add a one second timer to the "mouse in" event handler:

Listing 20.5: *app/templates/base.html*: Hover delay.

```
$(function() {
    var timer = null;
```

20.7. AJAX REQUESTS

```
    $('.user_popup').hover(
        function(event) {
            // mouse in event handler
            var elem = event.currentTarget;
            timer = setTimeout(function() {
                timer = null;
                // popup logic goes here
            }, 1000);
        },
        function(event) {
            // mouse out event handler
            var elem = event.currentTarget;
            if (timer) {
                clearTimeout(timer);
                timer = null;
            }
        }
    )
});
```

The `setTimeout()` function is available in the browser environment. It takes two arguments, a function and a time in milliseconds. The effect of `setTimeout()` is that the function is invoked after the given delay. So I added a function that for now is empty, which will be invoked one second after the hover event is dispatched. Thanks to closures in the JavaScript language, this function can access variables that were defined in an outer scope, such as `elem`.

I'm storing the timer object in a `timer` variable that I have defined outside of the `hover()` call, to make the timer object accessible also to the "mouse out" handler. The reason I need this is, once again, to make for a good user experience. If the user moves the mouse pointer into one of these user links and stays on it for, say, half a second before moving it away, I do not want that timer to still go off and invoke the function that will display the popup. So my mouse out event handler checks if there is an active timer object, and if there is one, it cancels it.

20.7 Ajax Requests

Ajax requests are not a new topic, as I have introduced this topic back in Chapter 14 as part of the live language translation feature. When using jQuery, the `$.ajax()` function sends an asynchronous request to the server.

The request that I'm going to send to the server will have the */user/<username>/popup* URL, which I added to the application at the start of this chapter. The response from this request is going to contain the HTML that I need to insert in the popup.

My immediate problem regarding this request is to know what is the value of `username` that

I need to include in the URL. The mouse in event handler function is generic, it's going to run for all the user links that are found in the page, so the function needs to determine the username from its context.

The `elem` variable contains the target element from the hover event, which is the `<span>` element that wraps the `<a>` element. To extract the username, I can navigate the DOM starting from the `<span>`, moving to the first child, which is the `<a>` element, and then extracting the text from it, which is the username that I need to use in my URL. With jQuery's DOM traversal functions, this is actually easy:

```
elem.first().text().trim()
```

The `first()` function applied to a DOM node returns its first child. The `text()` function returns the text contents of a node. This function doesn't do any trimming of the text, so for example, if you have the `<a>` in one line, the text in the following line, and the `</a>` in another line, `text()` will return all the whitespace that surrounds the text. To eliminate all that whitespace and leave just the text, I use the `trim()` JavaScript function.

And that is all the information I need to be able to issue the request to the server:

Listing 20.6: *app/templates/base.html*: XHR request.

```
$(function() {
    var timer = null;
    var xhr = null;
    $('.user_popup').hover(
        function(event) {
            // mouse in event handler
            var elem = $(event.currentTarget);
            timer = setTimeout(function() {
                timer = null;
                xhr = $.ajax(
                    '/user/' + elem.first().text().trim() + '/popup').done(
                        function(data) {
                            xhr = null
                            // create and display popup here
                        }
                    );
            }, 1000);
        },
        function(event) {
            // mouse out event handler
            var elem = $(event.currentTarget);
            if (timer) {
                clearTimeout(timer);
                timer = null;
            }
            else if (xhr) {
                xhr.abort();
```

20.8. POPOVER CREATION AND DESTRUCTION

```
                xhr = null;
            }
            else {
                // destroy popup here
            }
        }
    )
});
```

Here I defined a new variable in the outer scope, `xhr`. This variable is going to hold the asynchronous request object, which I initialize from a call to `$.ajax()`. Unfortunately when building URLs directly in the JavaScript side I cannot use the `url_for()` from Flask, so in this case I have to concatenate the URL parts explicitly.

The `$.ajax()` call returns a promise, which is this special JavaScript object that represents the asynchronous operation. I can attach a completion callback by adding `.done(function)`, so then my callback function will be invoked once the request is complete. The callback function will receive the response as an argument, which you can see I named `data` in the code above. This is going to be the HTML content that I'm going to put in the popover.

But before we get to the popover, there is one more detail related to giving the user a good experience that needs to be taken care of. Recall that I added logic in the "mouse out" event handler function to cancel the one second timeout if the user moved the mouse pointer out of the `<span>`. The same idea needs to be applied to the asynchronous request, so I have added a second clause to abort my `xhr` request object if it exists.

20.8 Popover Creation and Destruction

So finally I can create my popover component, using the `data` argument that was passed to me in the Ajax callback function:

Listing 20.7: *app/templates/base.html*: Display popover.

```
                function(data) {
                    xhr = null;
                    elem.popover({
                        trigger: 'manual',
                        html: true,
                        animation: false,
                        container: elem,
                        content: data
                    }).popover('show');
                    flask_moment_render_all();
                }
```

The actual creation of the popup is very simple, the `popover()` function from Bootstrap does all the work required to set it up. Options for the popover are given as an argument. I have configured this popover with the "manual" trigger mode, HTML content, no fade animation (so that it appears and disappears more quickly), and I have set the parent to be the `<span>` element itself, so that the hover behavior extends to the popover by inheritance. Finally, I'm passing the `data` argument to the Ajax callback as the `content` argument.

The return of the `popover()` call is the newly created popover component, which for a strange reason, had another method also called `popover()` that is used to display it. So I had to add a second `popover('show')` call to make the popup appear on the page.

The content of the popup includes the "last seen" date, which is generated through the Flask-Moment plugin as covered in Chapter 12. As documented[6] by the extension, when new Flask-Moment elements are added via Ajax, the `flask_moment_render_all()` function needs to be called to appropriately render those elements.

What remains now is to deal with the removal of the popup on the mouse out event handler. This handler already has the logic to abort the popover operation if it is interrupted by the user moving the mouse out of the target element. If none of those conditions apply, then that means that the popover is currently displayed and the user is leaving the target area, so in that case, a `popover('destroy')` call to the target element does the proper removal and cleanup.

Listing 20.8: *app/templates/base.html*: Destroy popover.

```
function(event) {
    // mouse out event handler
    var elem = $(event.currentTarget);
    if (timer) {
        clearTimeout(timer);
        timer = null;
    }
    else if (xhr) {
        xhr.abort();
        xhr = null;
    }
    else {
        elem.popover('destroy');
    }
}
```

---

[6]https://github.com/miguelgrinberg/Flask-Moment#ajax-support

Chapter 21

User Notifications

In this chapter I want to continue working on improving the user experience of my Microblog application. One aspect that applies to a lot of applications is the presentation of alerts or notifications to the user. Social applications show these notifications to let you know you've got new mentions or private messages, usually by showing a little badge with a number in the top navigation bar. While this is the most obvious usage, the notification pattern can be applied to a lot of other types of applications to inform the user that something requires their attention.

But to show you the techniques involved in building user notifications, I needed to extend Microblog with a feature that can benefit from them, so in the first part of this chapter I'm going to build a user messaging system that allows any user to send a private message to another user. This is actually simpler than it sounds, and it will be a good refresher on core Flask practices and a reminder of how lean, efficient and fun programming with Flask can be. And once the messaging system is in place, I'm going to discuss some options to implement a notification badge that shows a count of unread messages.

The GitHub links for this chapter are: Browse[1], Zip[2], Diff[3].

21.1 Private Messages

The private messaging feature that I'm going to implement is going to be very simple. When you visit the profile page of a user, there will be a link to send that user a private message. The link will take you to a new page in which a web form takes the message. To read messages sent

---

[1]https://github.com/miguelgrinberg/microblog/tree/v0.21
[2]https://github.com/miguelgrinberg/microblog/archive/v0.21.zip
[3]https://github.com/miguelgrinberg/microblog/compare/v0.20...v0.21

to you, the navigation bar at the top of the page will have a new "Messages" link, that will take you to a page that is similar in structure to the index or explore pages, but instead of showing blog posts it will show messages other users sent you.

The following sections describe the steps I took to implement this feature.

21.1.1 Database Support for Private Messages

The first task is to extend the database to support private messages. Here is a new `Message` model:

Listing 21.1: *app/models.py*: Message model.

```python
class Message(db.Model):
    id = db.Column(db.Integer, primary_key=True)
    sender_id = db.Column(db.Integer, db.ForeignKey('user.id'))
    recipient_id = db.Column(db.Integer, db.ForeignKey('user.id'))
    body = db.Column(db.String(140))
    timestamp = db.Column(db.DateTime, index=True, default=datetime.utcnow)

    def __repr__(self):
        return '<Message {}>'.format(self.body)
```

This model class is similar to the `Post` model, with the only difference that there are two user foreign keys, one for the sender and one for the recipient. The `User` model can get relationships for these two users, plus a new field that indicates what was the last time users read their private messages:

Listing 21.2: *app/models.py*: Private messages support in User model.

```python
class User(UserMixin, db.Model):
    # ...
    messages_sent = db.relationship('Message',
                                    foreign_keys='Message.sender_id',
                                    backref='author', lazy='dynamic')
    messages_received = db.relationship('Message',
                                        foreign_keys='Message.recipient_id',
                                        backref='recipient', lazy='dynamic')
    last_message_read_time = db.Column(db.DateTime)

    # ...

    def new_messages(self):
        last_read_time = self.last_message_read_time or datetime(1900, 1, 1)
        return Message.query.filter_by(recipient=self).filter(
            Message.timestamp > last_read_time).count()
```

21.1. PRIVATE MESSAGES

The two relationships will return messages sent and received for a given user, and on the `Message` side of the relationship will add `author` and `recipient` back references. The reason why I used a `author` backref instead of a maybe more appropriate `sender` is that by using `author` I can then render these messages using the same logic that I use for blog posts. The `last_message_read_time` field will have the last time the user visited the messages page, and will be used to determine if there are unread messages, which will all have a timestamp newer than this field. The `new_messages()` helper method actually uses this field to return how many unread messages the user has. By the end of this chapter I will have this number as a nice badge in the navigation bar at the top of the page.

That completes the database changes, so now it is time to generate a new migration and upgrade the database with it:

```
(venv) $ flask db migrate -m "private messages"
(venv) $ flask db upgrade
```

21.1.2 Sending a Private Message

Next I'm going to work on sending messages. I'm going to need a simple web form that accepts the message:

Listing 21.3: *app/main/forms.py*: Private message form class.

```python
class MessageForm(FlaskForm):
    message = TextAreaField(_l('Message'), validators=[
        DataRequired(), Length(min=0, max=140)])
    submit = SubmitField(_l('Submit'))
```

And I also need the HTML template that renders this form on a web page:

Listing 21.4: *app/templates/send_message.html*: Send private message HTML template.

```
{% extends "base.html" %}
{% import 'bootstrap/wtf.html' as wtf %}

{% block app_content %}
    <h1>{{ _('Send Message to %(recipient)s', recipient=recipient) }}</h1>
    <div class="row">
        <div class="col-md-4">
            {{ wtf.quick_form(form) }}
        </div>
    </div>
{% endblock %}
```

Next I'm going to add a new */send_message/<recipient>* route to handle the actual sending of the private message:

Listing 21.5: *app/main/routes.py*: Send private message route.

```python
from app.main.forms import MessageForm
from app.models import Message

# ...

@bp.route('/send_message/<recipient>', methods=['GET', 'POST'])
@login_required
def send_message(recipient):
    user = User.query.filter_by(username=recipient).first_or_404()
    form = MessageForm()
    if form.validate_on_submit():
        msg = Message(author=current_user, recipient=user,
                      body=form.message.data)
        db.session.add(msg)
        db.session.commit()
        flash(_('Your message has been sent.'))
        return redirect(url_for('main.user', username=recipient))
    return render_template('send_message.html', title=_('Send Message'),
                           form=form, recipient=recipient)
```

I think the logic in this view function should be mostly self-explanatory. The action of sending a private message is simply carried out by adding a new `Message` instance to the database.

The last change that ties everything together is the addition of a link to the above route in the user profile page:

Listing 21.6: *app/templates/user.html*: Send private message link in user profile page.

```
{% if user != current_user %}
<p>
    <a href="{{ url_for('main.send_message',
                    recipient=user.username) }}">
        {{ _('Send private message') }}
    </a>
</p>
{% endif %}
```

21.1.3 Viewing Private Messages

The second big part of this feature is the viewing of private messages. For that I'm going to add another route at */messages* that works in a fairly similar way to the index and explore pages, including full support for pagination:

21.1. PRIVATE MESSAGES

Listing 21.7: *app/main/routes.py*: View messages route.

```python
@bp.route('/messages')
@login_required
def messages():
    current_user.last_message_read_time = datetime.utcnow()
    db.session.commit()
    page = request.args.get('page', 1, type=int)
    messages = current_user.messages_received.order_by(
        Message.timestamp.desc()).paginate(
            page, current_app.config['POSTS_PER_PAGE'], False)
    next_url = url_for('main.messages', page=messages.next_num) \
        if messages.has_next else None
    prev_url = url_for('main.messages', page=messages.prev_num) \
        if messages.has_prev else None
    return render_template('messages.html', messages=messages.items,
                           next_url=next_url, prev_url=prev_url)
```

The first thing I do in this view function is update the `User.last_message_read_time` field with the current time. This is basically marking all the messages that were sent to this user as read. Then I'm querying the `Message` model for the list of messages, sorted by timestamp from newer to older. I decided to reuse the `POSTS_PER_PAGE` configuration item here since the pages with posts and messages are going to look very much alike, but of course if the pages were to diverge, it may make sense to add a separate configuration variable for messages. The pagination logic is identical to what I used for posts, so this should all be familiar to you.

The view function above ends by rendering a new */app/templates/messages.html* template file, which you can see below:

Listing 21.8: *app/templates/messages.html*: View messages HTML template.

```html
{% extends "base.html" %}

{% block app_content %}
    <h1>{{ _('Messages') }}</h1>
    {% for post in messages %}
        {% include '_post.html' %}
    {% endfor %}
    <nav aria-label="...">
        <ul class="pager">
            <li class="previous{% if not prev_url %} disabled{% endif %}">
                <a href="{{ prev_url or '#' }}">
                    <span aria-hidden="true">&larr;</span> {{ _('Newer messages') }}
                </a>
            </li>
            <li class="next{% if not next_url %} disabled{% endif %}">
                <a href="{{ next_url or '#' }}">
                    {{ _('Older messages') }} <span aria-hidden="true">&rarr;</span>
                </a>
            </li>
        </ul>
```

```
        </nav>
{% endblock %}
```

Here I resorted to another little trick. I noticed that `Post` and `Message` instances have pretty much the same structure, with the exception that `Message` gets an extra `recipient` relationship (that I don't need to show in the messages page, since it is always the current user). So I decided to reuse the *app/templates/_post.html* sub-template to also render private messages. For this reason, this template uses the strange for-loop `for post in messages`, so that all the references to `post` in the sub-template work with messages too.

To give users access to the new view function, the navigation page gets a new "Messages" link:

Listing 21.9: *app/templates/base.html*: Messages link in navigation bar.

```
{% if current_user.is_anonymous %}
...
{% else %}
<li>
    <a href="{{ url_for('main.messages') }}">
        {{ _('Messages') }}
    </a>
</li>
...
{% endif %}
```

The feature is now complete, but as part of all these changes there were some new texts that were added in a few places, and those need to be incorporated into the language translations. The first step is to update all the language catalogs:

```
(venv) $ flask translate update
```

Then each of the languages in *app/translations* need to have its *messages.po* file updated with the new translations. You can find the Spanish translations in the GitHub repository for this project or in the download zip file[4].

21.2 Static Message Notification Badge

Now the private messages feature is implemented, but of course there is nothing that tells a user that there are private messages waiting to be read. The simplest implementation of a navigation bar indicator can be rendered as part of the base template, using a Bootstrap badge widget:

---
[4]`https://github.com/miguelgrinberg/microblog/archive/version-0.21.zip`

21.3 DYNAMIC MESSAGE NOTIFICATION BADGE

Listing 21.10: *app/templates/base.html*: Static message count badge in navigation bar.

```
...
<li>
    <a href="{{ url_for('main.messages') }}">
        {{ _('Messages') }}
        {% set new_messages = current_user.new_messages() %}
        {% if new_messages %}
        <span class="badge">{{ new_messages }}</span>
        {% endif %}
    </a>
</li>
...
```

Here I'm invoking the `new_messages()` method I added to the `User` model above directly from the template, and storing that number in a `new_messages` template variable. Then if that variable is non-zero, I just add the badge with the number next to the Messages link. Here is how this looks on the page:

21.3 Dynamic Message Notification Badge

The solution presented in the previous section is a decent and simple way to show a notification, but it has the disadvantage that the badge only appears when a new page is loaded. If the user spends a long time reading the content on one page without clicking on any links, new messages that come during that time will not be shown until the user finally does click on a link and loads a new page.

To make this application more useful to my users, I want the badge to update the count of unread messages on its own, without the user having to click on links and load new pages. One problem with the solution from the previous section is that the badge is only rendered to the page when the message count at the time the page loaded was non-zero. What's really more convenient is to always include the badge in the navigation bar, and mark it as hidden when the message count is zero. This would make it easy to make the badge visible using JavaScript:

Listing 21.11: *app/templates/base.html*: A JavaScript friendly unread messages badge.

```
<li>
    <a href="{{ url_for('main.messages') }}">
```

```
                    {{ _('Messages') }}
                    {% set new_messages = current_user.new_messages() %}
                    <span id="message_count" class="badge"
                        style="visibility: {% if new_messages %}visible
                                          {% else %}hidden {% endif %};">
                        {{ new_messages }}
                    </span>
                </a>
            </li>
```

With this version of the badge, I always include it, but the `visibility` CSS property is set to `visible` when `new_messages` is non-zero, or `hidden` if it is zero. I also added an `id` attribute to the `<span>` element that represents the badge, to make it easy to address this element using a `$('#message_count')` jQuery selector.

Next, I can code a short JavaScript function that updates this badge to a new number:

Listing 21.12: *app/templates/base.html*: Static message count badge in navigation bar.

```
...
{% block scripts %}
    <script>
        // ...
        function set_message_count(n) {
            $('#message_count').text(n);
            $('#message_count').css('visibility', n ? 'visible' : 'hidden');
        }
    </script>
{% endblock %}
```

This new `set_message_count()` function will set the number of messages in the badge element, and also adjust the visibility so that the badge is hidden when the count is 0 and visible otherwise.

21.4 Delivering Notifications to Clients

What remains now is to add a mechanism by which the client receives periodic updates regarding the number of unread messages the user has. When one of these updates occur, the client will call the `set_message_count()` function to make the update known to the user.

There are actually two methods for the server to deliver these updates to the client, and as you can probably guess, both have pros and cons, so which one to choose is largely dependent on the project. In the first approach, the client periodically asks the server for updates by sending an asynchronous request. The response from this request is a list of updates, which the client

21.4. DELIVERING NOTIFICATIONS TO CLIENTS

can use to update different elements of the page such as the unread message count badge. The second approach requires a special type of connection between the client and the server that allows the server to freely push data to the client. Note that regardless of the approach, I want to treat notifications as generic entities, so that I can extend this framework to support other types of events besides the unread messages badge.

The biggest thing the first solution has is that it is easy to implement. All I need to do is add yet another route to the application, say */notifications*, which returns a JSON list of notifications. The client application then goes through the list of notifications and applies the necessary changes to the page for each one. The disadvantage of this solution is that there is going to be a delay between the actual event and the notification for it, because the client is going to request the list of notifications at regular intervals. For example, if the client is asking for notifications every 10 seconds, a notification can be received up to 10 seconds late.

The second solution requires changes at the protocol level, because HTTP does not have any provisions for a server to send data to the client without the client asking. By far the most common way to implement server initiated messages is by extending the server to support WebSocket[5] connections in addition to HTTP. WebSocket is a protocol that unlike HTTP, establishes a permanent connection between the server and the client. The server and the client can both send data to the other party at any time, without the other side asking for it. The advantage of this mechanism is that whenever an event that is of interest to the client occurs, the server can send a notification, without any delays. The disadvantage is that WebSocket requires a more complicated setup than HTTP, because the server needs to maintain a permanent connection with each and every client. Imagine that a server that, for example, has four worker processes can typically serve a few hundred HTTP clients, because connections in HTTP are short lived and are constantly being recycled. The same server would be able to handle just four WebSocket clients, which in the vast majority of cases is going to be insufficient. It is for this limitation that WebSocket applications are typically designed around *asynchronous servers*, because these servers are more efficient at managing a large number of workers and active connections.

The good news is that regardless of the method that you use, in the client you will have a callback function that will be invoked with the list of updates. So I could start with the first solution, which is much easier to implement, and later, if I find it insufficient, migrate to a WebSocket server, which can be configured to invoke the same client callback. In my opinion, for this type of application the first solution is actually acceptable. A WebSocket based implementation would be useful for an application that requires updates to be delivered with near zero-latency.

In case you are curious, Twitter also uses the first approach for their navigation bar notifications.

---

[5]https://en.wikipedia.org/wiki/WebSocket

Facebook uses a variation of it called long polling[6], which addresses some of the limitations of straight polling while still using HTTP requests. Stack Overflow and Trello are two sites that implement WebSocket for their notifications. You can find what type of background activity occurs on any site by looking in the Network tab of the browser's debugger.

So let's go ahead and implement the polling solution. First, I'm going to add a new model to keep track of notifications for all users, along with a relationship in the user model.

Listing 21.13: *app/models.py*: Notification model.

```python
import json
from time import time

# ...

class User(UserMixin, db.Model):
    # ...
    notifications = db.relationship('Notification', backref='user',
                                    lazy='dynamic')

    # ...

class Notification(db.Model):
    id = db.Column(db.Integer, primary_key=True)
    name = db.Column(db.String(128), index=True)
    user_id = db.Column(db.Integer, db.ForeignKey('user.id'))
    timestamp = db.Column(db.Float, index=True, default=time)
    payload_json = db.Column(db.Text)

    def get_data(self):
        return json.loads(str(self.payload_json))
```

A notification is going to have a name, an associated user, a Unix timestamp and a payload. The timestamp gets its default value from the `time.time()` function. The payload is going to be different for each type of notification, so I'm writing it as a JSON string, as that will allow me to write lists, dictionaries or single values such as numbers or strings. I added the `get_data()` method as a convenience, so that the caller doesn't have to worry about the JSON deserialization.

These changes need to be included in a new database migration:

```
(venv) $ flask db migrate -m "notifications"
(venv) $ flask db upgrade
```

As a matter of convenience, I'm going to add the new `Message` and `Notification` models

---

[6]https://en.wikipedia.org/wiki/Push_technology#Long_polling

21.4. DELIVERING NOTIFICATIONS TO CLIENTS

to the shell context, so that when I start a shell with the `flask shell` command, the model class is automatically imported for me:

Listing 21.14: *microblog.py*: Add Message model to shell context.

```python
# ...
from app.models import User, Post, Notification, Message

# ...

@app.shell_context_processor
def make_shell_context():
    return {'db': db, 'User': User, 'Post': Post, 'Message': Message,
            'Notification': Notification}
```

I'm also going to add a `add_notification()` helper method in the user model to make it easier to work with these objects:

Listing 21.15: *app/models.py*: Notification model.

```python
class User(UserMixin, db.Model):
    # ...

    def add_notification(self, name, data):
        self.notifications.filter_by(name=name).delete()
        n = Notification(name=name, payload_json=json.dumps(data), user=self)
        db.session.add(n)
        return n
```

This method not only adds a notification for the user to the database, but also ensures that if a notification with the same name already exists, it is removed first. The notification I'm going to work with is going to be called `unread_message_count`. If the database already has a notification with this name with, for example, a value of 3, whenever the user receives a new message and the message count goes to 4 I want to replace the old notification.

In any place where the unread message count changes, I need to call `add_notification()` so that I have my notifications for the user updated. There are two places where this changes. First, when the user receives a new private message, in the `send_message()` view function:

Listing 21.16: *app/main/routes.py*: Update user notification.

```python
@bp.route('/send_message/<recipient>', methods=['GET', 'POST'])
@login_required
def send_message(recipient):
    # ...
    if form.validate_on_submit():
```

```
        # ...
        user.add_notification('unread_message_count', user.new_messages())
        db.session.commit()
        # ...
    # ...
```

The second place where I need to notify the user is when the user goes to the messages page, at which point the unread count goes back to zero:

Listing 21.17: *app/main/routes.py*: View messages route.

```
@bp.route('/messages')
@login_required
def messages():
    current_user.last_message_read_time = datetime.utcnow()
    current_user.add_notification('unread_message_count', 0)
    db.session.commit()
    # ...
```

Now that all the notifications for users are maintained in the database, I can add a new route that the client can use to retrieve notifications for the logged in user:

Listing 21.18: *app/main/routes.py*: Notifications view function.

```
from app.models import Notification

# ...

@bp.route('/notifications')
@login_required
def notifications():
    since = request.args.get('since', 0.0, type=float)
    notifications = current_user.notifications.filter(
        Notification.timestamp > since).order_by(Notification.timestamp.asc())
    return jsonify([{
        'name': n.name,
        'data': n.get_data(),
        'timestamp': n.timestamp
    } for n in notifications])
```

This is a fairly simple function that returns a JSON payload with a list of notifications for the user. Each notification is given as a dictionary with three elements, the notification name, the additional data that pertains to the notification (such as the message count), and the timestamp. The notifications are delivered in the order they were created, from oldest to newest.

I do not want clients to get repeated notifications, so I'm giving them the option to only request notifications since a given time. The `since` option can be included in the query string of the

21.4. DELIVERING NOTIFICATIONS TO CLIENTS

request URL, with the unix timestamp of the starting time, as a floating point number. Only notifications that occurred after this time will be returned if this argument is included.

The final piece to complete this feature is to implement the actual polling in the client. The best place to do this is in the base template, so that all pages automatically inherit the behavior:

Listing 21.19: *app/templates/base.html*: Polling for notifications.

```
...
{% block scripts %}
    <script>
        // ...
        {% if current_user.is_authenticated %}
        $(function() {
            var since = 0;
            setInterval(function() {
                $.ajax('{{ url_for('main.notifications') }}?since=' + since).done(
                    function(notifications) {
                        for (var i = 0; i < notifications.length; i++) {
                            if (notifications[i].name == 'unread_message_count')
                                set_message_count(notifications[i].data);
                            since = notifications[i].timestamp;
                        }
                    }
                );
            }, 10000);
        });
        {% endif %}
    </script>
```

This function is enclosed in a template conditional, because I want to poll for new messages only when the user is logged in. For users that are not logged in, this function will not be included.

You've already seen jQuery's `$(function() { ...})` pattern in Chapter 20. This is how you register a function to execute after the page loads. For this feature, what I need to do on page load is to set up a regular timer that gets the notifications for the user. You've also seen the `setTimeout()` JavaScript function, which runs the function given as an argument after the specific time passes. The `setInterval()` function uses the same arguments as `setTimeout()`, but instead of firing the timer just once, it keeps calling the callback function at regular intervals. In this case my interval is set to 10 seconds (given in milliseconds), so I'm going to see the badge update with a resolution of roughly six times per minute.

The function associated with the interval timer issues an Ajax request for the new notifications route, and in its completion callback just iterates over the list of notifications. When a notification with name `unread_message_count` is received, the message count badge is adjusted by calling the function defined above with the count given in the notification.

The way I'm handling the `since` argument might be confusing. I start by initializing this argument to 0. The argument is always included in the request URL, but I can't generate the query string using Flask's `url_for()` like I've done before, because `url_for()` runs in the server once, and I need the `since` argument to dynamically update. The first time, the request is going to be sent to */notifications?since=0*, but as soon as I receive a notification, I update `since` to its timestamp. This ensures that I don't receive duplicates, since I'm always asking to receive notifications that occurred since the last notification I've seen. It's also important to note that I declared the `since` variable outside of the interval function, because I did not want this to be a local variable, I want the same variable to be used in all invocations.

The easiest way to try this out is to use two different browser. Log in to Microblog on both browsers using different users. Then from one of the browsers send one or more messages to the other user. The other browser's navigation bar should update to show the count of messages that you sent in less than 10 seconds. And when you click on the Messages link the unread message count resets back to zero.

Chapter 22

Background Jobs

This chapter is dedicated to the implementation of long or complex processes that need to run as part of the application. These processes cannot be executed synchronously in the context of a request because that would block the response to the client for the duration of the task. I briefly touched on this topic in Chapter 10, when I moved the sending of emails to background threads to prevent the client from having to wait during those 3-4 seconds that it takes to send an email. While using threads for emails is acceptable, this solution does not scale well when the processes in question are much longer. The accepted practice is to offload long tasks to a worker process, or more likely to a pool of them.

To justify the need for having long running tasks, I'm going to introduce an export feature to Microblog through which users will be able to request a data file with all their blog posts. When a user makes use of this option, the application is going to start an export task that will generate a JSON file with all the user's posts, and then send it to the user by email. All this activity is going to happen in a worker process, and while it happens the user will see a notification showing the percentage of completion.

The GitHub links for this chapter are: Browse[1], Zip[2], Diff[3].

22.1 Introduction to Task Queues

Task queues provide a convenient solution for the application to request the execution of a task by a *worker process*. Worker processes run independently of the application and can even be

---

[1] https://github.com/miguelgrinberg/microblog/tree/v0.22
[2] https://github.com/miguelgrinberg/microblog/archive/v0.22.zip
[3] https://github.com/miguelgrinberg/microblog/compare/v0.21...v0.22

located on a different system. The communication between the application and the workers is done through a *message queue*. The application submits a job, and then monitors its progress by interacting with the queue. The following diagram shows a typical implementation:

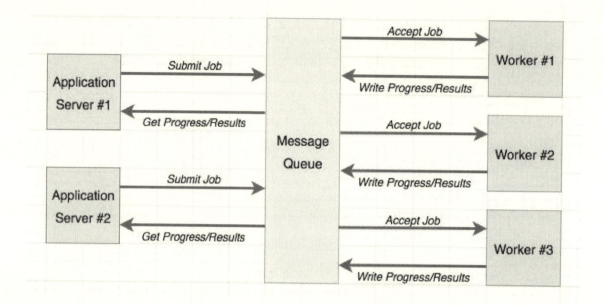

The most popular task queue for Python is Celery[4]. This is a fairly sophisticated package that has many options and supports several message queues. Another popular Python task queue is Redis Queue[5] or just RQ, which sacrifices some flexibility, such as only supporting a Redis[6] message queue, but in exchange it is much simpler to set up than Celery.

Both Celery and RQ are perfectly adequate to support background tasks in a Flask application, so my choice for this application is going to favor the simplicity of RQ. However, implementing the same functionality with Celery should be relatively easy. If you are interested in Celery more than RQ, you can read the Using Celery with Flask[7] article that I have on my blog.

22.2 Using RQ

RQ is a standard Python package, that is installed with `pip`:

---

[4] http://www.celeryproject.org/
[5] http://python-rq.org/
[6] https://redis.io/
[7] https://blog.miguelgrinberg.com/post/using-celery-with-flask

22.2. USING RQ

```
(venv) $ pip install rq
(venv) $ pip freeze > requirements.txt
```

As I mentioned earlier, the communication between the application and the RQ workers is going to be carried out in a Redis message queue, so you need to have a Redis server running. There are many options to get a Redis server installed and running, from one-click installers to downloading the source code and compiling it directly on your system. If you are using Windows, Microsoft maintains installers here[8]. On Linux, you can likely get it as a package through your operating system's package manager. Mac OS X users can run `brew install redis` and then start the service manually with the `redis-server` command.

You will not need to interact with Redis at all outside of just ensuring that the service is running and accessible to RQ.

22.2.1 Creating a Task

I'm going to show you how to run a simple task through RQ so that you familiarize with it. A task, is nothing more than a Python function. Here is an example task, that I'm going to put in a new *app/tasks.py* module:

Listing 22.1: *app/tasks.py*: Example background task.

```python
import time

def example(seconds):
    print('Starting task')
    for i in range(seconds):
        print(i)
        time.sleep(1)
    print('Task completed')
```

This task takes a number of seconds as an argument, and then waits that amount of time, printing a counter once a second.

22.2.2 Running the RQ Worker

Now that the task is ready, a worker can be starter. This is done with the `rq worker` command:

---
[8]https://github.com/MicrosoftArchive/redis/releases

```
(venv) $ rq worker microblog-tasks
18:55:06 RQ worker 'rq:worker:miguelsmac.90369' started, version 0.9.1
18:55:06 Cleaning registries for queue: microblog-tasks
18:55:06
18:55:06 *** Listening on microblog-tasks...
```

The worker process is now connected to Redis, and watching for any jobs that may be assigned to it on a queue named `microblog-tasks`. In cases where you want to have multiple workers to have more throughput, all you need to do is run more instances of `rq worker`, all connected to the same queue. Then when a job shows up in the queue, any of the available worker processes will pick it up. In a production environment you will probably want to have at least as many workers as available CPUs.

22.2.3 Executing Tasks

Now open a second terminal window and activate the virtual environment on it. I'm going to use a shell session to kick off the `example()` task in the worker:

```
>>> from redis import Redis
>>> import rq
>>> queue = rq.Queue('microblog-tasks', connection=Redis.from_url('redis://'))
>>> job = queue.enqueue('app.tasks.example', 23)
>>> job.get_id()
'c651de7f-21a8-4068-afd5-8b982a6f6d32'
```

The `Queue` class from RQ represents the task queue as seen from the application side. The arguments it takes are the queue name, and a `Redis` connection object, which in this case I initialize with a default URL. If you have your Redis server running on a different host or port number, you will need to use a different URL.

The `enqueue()` method on the queue is used to add a job to the queue. The first argument is the name of the task you want to execute, given directly as a function object, or as an import string. I find the string option much more convenient, as that makes it unnecessary to import the function on the application's side. Any remaining arguments given to `enqueue()` are going to be passed to the function running in the worker.

As soon as you make the `enqueue()` call you are going to notice some activity on your first terminal window, the one running the RQ worker. You will see that the `example()` function is now running, and printing the counter once per second. At the same time, your other terminal is not blocked and you can continue evaluating expressions in the shell. In the example above, I called the `job.get_id()` method to obtain the unique identifier assigned to the task. Another

22.2. USING RQ

interesting expression you can try with the `job` object is to check if the function on the worker has finished:

```
>>> job.is_finished
False
```

If you passed a `23` like I did in my example above, then the function is going to run for about 23 seconds. After that time, the `job.is_finished` expression will become `True`. Isn't this pretty cool? I really like the simplicity of RQ.

Once the function completes, the worker goes back to waiting for new jobs, so you can repeat the `enqueue()` call with different arguments if you want to experiment more. The data that is stored in the queue regarding a task will stay there for some time (500 seconds by default), but eventually will be removed. This is important, the task queue does not preserve a history of executed jobs.

22.2.4 Reporting Task Progress

The example task I have used above is unrealistically simple. Normally, for a long running task you will want some sort of progress information to be made available to the application, which in turn can show it to the user. RQ supports this by using the `meta` attribute of the job object. Let me rewrite the `example()` task to write progress reports:

Listing 22.2: *app/tasks.py*: Example background task with progress.

```python
import time
from rq import get_current_job

def example(seconds):
    job = get_current_job()
    print('Starting task')
    for i in range(seconds):
        job.meta['progress'] = 100.0 * i / seconds
        job.save_meta()
        print(i)
        time.sleep(1)
    job.meta['progress'] = 100
    job.save_meta()
    print('Task completed')
```

This new version of `example()` uses RQ's `get_current_job()` function to get a job instance, which is similar to the one returned to the application when it submits the task. The `meta` attribute of the job object is a dictionary where the task can write any custom data that it wants to communicate to the application. In this example, I'm writing a `progress` item that represents the percentage of completion of the task. Each time the progress is updated I call `job.save_meta()` to instruct RQ to write the data to Redis, where the application can find it.

On the application side (currently just a Python shell), I can run this task and then monitor progress as follows:

```
>>> job = queue.enqueue('app.tasks.example', 23)
>>> job.meta
{}
>>> job.refresh()
>>> job.meta
{'progress': 13.043478260869565}
>>> job.refresh()
>>> job.meta
{'progress': 69.56521739130434}
>>> job.refresh()
>>> job.meta
{'progress': 100}
>>> job.is_finished
True
```

As you can see above, on this side the `meta` attribute is available to read. The `refresh()` method needs to be invoked for the contents to be updated from Redis.

22.3 Database Representation of Tasks

For the example above it was enough to start a task and watch it run. For a web application things get a bit more complicated, because once one of these task is started as part of a request, that request is going to end, and all the context for that task is going to be lost. Because I want the application to keep track of what tasks each user is running, I need to use a database table to maintain some state. Below you can see the new `Task` model implementation:

Listing 22.3: *app/models.py*: Task model.

```
# ...
import redis
import rq

class User(UserMixin, db.Model):
    # ...
    tasks = db.relationship('Task', backref='user', lazy='dynamic')

# ...
```

22.3. DATABASE REPRESENTATION OF TASKS

```
class Task(db.Model):
    id = db.Column(db.String(36), primary_key=True)
    name = db.Column(db.String(128), index=True)
    description = db.Column(db.String(128))
    user_id = db.Column(db.Integer, db.ForeignKey('user.id'))
    complete = db.Column(db.Boolean, default=False)

    def get_rq_job(self):
        try:
            rq_job = rq.job.Job.fetch(self.id, connection=current_app.redis)
        except (redis.exceptions.RedisError, rq.exceptions.NoSuchJobError):
            return None
        return rq_job

    def get_progress(self):
        job = self.get_rq_job()
        return job.meta.get('progress', 0) if job is not None else 100
```

An interesting difference between this model and the previous ones is that the `id` primary key field is a string, not an integer. This is because for this model, I'm not going to rely on the database's own primary key generation and instead I'm going to use the job identifiers generated by RQ.

The model is going to store the task's fully qualified name (as passed to RQ), a description for the task that is appropriate for showing to users, a relationship to the user that requested the task, and a boolean that indicates if the task completed or not. The purpose of the `complete` field is to separate tasks that ended from those that are actively running, as running tasks require special handling to show progress updates.

The `get_rq_job()` method is a helper method that loads the RQ `Job` instance, from a given task id, which I can get from the model. This is done with `Job.fetch()`, which loads the `Job` instance from the data that exists in Redis about it. The `get_progress()` method builds on top of `get_rq_job()` and returns the progress percentage for the task. This method has a couple of interesting assumptions. If the job id from the model does not exist in the RQ queue, that means that the job already finished and the data expired and was removed from the queue, so in that case the percentage returned is 100. On the other extreme, if the job exists, but there is no information associated with the `meta` attribute, then it is safe to assume that the job is scheduled to run, but did not get a chance to start yet, so in that situation a 0 is returned as progress.

To apply the changes to the database schema, a new migration needs to be generated, and then the database upgraded:

```
(venv) $ flask db migrate -m "tasks"
(venv) $ flask db upgrade
```

The new model can also be added to the shell context, to make it accessible in shell sessions without having to import it:

> **Listing 22.4:** *microblog.py*: Add Task model to shell context.
>
> ```
> from app import create_app, db, cli
> from app.models import User, Post, Message, Notification, Task
>
> app = create_app()
> cli.register(app)
>
> @app.shell_context_processor
> def make_shell_context():
>     return {'db': db, 'User': User, 'Post': Post, 'Message': Message,
>             'Notification': Notification, 'Task': Task}
> ```

22.4 Integrating RQ with the Flask Application

The connection URL for the Redis service needs to be added to the configuration:

```
class Config(object):
    # ...
    REDIS_URL = os.environ.get('REDIS_URL') or 'redis://'
```

As always, the Redis connection URL will be sourced from an environment variable, and if the variable isn't defined, a default URL that assumes the service is running on the same host and in the default port will be used.

The application factory function will be in charge of initializing Redis and RQ:

> **Listing 22.5:** *app/__init__.py*: RQ integration.
>
> ```
> # ...
> from redis import Redis
> import rq
>
> # ...
>
> def create_app(config_class=Config):
>     # ...
>     app.redis = Redis.from_url(app.config['REDIS_URL'])
>     app.task_queue = rq.Queue('microblog-tasks', connection=app.redis)
>
>     # ...
> ```

22.4. INTEGRATING RQ WITH THE FLASK APPLICATION

The `app.task_queue` is going to be the queue where tasks are submitted. Having the queue attached to the application is convenient because anywhere in the application I can use `current_app.task_queue` to access it. To make it easy for any part of the application to submit or check on a task, I can create a few helper methods in the `User` model:

Listing 22.6: *app/models.py*: Task helper methods in the user model.

```python
# ...
class User(UserMixin, db.Model):
    # ...

    def launch_task(self, name, description, *args, **kwargs):
        rq_job = current_app.task_queue.enqueue('app.tasks.' + name, self.id,
                                                *args, **kwargs)
        task = Task(id=rq_job.get_id(), name=name, description=description,
                    user=self)
        db.session.add(task)
        return task

    def get_tasks_in_progress(self):
        return Task.query.filter_by(user=self, complete=False).all()

    def get_task_in_progress(self, name):
        return Task.query.filter_by(name=name, user=self,
                                    complete=False).first()
```

The `launch_task()` method takes care of submitting a task to the RQ queue, along with adding it to the database. The `name` argument is the function name, as defined in *app/tasks.py*. When submitting to RQ, the function prepends `app.tasks.` to this name to build the fully qualified function name. The `description` argument is a friendly description of the task that can be presented to users. For the function that export the blog posts, I will set the name to `export_posts` and the description to `Exporting posts...`. The remaining arguments are positional and keyword arguments that will be passed to the task. The function begins by calling the queue's `enqueue()` method to submit the job. The job object that is returned contains the task id assigned by RQ, so I can use that to create a corresponding `Task` object in my database.

Note that `launch_task()` adds the new task object to the session, but it does not issue a commit. In general, it is best to operate on the database session in the higher level functions, as that allows you to combine several updates made by lower level functions in a single transaction. This is not a strict rule, and in fact, you are going to see an exception where a commit is issued in a child function later in this chapter.

The `get_tasks_in_progress()` method returns the complete list of functions that are outstanding for the user. You will see later that I use this method to include information about running tasks in the pages that are rendered to the user.

Finally, the `get_task_in_progress()` is a simpler version of the previous one that returns a specific task. I prevent users from starting two or more tasks of the same type concurrently, so before I launch a task, I can use this method to find out if a previous task is currently running.

22.5 Sending Emails from the RQ Task

This may seem like a distraction from the main topic, but I said above that when the background export task completes, an email is going to be sent to the user with a JSON file that contains all the posts. The email functionality that I built in Chapter 11 needs to be extended in two ways. First, I need to add support for file attachments, so that I can attach a JSON file. Second, the `send_email()` function always sends emails asynchronously, using a background thread. When I'm going to send an email from a background task, which is already asynchronous, having a second level background task based on a thread makes little sense, so I need to support both synchronous and asynchronous email sending.

Luckily, Flask-Mail supports attachments, so all I need to do is extend the `send_email()` function to take them in an additional argument, and then configure them in the `Message` object. And to optionally send the email in the foreground, I just need to add a boolean `sync` argument:

Listing 22.7: *app/email.py*: Send emails with attachments.

```python
# ...
def send_email(subject, sender, recipients, text_body, html_body,
               attachments=None, sync=False):
    msg = Message(subject, sender=sender, recipients=recipients)
    msg.body = text_body
    msg.html = html_body
    if attachments:
        for attachment in attachments:
            msg.attach(*attachment)
    if sync:
        mail.send(msg)
    else:
        Thread(target=send_async_email,
            args=(current_app._get_current_object(), msg)).start()
```

The `attach()` method of the `Message` class accepts three arguments that define an attachment: the filename, the media type, and the actual file data. The filename is just the name that the recipient will see associated with the attachment, it does not need to be a real file. The media type defines what type of attachment is this, which helps email readers render it appropriately. For example, if you send `image/png` as the media type, an email reader will know

22.6. TASK HELPERS

that the attachment is an image, in which case it can show it as such. For the blog post data file I'm going to use the JSON format, which uses a `application/json` media type. The third and last argument is a string or byte sequence with the contents of the attachment.

To make it simple, the `attachments` argument to `send_email()` is going to be a list of tuples, and each tuple is going to have three elements which correspond to the three arguments of `attach()`. So for each element in this list, I need to send the tuple as arguments to `attach()`. In Python, if you have a list or tuple with arguments that you want to send to a function, you can use `func(*args)` to have that list expanded into the actual argument list, instead of having to use a more tedious syntax such as `func(args[0], args[1], args[2])`. So for example, if you have `args = [1, 'foo']`, the call will send two arguments, same as if you called `func(1, 'foo')`. Without the `*`, the call would have a single argument which would be the list.

As far as the synchronous sending of the email, what I needed to do is just revert back to calling `mail.send(msg)` directly when `sync` is `True`.

22.6 Task Helpers

While the `example()` task I used above was a simple standalone function, the function that exports blog posts is going to need some of the functionality I have in the application, like access to the database and the email sending function. Because this is going to run in a separate process, I need to initialize Flask-SQLAlchemy and Flask-Mail, which in turn need a Flask application instance from which to get their configuration. So I'm going to add a Flask application instance and application context at the top of the *app/tasks.py* module:

Listing 22.8: *app/tasks.py*: Create application and context.

```
from app import create_app

app = create_app()
app.app_context().push()
```

The application is created in this module because this is the only module that the RQ worker is going to import. When you use the `flask` command, the *microblog.py* module in the root directory creates the application, but the RQ worker knows nothing about that, so it needs to create its own application instance if the task functions need it. You have seen the `app.app_context()` method in a couple of places already, pushing a context makes the application be the "current" application instance, and this enables extensions such as Flask-

SQLAlchemy to use `current_app.config` to obtain their configuration. Without the context, the `current_app` expression would return an error.

I then started thinking about how I was going to report progress while this function is running. In addition to passing progress information through the `job.meta` dictionary, I'd like to push notifications to the client, so that the completion percentage can be updated dynamically without the user having to refresh the page. For this I'm going to use the notification mechanisms I built in Chapter 21. The updates are going to work in a very similar way to the unread messages badge. When the server renders a template, it will include "static" progress information obtained from `job.meta`, but then once the page is on the client's browser, the notifications are going to dynamically update the percentage using notifications. Because of the notifications, updating the progress of a running task is going to be slightly more involved than how I did it in the previous example, so I'm going to create a wrapper function dedicated to updating progress:

Listing 22.9: *app/tasks.py*: Set task progress.

```
from rq import get_current_job
from app import db
from app.models import Task

# ...

def _set_task_progress(progress):
    job = get_current_job()
    if job:
        job.meta['progress'] = progress
        job.save_meta()
        task = Task.query.get(job.get_id())
        task.user.add_notification('task_progress', {'task_id': job.get_id(),
                                                    'progress': progress})
        if progress >= 100:
            task.complete = True
        db.session.commit()
```

The export task can call `_set_task_progress()` to record the progress percentage. The function first writes the percentage to the `job.meta` dictionary and saves it to Redis, then it loads the corresponding task object from the database and uses `task.user` to push a notification to the user that requested the task, using the existing `add_notification()` method. The notification is going to be named `task_progress`, and the data associated with it is going to be a dictionary with two items, the task identifier and the progress number. Later I will add JavaScript code to act on this new notification type.

The function checks if the progress indicates that the function has completed, and in that case also updates the `complete` attribute of the task object in the database. The database commit call ensures that the task and the notification object added by `add_notification()` are both

22.7 Implementing the Export Task

saved immediately to the database. I needed to be very careful in how I designed the parent task to not make any database changes, since this commit call would write those as well.

Now all the pieces are in place for me to write the export function. The high level structure of this function is going to be as follows:

Listing 22.10: *app/tasks.py*: Export posts general structure.

```
def export_posts(user_id):
    try:
        # read user posts from database
        # send email with data to user
    except:
        # handle unexpected errors
```

Why wrap the whole task in a try/except block? The application code that exists in request handlers is protected against unexpected errors because Flask itself catches exceptions and then handles them observing any error handlers and logging configuration I have set up for the application. This function, however, is going to run in a separate process that is controlled by RQ, not Flask, so if any unexpected errors occur the task will abort, RQ will display the error to the console and then will go back to wait for new jobs. So basically, unless you are watching the output of the RQ worker or logging it to a file, you will never find out there was an error.

Let's start looking at the three sections indicated with comments above with the simplest one, which is the error handling at the end:

Listing 22.11: *app/tasks.py*: Export posts error handling.

```
import sys
# ...

def export_posts(user_id):
    try:
        # ...
    except:
        _set_task_progress(100)
        app.logger.error('Unhandled exception', exc_info=sys.exc_info())
```

Whenever an unexpected error occurs, I'm going to mark the task as finished by setting the progress to 100%, and then use the logger object from the Flask application to log the error, along with the stack trace, information which is provided by the `sys.exc_info()` call. The nice thing about using the Flask application logger to log errors here as well is that any logging mechanisms you have implemented for the Flask application will be observed. For example, in Chapter 7 I configured errors to be sent out to the administrator email address. Just by using `app.logger` I also get that behavior for these errors.

Next, I'm going to code the actual export, which simply issues a database query and walks through the results in a loop, accumulating them in a dictionary:

Listing 22.12: *app/tasks.py*: Read user posts from the database.

```python
import time
from app.models import User, Post

# ...

def export_posts(user_id):
    try:
        user = User.query.get(user_id)
        _set_task_progress(0)
        data = []
        i = 0
        total_posts = user.posts.count()
        for post in user.posts.order_by(Post.timestamp.asc()):
            data.append({'body': post.body,
                         'timestamp': post.timestamp.isoformat() + 'Z'})
            time.sleep(5)
            i += 1
            _set_task_progress(100 * i // total_posts)

        # send email with data to user
    except:
        # ...
```

For each post, the function is going to include a dictionary with two elements, the post body and the time the post was written. The time is going to be written in the ISO 8601[9] standard. The Python's `datetime` objects that I'm using do not store a timezone, so after I export the time in the ISO format I add the 'Z', which indicates UTC.

The code gets slightly complicated due to the need to keep track of progress. I maintain the counter `i`, and I need to issue an extra database query before I enter the loop for `total_posts` to have the number of posts. Using `i` and `total_posts`, each loop iteration can update the task progress with a number from 0 to 100.

You may have noticed that I also added a `time.sleep(5)` call in each loop iteration. The main reason I added the sleep is to make the export task last longer, and be able to see the progress go up even when the export covers just a handful of blog posts.

---
[9]https://en.wikipedia.org/wiki/ISO_8601

22.7. IMPLEMENTING THE EXPORT TASK

Below you can see the last part of the function, which sends an email to the user with all the information collected in `data` as an attachment:

Listing 22.13: *app/tasks.py*: Email posts to user.

```
import json
from flask import render_template
from app.email import send_email

# ...

def export_posts(user_id):
    try:
        # ...
        send_email('[Microblog] Your blog posts',
                sender=app.config['ADMINS'][0], recipients=[user.email],
                text_body=render_template('email/export_posts.txt', user=user),
                html_body=render_template('email/export_posts.html', user=user),
                attachments=[('posts.json', 'application/json',
                              json.dumps({'posts': data}, indent=4))],
                sync=True)
    except:
        # ...
```

This is simply a call to the `send_email()` function. The attachment is defined as a tuple with the three elements that are then passed to the `attach()` method of Flask-Mail's `Message` object. The third element in the tuple is the attachment contents, which are generated with Python's `json.dumps()` function.

There are a pair of new templates referenced here, which provide the contents of the email body in plain text and HTML form. Here is the text template:

Listing 22.14: *app/templates/email/export_posts.txt*: Export posts text email template.

```
Dear {{ user.username }},

Please find attached the archive of your posts that you requested.

Sincerely,

The Microblog Team
```

Here is the HTML version of the email:

Listing 22.15: *app/templates/email/export_posts.html*: Export posts HTML email template.

```
<p>Dear {{ user.username }},</p>
<p>Please find attached the archive of your posts that you requested.</p>
<p>Sincerely,</p>
<p>The Microblog Team</p>
```

22.8 Export Functionality in the Application

All the core pieces to support the background export tasks are now in place. What remains is to hook up this functionality to the application, so that users can place requests for their posts to be emailed to them.

Below you can see a new `export_posts` view function:

Listing 22.16: *app/main/routes.py*: Export posts route and view function.

```
@bp.route('/export_posts')
@login_required
def export_posts():
    if current_user.get_task_in_progress('export_posts'):
        flash(_('An export task is currently in progress'))
    else:
        current_user.launch_task('export_posts', _('Exporting posts...'))
        db.session.commit()
    return redirect(url_for('main.user', username=current_user.username))
```

The function first checks if the user has an outstanding export task, and in that case just flashes a message. It really makes no sense to have two export tasks for the same user at the same time, so this is prevented. I can check for this condition using the `get_task_in_progress()` method I implemented earlier.

If the user isn't already running an export, then `launch_task()` is invoked to start a one. The first argument is the name of the function that will be passed to the RQ worker, prefixed with `app.tasks.`. The second argument is just a friendly text description that will be shown to the user. Both values are written to the `Task` object in the database. The function ends with a redirect to the user profile page.

Now I need to expose a link to this route that the user can access to request the export. I think the most appropriate place to do this is in the user profile page, where the link can only be shown when users view their own page, right below the "Edit your profile" link:

Listing 22.17: *app/templates/user.html*: Export link in user profile page.

```
...
<p>
    <a href="{{ url_for('main.edit_profile') }}">
        {{ _('Edit your profile') }}
    </a>
</p>
{% if not current_user.get_task_in_progress('export_posts') %}
<p>
    <a href="{{ url_for('main.export_posts') }}">
        {{ _('Export your posts') }}
    </a>
</p>
...
{% endif %}
```

This link is tied to a conditional, because I don't want it to appear when the user already has an export in progress.

At this point the background jobs should be functional, but without giving any feedback to the user. If you want to try this out, you can start the application and the RQ worker as follows:

- Make sure you have Redis running

- In a first terminal window, start one or more instances of the RQ worker. For this you have to use the command `rq worker microblog-tasks`

- In a second terminal window, start the Flask application with `flask run` (remember to set `FLASK_APP` first)

22.9 Progress Notifications

To wrap up this feature I want to inform the user when a background task is running, including a percentage of completion. In looking through the Bootstrap component options, I decided to use an alert below the navigation bar for this. Alerts are these color horizontal bars that display information to the user. The blue alert boxes are what I'm using to render flashed messages. Now I'm going to add a green one to show progress status. Below you can see how that is going to look:

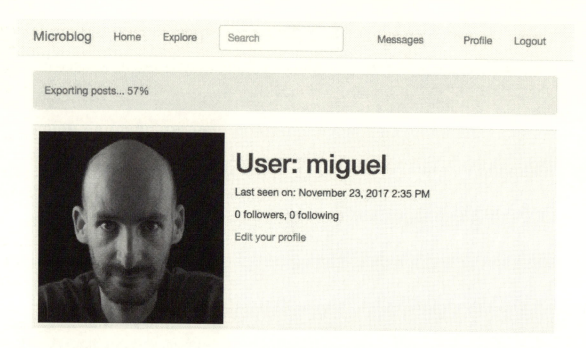

Listing 22.18: *app/templates/base.html*: Export progress alert in base template.

```
...
{% block content %}
    <div class="container">
        {% if current_user.is_authenticated %}
        {% with tasks = current_user.get_tasks_in_progress() %}
        {% if tasks %}
            {% for task in tasks %}
            <div class="alert alert-success" role="alert">
                {{ task.description }}
                <span id="{{ task.id }}-progress">{{ task.get_progress() }}</span>%
            </div>
            {% endfor %}
        {% endif %}
        {% endwith %}
        {% endif %}
        ...
{% endblock %}
...
```

The method to render the task alerts is almost identical to the flashed messages. The outer conditional skips all the alert related markup when the user is not logged in. For logged in users, I get the currently in-progress task list by calling the `get_tasks_in_progress()` method I created earlier. In the current version of the application I will only get one result at the most, since I don't allow more than one active export at a time, but in the future I may want to support other types of tasks that can coexist, so writing this in a generic way could save me time later.

22.9. PROGRESS NOTIFICATIONS

For each task I write an alert element to the page. The color of the alert is controlled with the second CSS style, which in this case is `alert-success`, while in the case of the flashed messages was `alert-info`. The Bootstrap documentation[10] includes the details on the HTML structure for the alerts. The text of the alert includes the `description` field stored in the `Task` model, followed by the completion percentage.

The percentage is wrapped in a `<span>` element that has a `id` attribute. The reason for this is that I'm going to refresh the percentage from JavaScript when notifications are received. The id that I'm using for a given task is constructed as the task id with `-progress` appended at the end. When a notification arrives, it will contain the task id, so I can easily locate the correct `<span>` element to update with a selector for `#<task.id>-progress`.

If you try the application at this point, you are going to see "static" progress updates, each time you navigate to a new page. You will notice that after you start an export task, you can freely navigate to different pages of the application, and the state of the running task is always recalled.

To prepare for applying dynamic updates to the percentage `<span>` elements, I'm going to write a little helper function in the JavaScript side:

Listing 22.19: *app/templates/base.html*: Helper function to dynamically update task progress.

```
...
{% block scripts %}
    ...
    <script>
        ...
        function set_task_progress(task_id, progress) {
            $('#' + task_id + '-progress').text(progress);
        }
    </script>
    ...
{% endblock %}
```

This function takes a task `id` and a progress value, and uses jQuery to locate the `<span>` element for this task and write the new progress as its contents. There is really no need to verify if the element exists on the page, because jQuery will do nothing if no elements are located with the given selector.

The notifications are already arriving to the browser because the `_set_task_progress()` function in *app/tasks.py* calls `add_notification()` each time the progress is updated. If you are confused about how these notifications could be reaching the browser without me

---

[10]https://getbootstrap.com/docs/3.3/components/#alerts

having to do anything, it's really because in Chapter 21 I was wise to implement the notifications feature in a completely generic way. Any notifications that are added through the `add_notification()` method will be seen by the browser when it periodically asks the server for notification updates.

But the JavaScript code that processes these notifications only recognizes those that have a `unread_message_count` name, and ignores the rest. What I need to do now is expand that function to also handle `task_progress` notifications by calling the `set_task_progress()` function I defined above. Here is an updated version of the loop that processes notifications from JavaScript:

Listing 22.20: *app/templates/base.html*: Notification handler.

```javascript
for (var i = 0; i < notifications.length; i++) {
    switch (notifications[i].name) {
        case 'unread_message_count':
            set_message_count(notifications[i].data);
            break;
        case 'task_progress':
            set_task_progress(
                notifications[i].data.task_id,
                notifications[i].data.progress);
            break;
    }
    since = notifications[i].timestamp;
}
```

Now that I need to handle two different notifications, I decided to replace the `if` statement that checked for the `unread_message_count` notification name with a `switch` statement that contains one section for each of the notifications I now need to support. If you are not very familiar with the "C" family of languages you may not have seen switch statements before. These provide a convenient syntax that replaces a long chain of `if/elseif` statements. This is nice because as I need to support more notifications, I can simply keep adding them as additional `case` blocks.

If you recall, the data that the RQ task attaches to the `task_progress` notification is a dictionary with two elements, `task_id` and `progress`, which are the two arguments that I need to use to invoke `set_task_progress()`.

If you run the application now, the progress indicator in the green alert box is going to refresh every 10 seconds, as notifications are delivered to the client.

Because I have introduced new translatable strings in this chapter, the translation files need to be updated. If you are maintaining a non-English language file, you need to use Flask-Babel to refresh your translation files and then add new translations:

```
(venv) $ flask translate update
```

If you are using the Spanish translation, then I have done the translation work for you, so you can just extract the *app/translations/es/LC_MESSAGES/messages.po* files from the download package[11] for this chapter and add it to your project.

After the translations are done, you have to compile the translation files:

```
(venv) $ flask translate compile
```

22.10 Deployment Considerations

To complete this chapter, I want to discuss how the deployment of the application changes. To support background tasks I have added two new components to the stack, a Redis server, and one or more RQ workers. Obviously these need to be included in your deployment strategy, so I'm going to briefly go over the different deployment options I covered in previous chapters and how they are affected by these changes.

22.10.1 Deployment on a Linux Server

If you are running your application on a Linux server, adding Redis should be as simple as installing this package from your operating system. For Ubuntu Linux, you have to run `sudo apt-get install redis-server`.

To run the RQ worker process, you can follow the "Setting Up Gunicorn and Supervisor" section in Chapter 17 to create a second Supervisor configuration in which you run `rq worker microblog-tasks` instead of `gunicorn`. If you want to run more than one worker (and you probably should for production), you can use Supervisor's `numprocs` directive to indicate how many instances you want to have running concurrently.

22.10.2 Deployment on Heroku

To deploy the application on Heroku you are going to need to add a Redis service to your account. This is similar to the process that I used to add the Postgres database. Redis also has

---

[11]https://github.com/miguelgrinberg/microblog/archive/version-0.22.zip

a free tier, which can be added with the following command:

```
$ heroku addons:create heroku-redis:hobby-dev
```

The access URL for your new redis service is going to be added to your Heroku environment as a REDIS_URL variable, which is exactly what the application expects.

The free plan in Heroku allows one web dyno and one worker dyno, so you can host a single rq worker along with your application without incurring into any expenses. For this you will need to declare the worker in a separate line in your procfile:

```
web: flask db upgrade; flask translate compile; gunicorn microblog:app
worker: rq worker microblog-tasks
```

After you deploy with these changes, you can start the worker with the following command:

```
$ heroku ps:scale worker=1
```

22.10.3 Deployment on Docker

If you are deploying the application to Docker containers, then you first need to create a Redis container. For this you can use one of the official Redis images from the Docker registry:

```
$ docker run --name redis -d -p 6379:6379 redis:3-alpine
```

When you run your application you will need to link the redis container and set the REDIS_URL environment variable, similar to how the MySQL container is linked. Here is a complete command to start the application including a redis link:

```
$ docker run --name microblog -d -p 8000:5000 --rm -e SECRET_KEY=my-secret-key \
    -e MAIL_SERVER=smtp.googlemail.com -e MAIL_PORT=587 -e MAIL_USE_TLS=true \
    -e MAIL_USERNAME=<your-gmail-username> -e MAIL_PASSWORD=<your-gmail-password> \
    --link mysql:dbserver --link redis:redis-server \
    -e DATABASE_URL=mysql+pymysql://microblog:<database-password>@dbserver/microblog \
    -e REDIS_URL=redis://redis-server:6379/0 \
    microblog:latest
```

22.10. DEPLOYMENT CONSIDERATIONS

Finally, you will need to run one or more containers for the RQ workers. Because the workers are based on the same code as the main application, you can use the same container image you use for your application, overriding the start up command so that the worker is started instead of the web application. Here is an example `docker run` command that starts a worker:

```
$ docker run --name rq-worker -d --rm -e SECRET_KEY=my-secret-key \
    -e MAIL_SERVER=smtp.googlemail.com -e MAIL_PORT=587 -e MAIL_USE_TLS=true \
    -e MAIL_USERNAME=<your-gmail-username> -e MAIL_PASSWORD=<your-gmail-password> \
    --link mysql:dbserver --link redis:redis-server \
    -e DATABASE_URL=mysql+pymysql://microblog:<database-password>@dbserver/microblog \
    -e REDIS_URL=redis://redis-server:6379/0 \
    --entrypoint venv/bin/rq \
    microblog:latest worker -u redis://redis-server:6379/0 microblog-tasks
```

Overriding the default start up command of a Docker image is a bit tricky because the command needs to be given in two parts. The `-entrypoint` argument takes just the executable name, but the arguments (if any) need to be given after the image and tag, at the end of the command line. Note that `rq` needs to be given as `venv/bin/rq` so that it works without having the virtual environment activated.

Chapter 23

Application Programming Interfaces (APIs)

All the functionality that I built so far for this application is meant for one specific type of client: the web browser. But what about other types of clients? If I wanted to build an Android or iOS app, for example, I have two main ways to go about it. The easiest solution would be to build a simple app with just a web view component that fills the entire screen, where the Microblog website is loaded, but this would offer little benefit over opening the application in the device's web browser. A better solution (though much more laborious) would be to build a native app, but how can this app interact with a server that only returns HTML pages?

This is the problem area where Application Programming Interfaces (or APIs) can help. An API is a collection of HTTP routes that are designed as low-level entry points into the application. Instead of defining routes and view functions that return HTML to be consumed by web browsers, APIs allow the client to work directly with the application's *resources*, leaving the decision of how to present the information to the user entirely to the client. For example, an API in Microblog could provide user and blog post information to the client, and it could also allow the user to edit an existing blog post, but only at the data level, without mixing this logic with HTML.

If you study all the routes currently defined in the application, you will notice that there are a few that could fit the definition of API I used above. Did you find them? I'm talking about the few routes that return JSON, such as the */translate* route defined in Chapter 14. This is a route that takes a text, source and destination languages, all given in JSON format in a `POST` request. The response to this request is the translation of that text, also in JSON format. The server only returns the requested information, leaving the client with the responsibility to present this information to the user.

While the JSON routes in the application have an API "feel" to them, they were designed to support the web application running in the browser. Consider that if a smartphone app wanted to use these routes, it would not be able to because they require a logged in user, and the log in can only happen through an HTML form. In this chapter I'm going to show how to build APIs that do not rely on the web browser and make no assumptions about what kind of client connects to them.

The GitHub links for this chapter are: Browse[1], Zip[2], Diff[3].

23.1 REST as a Foundation of API Design

Some people may strongly disagree with my statement above that */translate* and the other JSON routes are API routes. Others may agree, with the disclaimer that they consider them a badly designed API. So what are the characteristics of a well designed API, and why aren't the JSON routes in that category?

You may have heard the term REST API[4]. REST, which stands for Representational State Transfer, is an architecture proposed by Dr. Roy Fielding in his doctoral dissertation[5]. In his work, Dr. Fielding presents the six defining characteristics of REST in a fairly abstract and generic way.

There is no authoritative specification for REST besides Dr. Fielding's dissertation, and this leaves a lot of details to be interpreted by the reader. The topic of whether a given API complies with REST or not is often the source of heated debates between REST "purists", who believe that a REST API must observe all six characteristics and do so in a very specific way, versus the REST "pragmatists", who take the ideas presented by Dr. Fielding in his dissertation as guidelines or recommendations. Dr. Fielding himself sides with the purist camp, and has provided some additional insight into his vision in blog posts and online comments.

The vast majority of APIs currently implemented adhere to a "pragmatic" REST implementation. This includes most of the APIs from the "big players", such as Facebook, GitHub, Twitter, etc. There are very few public APIs that are unanimously considered to be pure REST, because most APIs miss certain implementation details that purists consider must-haves. In spite of the strict views Dr. Fielding and other REST purists have on what is or isn't a REST API, it is common in the software industry to refer to REST in the pragmatic sense.

---

[1] https://github.com/miguelgrinberg/microblog/tree/v0.23
[2] https://github.com/miguelgrinberg/microblog/archive/v0.23.zip
[3] https://github.com/miguelgrinberg/microblog/compare/v0.22...v0.23
[4] https://en.wikipedia.org/wiki/Representational_state_transfer
[5] http://www.ics.uci.edu/~fielding/pubs/dissertation/rest_arch_style.htm

23.1. REST AS A FOUNDATION OF API DESIGN

To give you an idea of what's in the REST dissertation, the following sections describe the six principles enumerated by Dr. Fielding.

23.1.1 Client-Server

The client-server principle is fairly straightforward, as it simply states that in a REST API the roles of the client and the server should be clearly differentiated. In practice, this means that the client and the server are in separate processes that communicate over a transport, which in the majority of the cases is the HTTP protocol over a TCP network.

23.1.2 Layered System

The layered system principle says that when a client needs to communicate with a server, it may end up connected to an intermediary and not the actual server. The idea is that for the client, there should be absolutely no difference in the way it sends requests if not connected directly to the server, in fact, it may not even know if it is connected to the target server or not. Likewise, this principle states that a server may receive client requests from an intermediary and not the client directly, so it must never assume that the other side of the connection is the client.

This is an important feature of REST, because being able to add intermediary nodes allows application architects to design large and complex networks that are able to satisfy a large volume of requests through the use of load balancers, caches, proxy servers, etc.

23.1.3 Cache

This principle extends the layered system, by indicating explicitly that it is allowed for the server or an intermediary to cache responses to requests that are received often to improve system performance. There is an implementation of a cache that you are likely familiar with: the one in all web browsers. The web browser cache layer is often used to avoid having to request the same files, such as images, over and over again.

For the purposes of an API, the target server needs to indicate through the use of *cache controls* if a response can be cached by intermediaries as it travels back to the client. Note that because for security reasons APIs deployed to production must use encryption, caching is usually not done in an intermediate node unless this node *terminates* the SSL connection, or performs decryption and re-encryption.

23.1.4 Code On Demand

This is an optional requirement that states that the server can provide executable code in responses to the client. Because this principle requires an agreement between the server and the client on what kind of executable code the client is able to run, this is rarely used in APIs. You would think that the server could return JavaScript code for web browser clients to execute, but REST is not specifically targeted to web browser clients. Executing JavaScript, for example, could introduce a complication if the client is an iOS or Android device.

23.1.5 Stateless

The stateless principle is one of the two at the center of most debates between REST purists and pragmatists. It states that a REST API should not save any client state to be recalled every time a given client sends a request. What this means is that none of the mechanisms that are common in web development to "remember" users as they navigate through the pages of the application can be used. In a stateless API, every request needs to include the information that the server needs to identify and authenticate the client and to carry out the request. It also means that the server cannot store any data related to the client connection in a database or other form of storage.

If you are wondering why REST requires stateless servers, the main reason is that stateless servers are very easy to scale, all you need to do is run multiple instances of the server behind a load balancer. If the server stores client state things get more complicated, as you have to figure out how multiple servers can access and update that state, or alternatively ensure that a given client is always handled by the same server, something commonly referred to as *sticky sessions*.

If you consider again the */translate* route discussed in the chapter's introduction, you'll realize that it cannot be considered *RESTful*, because the view function associated with that route relies on the `@login_required` decorator from Flask-Login, which in turn stores the logged in state of the user in the Flask user session.

23.1.6 Uniform Interface

The final, most important, most debated and most vaguely documented REST principle is the uniform interface. Dr. Fielding enumerates four distinguishing aspects of the REST uniform interface: unique resource identifiers, resource representations, self-descriptive messages, and hypermedia.

23.1. REST AS A FOUNDATION OF API DESIGN

Unique resource identifiers are achieved by assigning a unique URL to each resource. For example, the URL associated with a given user can be */api/users/<user-id>*, where *<user-id>* is the identifier assigned to the user in the database table's primary key. This is reasonably well implemented by most APIs.

The use of resource representations means that when the server and the client exchange information about a resource, they must use an agreed upon format. For most modern APIs, the JSON format is used to build resource representations. An API can choose to support multiple resource representation formats, and in that case the *content negotiation* options in the HTTP protocol are the mechanism by which the client and the server can agree on a format that both like.

Self-descriptive messages means that requests and responses exchanged between the clients and the server must include all the information that the other party needs. As a typical example, the HTTP request method is used to indicate what operation the client wants the server to execute. A `GET` request indicates that the client wants to retrieve information about a resource, a `POST` request indicates the client wants to create a new resource, `PUT` or `PATCH` requests define modifications to existing resources, and `DELETE` indicates a request to remove a resource. The target resource is indicated as the request URL, with additional information provided in HTTP headers, the query string portion of the URL or the request body.

The hypermedia requirement is the most polemic of the set, and one that few APIs implement, and those APIs that do implement it rarely do so in a way that satisfies REST purists. Since the resources in an application are all inter-related, this requirement asks that those relationships are included in the resource representations, so that clients can discover new resources by traversing relationships, pretty much in the same way you discover new pages in a web application by clicking on links that take you from one page to the next. The idea is that a client could enter an API without any previous knowledge about the resources in it, and learn about them simply by following hypermedia links. One of the aspects that complicate the implementation of this requirement is that unlike HTML and XML, the JSON format that is commonly used for resource representations in APIs does not define a standard way to include links, so you are forced to use a custom structure, or one of the proposed JSON extensions that try to address this gap, such as JSON-API[6], HAL[7], JSON-LD[8] or similar.

---

[6] http://jsonapi.org/
[7] http://stateless.co/hal_specification.html
[8] https://json-ld.org/

23.2 Implementing an API Blueprint

To give you a taste of what is involved in developing an API, I'm going to add one to Microblog. This is not going to be a complete API, I'm going to implement all the functions related to users, leaving the implementation of other resources such as blog posts to the reader as an exercise.

To keep things organized, and following the structure I described in Chapter 15, I'm going to create a new blueprint that will contain all the API routes. So let's begin by creating the directory where this blueprint will live:

```
(venv) $ mkdir app/api
```

The blueprint's *__init__.py* file creates the blueprint object, similar to the other blueprints in the application:

Listing 23.1: *app/api/__init__.py*: API blueprint constructor.

```python
from flask import Blueprint

bp = Blueprint('api', __name__)

from app.api import users, errors, tokens
```

You probably remember that it is sometimes necessary to move imports to the bottom to avoid circular dependency errors. That is the reason why the *app/api/users.py*, *app/api/errors.py* and *app/api/tokens.py* modules (that I'm yet to write) are imported after the blueprint is created.

The meat of the API is going to be stored in the *app/api/users.py* module. The following table summarizes the routes that I'm going to implement:

HTTP Method	Resource URL	Notes
GET	/api/users/<id>	Return a user.
GET	/api/users	Return the collection of all users.
GET	/api/users/<id>/followers	Return the followers of this user.
GET	/api/users/<id>/followed	Return the users this user is following.
POST	/api/users	Register a new user account.
PUT	/api/users/<id>	Modify a user.

For now I'm going to create a skeleton module with placeholders for all these routes:

23.2. IMPLEMENTING AN API BLUEPRINT

Listing 23.2: *app/api/users.py*: User API resource placeholders.

```python
from app.api import bp

@bp.route('/users/<int:id>', methods=['GET'])
def get_user(id):
    pass

@bp.route('/users', methods=['GET'])
def get_users():
    pass

@bp.route('/users/<int:id>/followers', methods=['GET'])
def get_followers(id):
    pass

@bp.route('/users/<int:id>/followed', methods=['GET'])
def get_followed(id):
    pass

@bp.route('/users', methods=['POST'])
def create_user():
    pass

@bp.route('/users/<int:id>', methods=['PUT'])
def update_user(id):
    pass
```

The *app/api/errors.py* module is going to define a few helper functions that deal with error responses. But for now, I'm also going to use a placeholder that I will fill out later:

Listing 23.3: *app/api/errors.py*: Error handling placeholder.

```python
def bad_request():
    pass
```

The *app/api/tokens.py* is the module where the authentication subsystem is going to be defined. This is going to provide an alternative way for clients that are not web browsers to log in. For now, I'm going to write a placeholder for this module as well:

Listing 23.4: *app/api/tokens.py*: Token handling placeholder.

```python
def get_token():
    pass

def revoke_token():
    pass
```

The new API blueprint needs to be registered in the application factory function:

Listing 23.5: *app/__init__.py*: Register API blueprint with the application.

```
# ...

def create_app(config_class=Config):
    app = Flask(__name__)

    # ...

    from app.api import bp as api_bp
    app.register_blueprint(api_bp, url_prefix='/api')

    # ...
```

23.3 Representing Users as JSON Objects

The first aspect to consider when implementing an API is to decide what the representation of its resources is going to be. I'm going to implement an API that works with users, so a representation for my user resources is what I need to decide on. After some brainstorming, I came up with the following JSON representation:

```
{
    "id": 123,
    "username": "susan",
    "password": "my-password",
    "email": "susan@example.com",
    "last_seen": "2017-10-20T15:04:27Z",
    "about_me": "Hello, my name is Susan!",
    "post_count": 7,
    "follower_count": 35,
    "followed_count": 21,
    "_links": {
        "self": "/api/users/123",
        "followers": "/api/users/123/followers",
        "followed": "/api/users/123/followed",
        "avatar": "https://www.gravatar.com/avatar/..."
    }
}
```

Many of the fields are directly coming from the user database model. The `password` field is special in that it is only going to be used when a new user is registered. As you remember from Chapter 5, user passwords are not stored in the database, only a hash is, so password are never returned. The `email` field is also treated specially, because I don't want to expose the email addresses of users. The `email` field is only going to be returned when users request their own entry, but not when they retrieve entries from other users. The `post_count`, `follower_count` and `followed_count` fields are "virtual" fields that do not exist as fields

23.3. REPRESENTING USERS AS JSON OBJECTS

in the database, but are provided to the client as a convenience. This is a great example that demonstrates that a resource representation does not need to match how the actual resource is defined in the server.

Note the `_links` section, which implements the hypermedia requirements. The links that are defined include links to the current resource, the list of users that follow this user, the list of users followed by the user, and finally a link to the user's avatar image. In the future, if I decide to add posts to this API, a link to the list of posts by the user should be included here as well.

One nice thing about the JSON format is that it always translates to a representation as a Python dictionary or list. The `json` package from the Python standard library takes care of converting the Python data structures to and from JSON. So to generate these representations, I'm going to add a method to the `User` model called `to_dict()`, which returns a Python dictionary:

Listing 23.6: *app/models.py*: User model to representation.

```python
from flask import url_for
# ...

class User(UserMixin, db.Model):
    # ...
    def to_dict(self, include_email=False):
        data = {
            'id': self.id,
            'username': self.username,
            'last_seen': self.last_seen.isoformat() + 'Z',
            'about_me': self.about_me,
            'post_count': self.posts.count(),
            'follower_count': self.followers.count(),
            'followed_count': self.followed.count(),
            '_links': {
                'self': url_for('api.get_user', id=self.id),
                'followers': url_for('api.get_followers', id=self.id),
                'followed': url_for('api.get_followed', id=self.id),
                'avatar': self.avatar(128)
            }
        }
        if include_email:
            data['email'] = self.email
        return data
```

This method should be mostly self-explanatory, the dictionary with the user representation I settled on is simply generated and returned. As I mentioned above, the `email` field needs special treatment, because I want to include the email only when users request their own data. So I'm using the `include_email` flag to determine if that field gets included in the representation or not.

Note how the `last_seen` field is generated. For date and time fields, I'm going to use the ISO

8601[9] format, which Python's `datetime` can generate through the `isoformat()` method. But because I'm using naive `datetime` objects that are UTC but do not have the timezone recorded in their state, I need to add the Z at the end, which is ISO 8601's timezone code for UTC.

Finally, see how I implemented the hypermedia links. For the three links that point to other application routes I use `url_for()` to generate the URLs (which currently point to the placeholder view functions I defined in *app/api/users.py*). The avatar link is special because it is a Gravatar URL, external to the application. For this link I use the same `avatar()` method that I've used to render the avatars in web pages.

The `to_dict()` method converts a user object to a Python representation, which will then be converted to JSON. I also need look at the reverse direction, where the client passes a user representation in a request and the server needs to parse it and convert it to a `User` object. Here is the `from_dict()` method that achieves the conversion from a Python dictionary to a model:

Listing 23.7: *app/models.py*: Representation to User model.

```python
class User(UserMixin, db.Model):
    # ...

    def from_dict(self, data, new_user=False):
        for field in ['username', 'email', 'about_me']:
            if field in data:
                setattr(self, field, data[field])
        if new_user and 'password' in data:
            self.set_password(data['password'])
```

In this case I decided to use a loop to import any of the fields that the client can set, which are `username`, `email` and `about_me`. For each field I check if I there is a value provided in the `data` argument, and if there is I use Python's `setattr()` to set the new value in the corresponding attribute for the object.

The `password` field is treated as a special case, because it isn't a field in the object. The `new_user` argument determines if this is a new user registration, which means that a `password` is included. To set the password in the user model, I call the `set_password()` method, which creates the password hash.

---

[9]https://en.wikipedia.org/wiki/ISO_8601

23.4 Representing Collections of Users

In addition to working with single resource representations, this API is going to need a representation for a group of users. This is going to be the format used when the client requests the list of users or followers, for example. Here is the representation for a collection of users:

```
{
    "items": [
        { ... user resource ... },
        { ... user resource ... },
        ...
    ],
    "_meta": {
        "page": 1,
        "per_page": 10,
        "total_pages": 20,
        "total_items": 195
    },
    "_links": {
        "self": "http://localhost:5000/api/users?page=1",
        "next": "http://localhost:5000/api/users?page=2",
        "prev": null
    }
}
```

In this representation, `items` is the list of user resources, each defined as described in the previous section. The `_meta` section includes metadata for the collection that the client might find useful in presenting pagination controls to the user. The `_links` section defines relevant links, including a link to the collection itself, and the previous and next page links, also to help the client paginate the listing.

Generating the representation of a collection of users is tricky because of the pagination logic, but the logic is going to be common to other resources I may want to add to this API in the future, so I'm going to implement this representation in a generic way that I can then apply to other models. Back in Chapter 16 I was in a similar situation with full-text search indexes, another feature that I wanted to implement generically so that it can be applied to any models. The solution that I used was to implement a `SearchableMixin` class that any models that need a full-text index can inherit from. I'm going to use the same idea for this, so here is a new mixin class that I named `PaginatedAPIMixin`:

Listing 23.8: *app/models.py*: Paginated representation mixin class.

```python
class PaginatedAPIMixin(object):
    @staticmethod
    def to_collection_dict(query, page, per_page, endpoint, **kwargs):
        resources = query.paginate(page, per_page, False)
```

```python
        data = {
            'items': [item.to_dict() for item in resources.items],
            '_meta': {
                'page': page,
                'per_page': per_page,
                'total_pages': resources.pages,
                'total_items': resources.total
            },
            '_links': {
                'self': url_for(endpoint, page=page, per_page=per_page,
                                **kwargs),
                'next': url_for(endpoint, page=page + 1, per_page=per_page,
                                **kwargs) if resources.has_next else None,
                'prev': url_for(endpoint, page=page - 1, per_page=per_page,
                                **kwargs) if resources.has_prev else None
            }
        }
        return data
```

The `to_collection_dict()` method produces a dictionary with the user collection representation, including the `items`, `_meta` and `_links` sections. You may need to review the method carefully to understand how it works. The first three arguments are a Flask-SQLAlchemy query object, a page number and a page size. These are the arguments that determine what are the items that are going to be returned. The implementation uses the `paginate()` method of the query object to obtain a page worth of items, like I did with posts in the index, explore and profile pages of the web application.

The complicated part is in generating the links, which include a self-reference and the links to the next and previous pages. I wanted to make this function generic, so I could not, for example, use `url_for('api.get_users', id=id, page=page)` to generate the self link. The arguments to `url_for()` are going to be dependent on the particular collection of resources, so I'm going to rely on the caller passing in the `endpoint` argument the view function that needs to be sent to `url_for()`. And because many routes have arguments, I also need to capture additional keyword arguments in `kwargs`, and pass those to `url_for()` as well. The `page` and `per_page` query string argument are given explicitly because these control pagination for all API routes.

This mixin class needs to be added to the `User` model as a parent class:

Listing 23.9: *app/models.py*: Add PaginatedAPIMixin to User model.

```python
class User(PaginatedAPIMixin, UserMixin, db.Model):
    # ...
```

In the case of collections I'm not going to need the reverse direction because I'm not going to have any routes that require the client to send lists of users.

23.5 Error Handling

The error pages that I defined in Chapter 7 are only appropriate for a user that is interacting with the application using a web browser. When an API needs to return an error, it needs to be a "machine friendly" type of error, something that the client application can easily interpret. So in the same way I defined representations for my API resources in JSON, now I'm going to decide on a representation for API error messages. Here is the basic structure that I'm going to use:

```
{
    "error": "short error description",
    "message": "error message (optional)"
}
```

In addition to the payload of the error, I will use the status codes from the HTTP protocol to indicate the general class of the error. To help me generate these error responses, I'm going to write the `error_response()` function in *app/api/errors.py*:

Listing 23.10: *app/api/errors.py*: Error responses.

```python
from flask import jsonify
from werkzeug.http import HTTP_STATUS_CODES

def error_response(status_code, message=None):
    payload = {'error': HTTP_STATUS_CODES.get(status_code, 'Unknown error')}
    if message:
        payload['message'] = message
    response = jsonify(payload)
    response.status_code = status_code
    return response
```

This function uses the handy `HTTP_STATUS_CODES` dictionary from Werkzeug (a core dependency of Flask) that provides a short descriptive name for each HTTP status code. I'm using these names for the `error` field in my error representations, so that I only need to worry about the numeric status code and the optional long description. The `jsonify()` function returns a Flask `Response` object with a default status code of 200, so after I create the response, I set the status code to the correct one for the error.

The most common error that the API is going to return is going to be the code 400, which is the error for "bad request". This is the error that is used when the client sends a request that has invalid data in it. To make it even easier to generate this error, I'm going to add a dedicated function for it that only requires the long descriptive message as an argument. This is the `bad_request()` placeholder that I added earlier:

Listing 23.11: *app/api/errors.py*: Bad request responses.

```
# ...
def bad_request(message):
    return error_response(400, message)
```

23.6 User Resource Endpoints

The support that I need to work with JSON representations of users is now complete, so I'm ready to start coding the API endpoints.

23.6.1 Retrieving a User

Let's start with the request to retrieve a single user, given by `id`:

Listing 23.12: *app/api/users.py*: Return a user.

```
from flask import jsonify
from app.models import User

@bp.route('/users/<int:id>', methods=['GET'])
def get_user(id):
    return jsonify(User.query.get_or_404(id).to_dict())
```

The view function receives the `id` for the requested user as a dynamic argument in the URL. The `get_or_404()` method of the query object is a very useful variant of the `get()` method you have seen before, that also returns the object with the given `id` if it exists, but instead of returning `None` when the `id` does not exist, it aborts the request and returns a 404 error to the client. The advantage of `get_or_404()` over `get()` is that it removes the need to check the result of the query, simplifying the logic in view functions.

The `to_dict()` method I added to `User` is used to generate the dictionary with the resource representation for the selected user, and then Flask's `jsonify()` function converts that dictionary to JSON format to return to the client.

If you want to see how this first API route works, start the server and then type the following URL in your browser's address bar:

23.6. USER RESOURCE ENDPOINTS

```
http://localhost:5000/api/users/1
```

This should show you the first user, rendered in JSON format. Also try to use a large `id` value, to see how the `get_or_404()` method of the SQLAlchemy query object triggers a 404 error (I will later show you how to extend the error handling so that these errors are also returned in JSON format).

To test this new route, I'm going to install HTTPie[10], a command-line HTTP client written in Python that makes it easy to send API requests:

```
(venv) $ pip install httpie
```

I can now request information about the user with a `id` of `1` (which is probably yourself) with the following command:

```
(venv) $ http GET http://localhost:5000/api/users/1
HTTP/1.0 200 OK
Content-Length: 457
Content-Type: application/json
Date: Mon, 27 Nov 2017 20:19:01 GMT
Server: Werkzeug/0.12.2 Python/3.6.3

{
    "_links": {
        "avatar": "https://www.gravatar.com/avatar/993c...2724?d=identicon&s=128",
        "followed": "/api/users/1/followed",
        "followers": "/api/users/1/followers",
        "self": "/api/users/1"
    },
    "about_me": "Hello! I'm the author of the Flask Mega-Tutorial.",
    "followed_count": 0,
    "follower_count": 1,
    "id": 1,
    "last_seen": "2017-11-26T07:40:52.942865Z",
    "post_count": 10,
    "username": "miguel"
}
```

23.6.2 Retrieving Collections of Users

To return the collection of all users, I can now rely on the `to_collection_dict()` method of `PaginatedAPIMixin`:

---

[10]https://httpie.org/

Listing 23.13: *app/api/users.py*: Return the collection of all users.

```
from flask import request

@bp.route('/users', methods=['GET'])
def get_users():
    page = request.args.get('page', 1, type=int)
    per_page = min(request.args.get('per_page', 10, type=int), 100)
    data = User.to_collection_dict(User.query, page, per_page, 'api.get_users')
    return jsonify(data)
```

For this implementation I first extract `page` and `per_page` from the query string of the request, using the defaults of 1 and 10 respectively if they are not defined. The `per_page` has additional logic that caps it at 100. Giving the client control to request really large pages is not a good idea, as that can cause performance problems for the server. The `page` and `per_page` arguments are then passed to the `to_collection_query()` method, along with the query, which in this case is simply `User.query`, the most generic query that returns all users. The last argument is `api.get_users`, which is the endpoint name that I need for the three links that are used in the representation.

To test this endpoint with HTTPie, use the following command:

```
(venv) $ http GET http://localhost:5000/api/users
```

The next two endpoints are the ones that return the follower and followed users. These are fairly similar to the one above:

Listing 23.14: *app/api/users.py*: Return followers and followed users.

```
@bp.route('/users/<int:id>/followers', methods=['GET'])
def get_followers(id):
    user = User.query.get_or_404(id)
    page = request.args.get('page', 1, type=int)
    per_page = min(request.args.get('per_page', 10, type=int), 100)
    data = User.to_collection_dict(user.followers, page, per_page,
                                   'api.get_followers', id=id)
    return jsonify(data)

@bp.route('/users/<int:id>/followed', methods=['GET'])
def get_followed(id):
    user = User.query.get_or_404(id)
    page = request.args.get('page', 1, type=int)
    per_page = min(request.args.get('per_page', 10, type=int), 100)
    data = User.to_collection_dict(user.followed, page, per_page,
                                   'api.get_followed', id=id)
    return jsonify(data)
```

23.6. USER RESOURCE ENDPOINTS

Since these two routes are specific to a user, they have the `id` dynamic argument. The `id` is used to get the user from the database, and then to provide the `user.followers` and `user.followed` relationship based queries to `to_collection_dict()`, so hopefully now you can see why spending a little bit of extra time and designing this method in a generic way really pays off. The last two arguments to `to_collection_dict()` are the endpoint name, and the `id`, which the method is going to take as an extra keyword argument in `kwargs`, and then pass it to `url_for()` when generating the links section of the representation.

Similar to the previous example, you can exercise these two routes with HTTPie as follows:

```
(venv) $ http GET http://localhost:5000/api/users/1/followers
(venv) $ http GET http://localhost:5000/api/users/1/followed
```

I should note that thanks to hypermedia, you do not need to remember these URLs, as they are included in the `_links` section of the user representation.

23.6.3 Registering New Users

The `POST` request to the */users* route is going to be used to register new user accounts. You can see the implementation of this route below:

Listing 23.15: *app/api/users.py*: Register a new user.

```python
from flask import url_for
from app import db
from app.api.errors import bad_request

@bp.route('/users', methods=['POST'])
def create_user():
    data = request.get_json() or {}
    if 'username' not in data or 'email' not in data or 'password' not in data:
        return bad_request('must include username, email and password fields')
    if User.query.filter_by(username=data['username']).first():
        return bad_request('please use a different username')
    if User.query.filter_by(email=data['email']).first():
        return bad_request('please use a different email address')
    user = User()
    user.from_dict(data, new_user=True)
    db.session.add(user)
    db.session.commit()
    response = jsonify(user.to_dict())
    response.status_code = 201
    response.headers['Location'] = url_for('api.get_user', id=user.id)
    return response
```

This request is going to accept a user representation in JSON format from the client, provided in the request body. Flask provides the `request.get_json()` method to extract the JSON from the request and return it as a Python structure. This method returns `None` if JSON data isn't found in the request, so I can ensure that I always get a dictionary using the expression `request.get_json() or {}`.

Before I can use the data I need to ensure that I've got all the information, so I start by checking that the three mandatory fields are included. These are `username`, `email` and `password`. If any of those are missing, then I use the `bad_request()` helper function from the *app/api/errors.py* module to return an error to the client. In addition to that check, I need to make sure that the `username` and `email` fields are not already used by another user, so for that I try to load a user from the database by the username and emails provided, and if any of those return a valid user, I also return an error back to the client.

Once I've passed the data validation, I can easily create a user object and add it to the database. To create the user I rely on the `from_dict()` method in the `User` model. The `new_user` argument is set to `True`, so that it also accepts the `password` field which is normally not part of the user representation.

The response that I return for this request is going to be the representation of the new user, so `to_dict()` generates that payload. The status code for a `POST` request that creates a resource should be 201, the code that is used when a new entity has been created. Also, the HTTP protocol requires that a 201 response includes a `Location` header that is set to the URL of the new resource.

Below you can see how to register a new user from the command line through HTTPie:

```
(venv) $ http POST http://localhost:5000/api/users username=alice password=dog \
    email=alice@example.com "about_me=Hello, my name is Alice!"
```

23.6.4 Editing Users

The last endpoint that I'm going to use in my API is the one that modifies an existing user:

Listing 23.16: *app/api/users.py*: Modify a user.

```
@bp.route('/users/<int:id>', methods=['PUT'])
def update_user(id):
    user = User.query.get_or_404(id)
    data = request.get_json() or {}
    if 'username' in data and data['username'] != user.username and \
            User.query.filter_by(username=data['username']).first():
```

23.7. API AUTHENTICATION

```
        return bad_request('please use a different username')
    if 'email' in data and data['email'] != user.email and \
            User.query.filter_by(email=data['email']).first():
        return bad_request('please use a different email address')
    user.from_dict(data, new_user=False)
    db.session.commit()
    return jsonify(user.to_dict())
```

For this request I receive a user `id` as a dynamic part of the URL, so I can load the designated user and return a 404 error if it is not found. Like in the case of a new user, I need to validate that the `username` and `email` fields provided by the client do not collide with other users before I can use them, but in this case the validation is a bit more tricky. First of all, these fields are optional in this request, so I need to check that a field is present. The second complication is that the client may be providing the same value, so before I check if the username or email are taken I need to make sure they are different than the current ones. If any of these validation checks fail, then I return a 400 error back to the client, as before.

Once the data has been validated, I can use the `from_dict()` method of the `User` model to import all the data provided by the client, and then commit the change to the database. The response from this request returns the updated user representation to the user, with a default 200 status code.

Here is an example request that edits the `about_me` field with HTTPie:

```
(venv) $ http PUT http://localhost:5000/api/users/2 "about_me=Hi, I am Miguel"
```

23.7 API Authentication

The API endpoints I added in the previous section are currently open to any clients. Obviously they need to be available to registered users only, and to do that I need to add *authentication* and *authorization*, or "AuthN" and "AuthZ" for short. The idea is that requests sent by clients provide some sort of identification, so that the server knows what user the client is representing, and can verify if the requested action is allowed or not for that user.

The most obvious way to protect these API endpoints is to use the `@login_required` decorator from Flask-Login, but that approach has some problems. When the decorator detects a non-authenticated user, it redirects the user to a HTML login page. In an API there is no concept of HTML or login pages, if a client sends a request with invalid or missing credentials, the server has to refuse the request returning a 401 status code. The server can't assume that the API client is a web browser, or that it can handle redirects, or that it can render and process

HTML login forms. When the API client receives the 401 status code, it knows that it needs to ask the user for credentials, but how it does that is really not the business of the server.

23.7.1 Tokens In the User Model

For the API authentication needs, I'm going to use a *token* authentication scheme. When a client wants to start interacting with the API, it needs to request a temporary token, authenticating with a username and password. The client can then send API requests passing the token as authentication, for as long as the token is valid. Once the token expires, a new token needs to be requested. To support user tokens, I'm going to expand the `User` model:

Listing 23.17: *app/models.py*: Support for user tokens.

```
import base64
from datetime import datetime, timedelta
import os

class User(UserMixin, PaginatedAPIMixin, db.Model):
    # ...
    token = db.Column(db.String(32), index=True, unique=True)
    token_expiration = db.Column(db.DateTime)

    # ...

    def get_token(self, expires_in=3600):
        now = datetime.utcnow()
        if self.token and self.token_expiration > now + timedelta(seconds=60):
            return self.token
        self.token = base64.b64encode(os.urandom(24)).decode('utf-8')
        self.token_expiration = now + timedelta(seconds=expires_in)
        db.session.add(self)
        return self.token

    def revoke_token(self):
        self.token_expiration = datetime.utcnow() - timedelta(seconds=1)

    @staticmethod
    def check_token(token):
        user = User.query.filter_by(token=token).first()
        if user is None or user.token_expiration < datetime.utcnow():
            return None
        return user
```

With this change I'm adding a `token` attribute to the user model, and because I'm going to need to search the database by it I make it unique and indexed. I also added `token_expiration`, which has the date and time at which the token expires. This is so that a token does not remain valid for a long period of time, which can become a security risk.

23.7. API AUTHENTICATION

I created three methods to work with these tokens. The `get_token()` method returns a token for the user. The token is generated as a random string that is encoded in base64 so that all the characters are in the readable range. Before a new token is created, this method checks if a currently assigned token has at least a minute left before expiration, and in that case the existing token is returned.

When working with tokens it is always good to have a strategy to revoke a token immediately, instead of only relying on the expiration date. This is a security best practice that is often overlooked. The `revoke_token()` method makes the token currently assigned to the user invalid, simply by setting the expiration date to one second before the current time.

The `check_token()` method is a static method that takes a token as input and returns the user this token belongs to as a response. If the token is invalid or expired, the method returns `None`.

Because I have made changes to the database, I need to generate a new database migration and then upgrade the database with it:

```
(venv) $ flask db migrate -m "user tokens"
(venv) $ flask db upgrade
```

23.7.2 Token Requests

When you write an API you have to consider that your clients are not always going to be web browsers connected to the web application. The real power of APIs comes when standalone clients such as smartphone apps, or even browser-based single page applications can have access to backend services. When these specialized clients need to access API services, they begin by requesting a token, which is the counterpart to the login form in the traditional web application.

To simplify the interactions between client and server when token authentication is used, I'm going to use a Flask extension called Flask-HTTPAuth[11]. Flask-HTTPAuth is installed with pip:

```
(venv) $ pip install flask-httpauth
```

Flask-HTTPAuth supports a few different authentication mechanisms, all API friendly. To begin, I'm going to use HTTP Basic Authentication[12], in which the client sends the user cre-

---
[11]https://flask-httpauth.readthedocs.io/
[12]https://en.wikipedia.org/wiki/Basic_access_authentication

dentials in a standard Authorization[13] HTTP Header. To integrate with Flask-HTTPAuth, the application needs to provide two functions: one that defines the logic to check the username and password provided by the user, and another that returns the error response in the case of an authentication failure. These functions are registered with Flask-HTTPAuth through decorators, and then are automatically called by the extension as needed during the authentication flow. You can see the implementation:

Listing 23.18: *app/api/auth.py*: Basic authentication support.

```python
from flask import g
from flask_httpauth import HTTPBasicAuth
from app.models import User
from app.api.errors import error_response

basic_auth = HTTPBasicAuth()

@basic_auth.verify_password
def verify_password(username, password):
    user = User.query.filter_by(username=username).first()
    if user is None:
        return False
    g.current_user = user
    return user.check_password(password)

@basic_auth.error_handler
def basic_auth_error():
    return error_response(401)
```

The `HTTPBasicAuth` class from Flask-HTTPAuth is the one that implements the basic authentication flow. The two required functions are configured through the `verify_password` and `error_handler` decorators respectively.

The verification function receives the username and password that the client provided and returns `True` if the credentials are valid or `False` if not. To check the password I rely on the `check_password()` method of the `User` class, which is also used by Flask-Login during authentication for the web application. I save the authenticated user in `g.current_user`, so that I can then access it from the API view functions.

The error handler function simply returns a 401 error, generated by the `error_response()` function in *app/api/errors.py*. The 401 error is defined in the HTTP standard as the "Unauthorized" error. HTTP clients know that when they receive this error the request that they sent needs to be resent with valid credentials.

Now I have basic authentication support implemented, so I can add the token retrieval route that clients will invoke when they need a token:

---

[13] https://developer.mozilla.org/en-US/docs/Web/HTTP/Headers/Authorization

23.7. API AUTHENTICATION

Listing 23.19: *app/api/tokens.py*: Generate user tokens.

```python
from flask import jsonify, g
from app import db
from app.api import bp
from app.api.auth import basic_auth

@bp.route('/tokens', methods=['POST'])
@basic_auth.login_required
def get_token():
    token = g.current_user.get_token()
    db.session.commit()
    return jsonify({'token': token})
```

This view function is decorated with the `@basic_auth.login_required` decorator from the `HTTPBasicAuth` instance, which will instruct Flask-HTTPAuth to verify authentication (through the verification function I defined above) and only allow the function to run when the provided credentials are valid. The implementation of this view function relies on the `get_token()` method of the user model to produce the token. A database commit is issued after the token is generated to ensure that the token and its expiration are written back to the database.

If you try to send a POST request to the tokens API route, this is what happens:

```
(venv) $ http POST http://localhost:5000/api/tokens
HTTP/1.0 401 UNAUTHORIZED
Content-Length: 30
Content-Type: application/json
Date: Mon, 27 Nov 2017 20:01:00 GMT
Server: Werkzeug/0.12.2 Python/3.6.3
WWW-Authenticate: Basic realm="Authentication Required"

{
    "error": "Unauthorized"
}
```

The HTTP response includes the 401 status code, and the error payload that I defined in my `basic_auth_error()` function. Here is the same request, this time including basic authentication credentials:

```
(venv) $ http --auth <username>:<password> POST http://localhost:5000/api/tokens
HTTP/1.0 200 OK
Content-Length: 50
Content-Type: application/json
Date: Mon, 27 Nov 2017 20:01:22 GMT
Server: Werkzeug/0.12.2 Python/3.6.3
```

```
{
    "token": "pClNu9wwyNt8VCjltrWilFdFI276AcbS"
}
```

Now the status code is 200, which is the code for a successful request, and the payload includes a newly generated token for the user. Note that when you send this request you will need to replace `<username>:<password>` with your own credentials. The username and password need to be provided with a colon as separator.

23.7.3 Protecting API Routes with Tokens

The clients can now request a token to use with the API endpoints, so what's left is to add token verification to those endpoints. This is something that Flask-HTTPAuth can also handle for me. I need to create a second authentication instance based on the `HTTPTokenAuth` class, and provide a token verification callback:

Listing 23.20: *app/api/auth.py*: Token authentication support.

```python
# ...
from flask_httpauth import HTTPTokenAuth

# ...
token_auth = HTTPTokenAuth()

# ...

@token_auth.verify_token
def verify_token(token):
    g.current_user = User.check_token(token) if token else None
    return g.current_user is not None

@token_auth.error_handler
def token_auth_error():
    return error_response(401)
```

When using token authentication, Flask-HTTPAuth uses a `verify_token` decorated function, but other than that, token authentication works in the same way as basic authentication. My token verification function uses `User.check_token()` to locate the user that owns the provided token. The function also handles the case of a missing token by setting the current user to `None`. The `True` or `False` return value determines if Flask-HTTPAuth allows the view function to run or not.

To protect API routes with tokens, the `@token_auth.login_required` decorator needs to be added:

23.7. API AUTHENTICATION

Listing 23.21: *app/api/users.py*: Protect user routes with token authentication.

```python
from app.api.auth import token_auth

@bp.route('/users/<int:id>', methods=['GET'])
@token_auth.login_required
def get_user(id):
    # ...

@bp.route('/users', methods=['GET'])
@token_auth.login_required
def get_users():
    # ...

@bp.route('/users/<int:id>/followers', methods=['GET'])
@token_auth.login_required
def get_followers(id):
    # ...

@bp.route('/users/<int:id>/followed', methods=['GET'])
@token_auth.login_required
def get_followed(id):
    # ...

@bp.route('/users', methods=['POST'])
def create_user():
    # ...

@bp.route('/users/<int:id>', methods=['PUT'])
@token_auth.login_required
def update_user(id):
    # ...
```

Note that the decorator is added to all the API view functions except `create_user()`, which obviously cannot accept authentication since the user that will request the token needs to be created first.

If you send a request to any of these endpoints as shown previously, you will get back a 401 error response. To gain access, you need to add the `Authorization` header, with a token that you received from a request to */api/tokens*. Flask-HTTPAuth expects the token to be sent as a "bearer" token, which isn't directly supported by HTTPie. For basic authentication with username and password, HTTPie offers a `-auth` option, but for tokens the header needs to be explicitly provided. Here is the syntax to send the bearer token:

```
(venv) $ http GET http://localhost:5000/api/users/1 \
    "Authorization:Bearer pC1Nu9wwyNt8VCj1trWilFdFI276AcbS"
```

23.7.4 Revoking Tokens

The last token related feature that I'm going to implement is the token revocation, which you can see below:

> **Listing 23.22:** *app/api/tokens.py*: Revoke tokens.
>
> ```
> from app.api.auth import token_auth
>
> @bp.route('/tokens', methods=['DELETE'])
> @token_auth.login_required
> def revoke_token():
>     g.current_user.revoke_token()
>     db.session.commit()
>     return '', 204
> ```

Clients can send a `DELETE` request to the */tokens* URL to invalidate the token. The authentication for this route is token based, in fact the token sent in the `Authorization` header is the one being revoked. The revocation itself uses the helper method in the `User` class, which resets the expiration date on the token. The database session is committed so that this change is written to the database. The response from this request does not have a body, so I can return an empty string. A second value in the return statement sets the status code of the response to 204, which is the code to use for successful requests that have no response body.

Here is an example token revocation request sent from HTTPie:

```
(venv) $ http DELETE http://localhost:5000/api/tokens \
    Authorization:"Bearer pC1Nu9wwyNt8VCj1trWilFdFI276AcbS"
```

23.8 API Friendly Error Messages

Do you recall what happened early in this chapter when I asked you to send an API request from the browser with an invalid user URL? The server returned a 404 error, but this error was formatted as the standard 404 HTML error page. Many of the errors the API might need to return can be overriden with JSON versions in the API blueprint, but there are some errors handled by Flask that still go through the error handlers that are globally registered for the application, and these continue to return HTML.

The HTTP protocol supports a mechanism by which the client and the server can agree on the best format for a response, called *content negotiation*. The client needs to send an `Accept`

23.8. API FRIENDLY ERROR MESSAGES

header with the request, indicating the format preferences. The server then looks at the list and responds using the best format it supports from the list offered by the client.

What I want to do is modify the global application error handlers so that they use content negotiation to reply in HTML or JSON according to the client preferences. This can be done using the `request.accept_mimetypes` object from Flask:

Listing 23.23: *app/errors/handlers.py*: Content negotiation for error responses.

```python
from flask import render_template, request
from app import db
from app.errors import bp
from app.api.errors import error_response as api_error_response

def wants_json_response():
    return request.accept_mimetypes['application/json'] >= \
        request.accept_mimetypes['text/html']

@bp.app_errorhandler(404)
def not_found_error(error):
    if wants_json_response():
        return api_error_response(404)
    return render_template('errors/404.html'), 404

@bp.app_errorhandler(500)
def internal_error(error):
    db.session.rollback()
    if wants_json_response():
        return api_error_response(500)
    return render_template('errors/500.html'), 500
```

The `wants_json_response()` helper function compares the preference for JSON or HTML selected by the client in their list of preferred formats. If JSON rates higher than HTML, then I return a JSON response. Otherwise I'll return the original HTML responses based on templates. For the JSON responses I'm going to import the `error_response` helper function from the API blueprint, but here I'm going to rename it to `api_error_response()` so that it is clear what it does and where it comes from.

Made in the USA
Lexington, KY
22 August 2018